An excellent solution to the [illegible]
with three feet, each planted [illegible], Beckett.
An appropriate marriage of BA Physics & PhD in English.
(an otherwise ambitious & difficult road!)

NO-THING IS LEFT TO TELL

Zen/Chaos Theory in the Dramatic Art of Samuel Beckett

John Leeland Kundert-Gibbs

Madison • Teaneck
Fairleigh Dickinson University Press
London: Associated University Presses

Associated University Presses
440 Forsgate Drive
Cranbury, NJ 08512

Associated University Presses
16 Barter Street
London WC1A 2AH, England

Associated University Presses
P.O. Box 338, Port Credit
Mississauga, Ontario
Canada L5G 4L8

The paper used in this publication meets the requirements of the American National Standard for Permanence of Paper for Printed Library Materials Z39.48-1984.]

Library of Congress Cataloging-in-Publication Data

Kundert-Gibbs, John L.
No-thing is left to tell : Zen/Chaos theory in the dramatic art of Samuel Beckett / John Leeland Kundert-Gibbs.
p. cm.
Includes bibliographical references and index.
ISBN 0-8386-3762-0 (alk. paper)
1. Beckett, Samuel, 1906– —Dramatic works. 2. Literature and science—Ireland—History—20th century. 3. Beckett, Samuel, 1906– —Knowledge—Science. 4. Chaotic behavior in systems in literature. 5. Complexity (Philosophy) in literature. 6. English drama--Oriental influences. 7. Beckett, Samuel, 1906– —Religion. 8. Zen Buddhism in literature. I. Title.
PR6003.E282Z77124 1999
842'.914—dc21 98-25241
CIP

PRINTED IN THE UNITED STATES OF AMERICA

For Kristin, Joshua, and Kenlee . . .

A peach petal poised
falling brown brush strokes behind
white parchment field—Spring!

The detail of the pattern is movement,
As in the figure of the ten stairs.
Desire itself is movement
Not in itself desirable . . .

—T. S. Eliot

. . . and constant craving has always been . . .

—k. d. lang

Everything must hinge on the art of archery. . . .

—Eugen Herrigel

Contents

Illustrations

Figures:

Except where otherwise noted, the author has generated all figures and tables in this work, and any inaccuracies or errors are his responsibility.

Acknowledgments

I would like to thank all those who helped to make this work what it is, but I only have space to mention a special few. First, I must thank Katherine H. Burkman for being mentor, colleague, and friend throughout the journey that has produced this work. I am also very much indebted to Grand Master Choi Joon Pyo of the Oriental Martial Arts College for his years of expert guidance in the physical, mental, and spiritual art of Tae Kwon Do: my understanding of Zen has been profoundly influenced by his teaching and friendship. I am also indebted to Judy Kundert, who sacrificed several weeks of her life to come to a strange city and watch our infant son; without this precious writing time, this book would still be unfinished. To my parents, Lee and Joan, I am deeply indebted not only for this work but for being wonderful, nurturing role models. Finally, my humble thanks to my wife, Kristin, and sons, Joshua and Kenlee, whose love and faith have been my guide to completing this work.

NO-THING IS LEFT TO TELL

1
Introduction

> In a way, art is a theory about the way the world looks to human beings. It's abundantly obvious that one doesn't know the world around us in detail. What artists have accomplished is realizing that there's only a small amount of stuff that's important, and then seeing what it was.
>
> —Mitchell Feigenbaum

> Then comes the supreme and ultimate miracle: art becomes "artless," shooting becomes not-shooting, a shooting without bow and arrow; the teacher becomes a pupil again, the Master a beginner, the end a beginning, and the beginning perfection.
>
> —Eugen Herrigel

"Nothing is left to tell." So saying, R closes the "worn volume" in Samuel Beckett's short play *Ohio Impromptu*, a move claiming at once closure and ending, and—given its context—leaving characters and audience in some "other" realm of "Profounds of mind. Of mindlessness." Seemingly contrary signals of finality and ever-opening horizons exist simultaneously in a work whose dramatic impact far outweighs its small size. R's words, following a period of quasi-meditative ritual readings, apparently close off any further development for both *Ohio Impromptu* and drama as a whole; for, when "Nothing is left to tell," what is there to say? Yet this very act of finality is generative, the unclosed pieces of the play re-membering[1] and reconfiguring themselves in manifold ways within the potential space left by the final "stone" stare R and L share. This final moment in *Ohio Impromptu* is emblematic of Beckett's entire dramatic oeuvre in its compression of apparent polarities into a fluid union; it is a re-placement, or re-centering, of complex "fringe" elements into a generative phenomenology where meaning gives way to patterns of information—a central theme for both Zen Buddhism and Chaos theory, as well as Beckett's plays. Instead of comprehending Beckett's drama in terms of an expanding entropy that will ultimately lead to what Clov calls a "silent stillness," Zen and Chaos theory help us to apprehend the plays in terms of a prereflective patterning that reorganizes itself on a higher informational plane.

Is there, then, something more to say than "Nothing"? Certainly audiences and critics alike have found Beckett's work rich ground for discussion and deep contemplation. In fact, in recent years, his first produced play, *Waiting for Godot*, has taken on quasi-iconic stature in pop culture, as a recent MTV video indicates.[2] In the world of academia, Beckett's plays and fiction have caused near hysteria, generating hundreds of books and well over a thousand articles.[3] Given the popularity and intense scrutiny Beckett's plays have evoked, there is reason enough to weigh the value of another study devoted to this subject. Yet if we examine the issue from the reverse angle—that Beckett's plays have generated such interest and study because they are so richly and succinctly created—then justification for another examination of his plays is simply that it must unveil more layers and beauty within his works. Considering this "prime directive," I have opted here for a set of rather unusual, yet highly revealing, tools through which to re-view Beckett's drama: in order to better understand Beckett's plays we will work with and through the uneasy coupling of Zen Buddhism and Chaos theory.

This unlikely pair of far different disciplines that arise from very different cultural milieus seems, at first glance, arbitrary. What, after all, can a branch of modern Western physics and mathematics have to do with an ancient Oriental philosophical and religious tradition? Contrary to what we might expect, however, exploration of this not only reveals a remarkable, dynamic parallelism between these two disciplines, it also points the way to a new reading of Beckett's plays. The defense, then, for pressing Zen Buddhism and Chaos theory into a dialogue with each other and with Beckett's dramatic work is that new substructures and patterns will come to light in all three subjects—and these patterns will, in turn, provide a new, more positive—or at least less despairing—reading of Beckett's dramatic work.

To see where the intersection of Zen and Chaos theory with Beckett's plays might lead, let us briefly examine the vast landscape of Beckett criticism. With the amazing amount of work that has already been done to explicate, interpret, and even denounce Beckett's writings, there is little surprise that almost every major critical tool has been leveled at his work—often even at the author himself. Beginning with Esslin's *The Theatre of the Absurd*, Beckett's work has been characterized in terms of absurdist writing, psychological models,[4] modernist subjectivity,[5] postmodernist fragmentation and lack of subjectivity,[6] decentering and deconstruction,[7] reader-response theory,[8] phenomenology,[9] speech-act theory,[10] nihilism,[11] semiotics,[12] mythological structures,[13] and many others. As for the critical tools utilized in these pages, Buddhism in fact has been utilized from early on in Beckett criticism.[14] Recently an entire book, Paul Foster's *Beckett and Zen*, employed Zen as a tool to probe the portrayal of dilemma in Beckett's fiction.[15] Elsewhere the sciences have shed their own interpretive light on the author's work.[16] Thus, both the religio-philosophical point of view of Zen Buddhism and the methodology and analogy of modern science have been used to explore Beckett's oeuvre.

Use of such wide-ranging critical points of view makes it nearly impossible to characterize *the* interpretation of Beckett's work; indeed, there should never be such a consensus about work of this complexity and power. There are, however, some common threads in many of the critical works centered on Beckett. One thread is that Beckett's work is more exposition than explication: as author—and often as critic—Beckett paints a picture of a situation rather than explaining it in analytic language. Another thread is that Beckett concerns himself mainly with the subject qua subject: plays, fiction, and poetry tend to center their narrative around the narrator himself. Furthermore, there is a general sense in Beckett's work that the characters, as well as the world itself, exist contingently at the edge (or perhaps in the middle) of an abyss or void that ostensibly constitutes the "true" nature of the world. Compositing these three elements leads to the conclusion that most interpreters of Beckett's work see it as creating a collapsing, subjective, existential portrait of subjectivity on the edge of disintegration. Often, as with deconstructive readings of his work, this subjectivity is based on language usage, a contingency that immediately decenters and destabilizes the subject, forcing him to fulfill his "pensum" even though he "can't go on" creating himself through plain (that is, non-narrative) language. Other readings, notably Garner's recent phenomenological one, see the subject in Beckett's work (especially, but not limited to, the physically manifested subject) in terms that pass beyond the merely linguistic, arguing that the central characters are indeed existentially destabilized but that the destabilization takes place in both physiological and logocentric fashion. Despite the diversity of approaches and agendas, most of Beckett's critics agree that his work is about the difficulty and/or triumph of existing and creating in a world devoid of extranatural (or extratextual) direction and purpose.

Certainly there is no need to dispute the verity of these major interpretive observations, which have revealed much of the vast and complex workings of Beckett's oeuvre. My object here is to use the dynamic relational context of Zen Buddhism and Chaos theory to engender an understanding of Beckett's work in terms of a progression or evolution toward "lessness," or the marginalized—a progression that eventually brings to the fore a different, more positive understanding of "reality." Although critics have often noted the trend toward minimalization in Beckett's work, the progressively shrinking scale his works exhibit is usually construed as the playwright's confrontation with the "ultimate failure" of creative language "to encompass the mystery and chaos of being" (Knowlson and Pilling 1980, 103). Thus, each of Beckett's plays (novels, and/or poems) is seen as moving one step closer to the chaos of silence and, implicitly, nonbeing.

The work we will do in the following pages, however, while accepting all the above arguments, will place them in a different light, so to speak. I will show that this ostensibly negative drive toward a ground zero where nothing can be said or done is, instead, an essentially positive (better yet, non-negative) movement: it is a paradigm shift, a displacement of the standard (Western) solutions to the existential riddle (solutions that lead to an impasse of suffering) that reveals a potential richness and beauty in the patterning of Beckett's plays. These plays are particularly suited to a re-vision that centralizes the supposedly marginal and inverts the primacy of narrative, logic, and causality as they devalue and destabilize traditional plot and character. In the circular eddies and swirls of a Chaotic system,[17] as well as in the apparently disjointed acausal world of Zen, Beckett's drama finds its ideal reflection. This different vision—ultimately it is only a change of point of view, not of what is there in the plays—arises from character and audience acceptance that what has been considered from the "normal" point of view as marginal, unsolvable, and therefore unimportant is, instead, central, definable, and of vital importance. To re-view Beckett's plays in light of two systems that eschew causal analysis may not be intuitive at first, but it is exactly this nondeterministic element in Zen and Chaos theory that uncovers important new layers and patterns within the plays.

In light of this conceptual difficulty, as well as the pro-regression in Beckett's plays, I have chosen to associate the chapters metaphorically with Eugen Herrigel's famous work, *Zen in the Art of Archery*, which describes the relation of Zen Buddhism to the activity of archery. Briefly, in order to perfect the "art" of archery (which is itself essentially a metaphor for attainment of a Zen attitude toward the "artless art" [Herrigel 1953, 65] of life), the student must learn to reject such conceptual dualisms as bow-and-arrow versus target, or Self versus Other. As the student approaches enlightenment, the distance between bow-versus-arrow and target decreases until conscious differences are forgotten and all become one. As his master teaches Professor Herrigel,

> You can learn from an ordinary bamboo leaf what ought to happen. It bends lower and lower under the weight of snow. Suddenly the snow slips to the ground without the leaf having stirred. . . . So, indeed, it is: when the tension [from drawing the bow] is fulfilled, the shot *must* fall from the archer like snow from a bamboo leaf. . . . (1953, 47–48)

Although choosing this archery metaphor is to some extent arbitrary, it does provide a context with which many Westerners are familiar, in addition to making more intuitive the affirming directionality-through-lessness of Beckett's work as seen through the lenses of Zen and Chaos theory. This metaphor is not intended to encapsulate the work of each chapter; instead, like a finger pointing at the moon,[18] it indicates the path taken both by Beckett's play(s) and by this analysis.

Between the claims put forth for this work and the unusual nature of the critical tools to be used, an examination of the salient points of Zen Buddhism and Chaos theory is important in order to lay the foundation for their application to Beckett's drama. The following chapter will first look at Zen and, to some extent, its place in the arena of comparative philosophy, then will proceed to elaborate to a small extent the discipline of Chaos (or dynamic systems) theory, indicating the significance of this new science to this project. Finally, the chapter will delve very briefly into the resultant mix of science and religio-philosophy to contextualize the interaction of Zen and Chaos theory. Later chapters will review several of Beckett's major plays in chronological fashion, focusing on the unique issues of each play, but at the same time placing each in a framework of similarity and movement—the arrow flying to a target of diminishing importance (as separate object)—indicating that "Beckett's theater has evolved consistently in the direction of reduction, compression, and the economy of artistic means" (Hale 1987, 145). Chapters 6 and 7—which concentrate on *Footfalls* and *Ohio Impromptu*, two of Beckett's late plays—reveal the resultant stark, mythical landscape that destabilizes our usual paradigmatic view of stage and life,[19] and centralizes the fringe elements of our "reality." The final chapter gives a brief overview of the results of the study.

What we will find in these chapters is that Zen, Chaos theory, and Beckett conjoin in their unusual, even radical, revisions of the traditionally marginal void that, for better or worse, surrounds our lives. All three indicate a needed paradigm shift toward—a re-visioning of—the void or emptiness that, of necessity, seems to lie at the fringe of the status quo. For Zen, as for Taoism, the Void *(Mu),* or emptiness (or *Sunya* in Sanskrit), is a "maelstrom," or chaos (Kasulis 1981, 28) around our puny constructed order; but this maelstrom is at heart a "source"—the source, in fact, of the universe. As the opening lines of the *Tao Te Ching* indicate, the ineffable void of the Tao is at once nothing and the progenitor of the world:

> The tao that can be told
> is not the eternal Tao.
> The name that can be named
> is not the eternal Name.

The unnamable is the eternally real.
Naming is the origin
of all particular things.

(Lao Tzu 1988, 1)

Nothingness—the eternally unnamable Tao—is, in fact, the source of all that is namable. "As the equivalent of the absolute Tao, Nonbeing or nothingness (Chinese *Wu*; Japanese *Mu*) is more than the mere opposite of Being. It is in fact ontologically *prior* to Being; it is the ultimate source of all things" (Kasulis 1981, 32). The void is thus associated with "*Hun-Dun*," the old Chinese character of chaos, whose allegorical hospitality allows order to thrive (and who can be destroyed by an overzealous attempt to polarize order and chaos as value-laden opposites). The void is a positive, plenary negative that gives birth (as the etymology of the Sanskrit term, *Sunya* indicates) to order and the "ten thousand things."

A similar revision takes place in Chaos theory. No longer is the unsolvable and "noisy" void of chaotic behavior the marginalized opposite of well-behaved systems and equations; now it is seen as a vast source of creative information. "The more chaotic a system is, the more information it produces. This perception is at the heart of the transvaluation of chaos, for it enables chaos to be conceived as an inexhaustible ocean of information rather than as a void signifying absence" (Hayles 1990, 8). With obvious ties to the Zen vision of the world, Chaos theory, on an ethical plane, alters our judgment of the chaotic void: ". . . chaos is envisioned not as an absence or void but as a positive force in its own right" (Hayles 1990, 3). The potential nihilism associated with the "death of order" brought on by quantum dynamics is shifted to a more positive potentiality as the excitement and energy of a vast new untapped source of information and creativity is perceived in Chaotic systems. This shift, in fact, even potentiates a new look at the postmodern *Zeitgeist:* "The reconceptualization of the void as a space of creation has deep affinities with the postmodern idea of a constructed reality [and thus with its potential deconstruction]" (Hayles 1991, 14). As with Zen, the "void" of Chaotic behavior is the same; it is only the way we perceive it that has changed. Far from being a negative or nihilistic shift, as would be expected on cursory examination, the change is a more positive one, where the knowledge of a socially created reality allows us, à la Zen, to step back from the bipolar categories of order/disorder, creation/destruction, etc., and see our world as essentially unitary instead.

If next we try to define the void in Beckett's plays (essentially an impossible job, as the void is indefinable), we might consider such elements as Godot in *Waiting for Godot*, the "without" in *Endgame*, the apparently malevolent force behind the "bell for waking" in *Happy Days*, "It all" in

"Hun-Dun"

Footfalls, or “The Dear Name” in *Ohio Impromptu*—all of which have only a tangential existence onstage but which destabilize and re-center the plays. By operating outside standard dramatic and narrative norms, these third “characters” slip the constraints of dramatic delimitation, acting instead as the unnamable (or better, uncharacterizable) operands who influence the pairs of characters on stage in more profound ways in this manner than any realizable character possibly could.

The void in Beckett's plays—which might be generalizable to the “world” around the characters, as it is, in whatever manifestation it takes in the individual play, the milieu from which those on stage take their existence—is, at the same time, a potentially nihilistic force driving toward annihilation of characters and world, and a source of extreme creative energy and (potential) positive change. The first valuation is from the traditional Western philosophical and theatrical traditions, whose polar conceptualization of order and chaos is threatened by Beckett's work; the second arises within the potential space of the twin paradigms of Zen Buddhism and Chaos theory. The foundations of Chaos theory and Zen Buddhism allow an understanding of Beckett's plays as an exploration of a “noisy,” “without-dualistic” world of vast positive potential. Rejecting the common, “centralized” paradigms of stage and life, Beckett was and is at the forefront of a re-visioning of theater and reality.

2

Zeno, Zen, and $z^2 + c$: The Unlikely Bow, Arrow, and Target

> I am an old man now, and when I die and go to Heaven there are two matters on which I hope for enlightenment. One is quantum electrodynamics, and the other is the turbulent motion of fluids. And about the former I am really rather optimistic.
>
> — Sir Horace Lamb

> This opened the pupil's mind to the secrets of the art, which had hitherto been kept from him.
>
> — Eugen Herrigel

Zen Buddhism is a grafting of two distinct religio-philosophies—Mahayana Buddhism, which was imported to China from India, and Taoism, which was native to China.[1] Although we in the West now think of Zen mostly as a Japanese phenomenon, it was developed and flowered first in China, where it was and is called Ch'an Buddhism, and was only later exported to the Japanese islands. Of the two root religio-philosophies, each is fairly equally represented in Zen, though Buddhism is the only one explicitly named.

Buddhism is, at heart, founded on the Buddha's "waking up" and achieving enlightenment (*nirvana* in Sanskrit, or *satori* in Japanese), then returning to the normal, "sleeping" world of men and teaching them/us how to achieve the awakened state. However, during the hundreds of years after the Buddha appeared, the religion became highly philosophical, literary, and academic, as schools of Buddhist monks first wrote and then dogmatized writings like the famous *Diamond Sutra*. By the time Buddhism crossed the Himalayas to China, it had become mired down (as Zen Buddhists would say) in ritual and scholastic argumentation over exact interpretations of minor passages in Buddhist writings (similar to heated arguments over relatively minor points of Christian dogma in Protestant religions). In founding the Zen tradition, Dogen, Hakuin[2] and others followed Nagarjuna's path to eliminate the confusion and irrelevance of the Buddhist tradition by going back to the primary experience of Buddhism: the Buddha's enlightenment. If, as many scholars, and the Buddha himself, had said, everything had "Buddha nature," then our only true mission in life should be to "wake up," or become enlightened to our true selves.

At the same time, Taoism, which had existed in China for hundreds of years before Buddhism arrived, had a major effect on how the Chinese responded to the Buddhist tradition. Taoism itself is extremely difficult to define, since it actually is a conglomeration of several religions and philosophical systems centered on the concept of the Tao. Again, to simplify the matter a great deal, the main focus of "pure" philosophical Taoism is to separate oneself from the everyday, striving world of men.[3] Thus, its devotees live obscurely and anonymously and do not concern themselves with taking sides on issues of even the greatest seeming importance (Kaltenmark 1969, 10). Primarily a "quietist" school (followers believing that lack of mental concern over anything, including their own death, is the key to a peaceful and harmonious life) Taoism leads its followers to accept death rather than a hectic life filled with empty ritual.

What, then, is this word, *Tao,* to which followers devote such faith? As with the system as a whole, the term *Tao* itself is not precisely definable. Through changes in script (the manner in which the word is written), context, or author, the word changes its meaning. Max Kaltenmark explores these meanings extensively:

> The root meaning of Tao is "path" or "way." When used as a verb, the same word (with sometimes a slight variation in the script) means "to direct," "to guide," or "to establish communication." A person directs another by telling him the way he has to follow, so Tao also means "to say" or "to tell." And insofar as saying or telling is the same as informing and teaching, Tao has the further meaning "Doctrine."
>
> Above all, then, the word Tao suggests a way to be followed and, by extension, moral guidance or a code of behavior. (1969, 22)

Yet, lest we think that the Tao can be reduced to a series of directions or rites, the *Tao Te Ching* opens with the lines, "The Tao that can be told / is not the eternal Tao" (1988, 1)—the true Tao is beyond the power of speech to signify.[4] It is, in reality, more than a doctrine or teaching, "it is a reality behind the origin of the universe" (Kaltenmark 1969, 28), also defined as the Void or "the mother of the universe" (Lao Tzu 1988, 25). Just to make matters more complex, this concept is called *Wu* by Chuang Tzu (Kaltenmark 1969, 40; this is the same term that is pronounced *Mu* in Japanese and that basically means "no-thing").

Essentially, then, these ancient philosophers were searching for a way to express in words a concept practically impossible to explain to others.

From the glimpses of deeper meaning we receive from the multiple definitions of Tao, however, we can see that the "void," "prime mover" (to use Plato's terminology), or unity that gives birth to multiplicity lies at the heart of Taoist thought and provides the basic "concept" on which Taoists depend to achieve transcendence over the desires and drives of society and nature. Sometimes referred to as the absolute, the Tao, leading to this state of mind, is "movement and stillness without beginning, yin and yang without beginning" (Cleary 1989, 3). It is beyond conception in this world of multiplicity and in our normal frame of mind (if this sounds similar to Zen Buddhist thought and expression, there is good reason—as will be explained below). Thus, the Tao is both the path to be followed and the goal to be reached, a doctrine and a reality, multiplicity and unity.

Is there any way to encapsulate all the different aspects of Taoist thought found in the *Tao Te Ching*? In his introduction to his translation of the work, Stephen Mitchell provides a key:

> The teaching of the Tao Te Ching is moral in the deepest sense. Unencumbered by any concept of sin, the Master doesn't see evil as a force to resist, but simply as an opaqueness, a state of self-absorption which is in disharmony with the universal process. . . . This freedom from moral categories allows him his great compassion for the wicked and the selfish. (Mitchell 1988, ix)

The objective, ego-self is the obstacle to living in harmony—the obstacle to *Wei-wu-wei*, or doing-not-doing, acting in harmony with the "flow" of nature. It is also important to note that this most important of Taoist (and Zen) terms, *Wu*, which is roughly translated as non-being or nothingness, "is more than the mere opposite of Being. It is in fact ontologically *prior* to Being; it is the ultimate source of all things." This property makes *Wu* "essentially positive rather than negative" (Kasulis 1981, 32). Thus, the void, or Tao, is, in effect, plenary rather than empty.

When, several centuries later, Buddhism crossed over into China, Taoist thought already had a strong hold on the imaginations of the Chinese, and thus had a profound influence on how Buddhism evolved there. In addition to its Mahayana Buddhist background, Zen draws heavily on these native Taoist teachings in its formulation of the path (or way, or Tao) to enlightenment, as D. T. Suzuki (1949, 41n), Herrlee G. Creel (1970, 23) and others have pointed out. "[T]he philosophy of Ch'an (or Zen) Buddhism is remarkably similar to philosophic Taoism" (Creel 1970, 23), so much so that many uninitiates have difficulty seeing a distinction between the two. Why is this so? First because much of the terminology is the same, and second because many of the aims of the two systems are the same. Both seek to purify and control the mind (Lu 1961, 17), both attempt to relieve the personal suffering caused by the common world, and both profess a unary substrate (Void, Tao, Satori—what you will) under the multiplicity of everyday life.

If we again reduce their complex nature somewhat, we can point out the two distinctive elements of Zen, the first of which arises from its Buddhist tradition (specifically in the writings of the great thinker Nagarjuna), the second coming from its Taoist influences. The mix of these two elements provides many of the unique features of Zen itself.

Nagarjuna, in his most important work, the *Mulamadhyamakakarika* (or Fundamentals of the Middle Way), set out to transcend scholastic infighting between Buddhist sects by demonstrating that "the problems of abhidharmic analysis are intrinsically irresolvable; that is, the various philosophical sects of Buddhism were founded on distinctions that must be seen as tentative rather than absolute" (Kasulis 1981, 17). The outcome of Nagarjuna's work is the demonstration that language itself cannot adequately describe reality as we experience it. Nagarjuna terms the "logical interdependence" of supposedly opposite categories which underlies this inadequacy as *sunyata*, or emptiness (see T. P. Kasulis 1981, 16–19, 21–24).[5] Basically, then, language and the resultant bipolar philosophies that arise from language are highly suspect, because they conceal great trenches of illusion and separate us from experiencing reality directly. Thus if we look into language and concepts closely enough, we will see the chaos, which, of necessity, lurks beneath the supposedly ordered world of language.[6]

The second tenet, which flows more from the Taoist tradition yet goes hand-in-hand with Nagarjuna's work, is basically the claim (which must of necessity lack rational, linguistic proof, as noted above) that experience arises from a source that cannot be described either in terms of being or nonbeing, as it is ontologically prior to either. At the same time, however, this distinctionless Tao (the Tao that cannot be told) can participate, through language and/or conceptualization, in distinguishable reality at any time or place. In other words, a rational, experimental, multipolar order can arise from this nondistinguishable source. Therefore, while we can, and generally do, speak of categories and distinctions, we should always do so in the knowledge that essentially these distinctions are only relative and not absolute, as the source of being (and nonbeing) exists before these distinctions. In order to clarify references to this a priori state, I will follow Kasulis's convention of prefixing terms dealing with this "pre-reflective" state with the term *without*. Thus, for example, the state that precedes the two distinctual states, being and nonbeing, can be termed "without-being" (thus it follows that the term *Mu*, which is most often translated as "no-thing," would be "without-thing"). Although we must always keep in mind Nagarjuna's warning that any conceptualization of a fundamentally "without-conceptual" state is highly suspect, this prefix does avoid the bipolar connotative baggage that the prefix *non* would of necessity carry with it.

In Zen, these two interdependent points intermix, resulting in Zen's cynical rejection of the efficacy of language and at the same time its promotion of the search for enlightenment as a way to bypass the pitfalls of conceptualization and perceive reality (the void, or emptiness, or Tao) in its plenary, primal state: the vision the Buddha had upon "awakening." Thus, Zen, even more than Taoism, defies description and categorization: "Zen refuses even tentatively to be defined or described in any manner" (Suzuki 1949, 267). "It is neither a religion nor a philosophy. It is a path of liberation"—a means to an end (Foster 1989, 28). One of the reasons it is so difficult to define Zen is that it "is ultimately a state of mind" (Foster 1989, 30); all the writings and sayings associated with it are, and can only be, indications of how to achieve this state. Once the ideal state of mental perception—satori or enlightenment—is fully realized, there is no further need of any of the tools Zen provides to help one along.[7] As noted above, one of the great mistakes in Zen is to pay too much attention to the literature and teachings associated with it: "[T]o point at the moon a finger is needed, but woe to those who take the finger for the moon" (Suzuki 1949, 19); or, as Dogen would characterize life and dogma, "Do not accept any view on mere faith; authenticate it within your own experience" (Kasulis 1981, 102).[8] Thus, in the literature associated with Zen, an overly logical framework of thought and careful analysis are not only useless for finding and defining Zen, they are detrimental in the extreme. Pretty much the only way to uncover the truths of Zen is to study it by practicing zazen "some years" with a master (Suzuki 1949, 267)—a feat beyond the capabilities or inclinations of most people (and a rather nice way to counter criticism from the casual, causal observer).[9]

Does this mean that there is no way for the uninitiate to even get a glimpse into what Zen is and means? Not necessarily. As Zen disclaims any absolute dependence on scripture or ritual (Stryk 1968, 334), all one need do is "think the right way" in order to understand Zen (although thinking this way involves discarding one's ego-centered way of life—Hakuin's "Great Death"—which is something of a stumbling block). In fact, all of life, if seen correctly, embodies Zen. Thus, as myriad masters have pointed out, there is a Zen way to approach *everything* we do. Thus, Zen—as a particular way of seeing and interacting with the world—may appear in religions besides Buddhism (see Suzuki 1949, 318–19, as well as the writings of Thomas Merton). "Essentially Ch'an [Zen] is an intuitive method of spiritual *training* whose aim is the discovery of the reality within, which can be described as the fundamental unity in all that makes up the world. This reality is the Buddha-nature or . . . the Void" (Stryk 1968, 335; my emphasis). Once a person intuits this unity, this master's life will be complete in everything he (or she—though women traditionally have been excluded from Zen teaching and enlightenment) does: the master eats when he eats; he sleeps when he sleeps (Suzuki 1949, 24). Although these circular statements may sound trivial, it is the focus and concentration of doing each thing wholly and without reserve that exemplifies a master's transcendence of the world of conceptual mediation and multiplicity.

Why is the great effort of will and training required to achieve this state of detachment and perception necessary? According to Zen teachers, these years of training and concentrated effort are the only way out of the cycle of birth-desire-death that is the source of all our suffering (*dukkha* in Sanskrit).

> Life, as most of us live it, is suffering. . . . As long as life is a form of struggle, it cannot be anything but pain. . . . One may not be conscious of all this, and may go on indulging in those momentary pleasures that are afforded by the senses. But this being unconscious does not in the least alter the facts of life. (Suzuki 1949, 15)

Desiring an escape from the suffering of life, however, precludes our getting away from it. As one of the original Mahayana Buddhist sutras—the *Lankávatára Sutra*[10]—states,

> Those who are suffering or who fear suffering, think of *Nirvana* as an escape and a recompense. They imagine that *Nirvana* consists in the future annihilation of the senses and the sense-minds; they are not aware that Universal Mind and *Nirvana* are One, and that this life-and-death world and *Nirvana* are not to be separated. These ignorant ones, instead of meditating on the meaninglessness of *Nirvana*, talk of different ways of emancipation. (Stryk 1968, 277)

A thirst (*tanha*) for anything—even for release from it—causes us to fall deeper into the world of desire and suffering. For Zen, as for Taoism, the solution to this problem is an abandonment of all desire (Foster 1989, 29). Where Taoist thought proclaims the ideal of *Wei-wu-wei,* Zen states that

> 'The abandonment of everything' means the transcending of the dualism of soul and body, of subject and object, or that which knows and that which is known, of 'it is' and 'it is not,' of soul and soul-lessness. . . . (Suzuki 1949, 159)

This is, in fact, the state which T. P. Kasulis indicates by use of the prefix *without.* The "Great Death," as Hakuin describes it, of the ego-driven self is not an escape from the world but a release from the tyranny of dualistic thinking and the illusion of causality, and this leads ultimately to the state described in Sanskrit as *nirvana* and in Japanese as *satori*, which is "the Alpha and Omega of Zen Buddhism" (Suzuki 1949, 230).

> There is only one reality—this world, right here and now—but this world may be experienced in two different ways. Samsara is the relative, phenomenal world as usually experienced, which is delusively understood to consist of a collection of discrete objects (including "me") that interact causally in space and time. *Nirvana* is that *same world but as it is in itself*, nondually incorporating both subject and object into a whole. (Loy 1988, 11; my emphasis)

That the state of nirvana (or satori) is identical to the suffering state of Samsara cannot be overemphasized: there is no difference at all in the world itself when one becomes enlightened; there is only difference in the "self"—or, better yet, in one's vision. The alogical, intuitive understanding of the world that is nirvana removes the distinction between observer and actor in the world, and thus, the master breaks free of the dualistic world.

Along these lines, one of the most celebrated methods of freeing oneself from the tyranny of the dualistic world is to make use of the Zen koan—something akin to a joke or riddle that has no logical solution. While this existential riddle is most often associated with the Rinzai school (Hakuin's branch), which advocates a quick, violent conversion to the state of satori, the Soto school (Dogen's branch) occasionally utilizes this method with certain students. In any case, the most famous collection of Zen koans is the *(Zen Shu) Mu Mon Kwan* (or the "Gateless [or "without-gate"] Barrier to Zen Experience"), a collection of forty-eight legendary anecdotal riddles, together with commentary by Zen master Mumon Ekai.[11] When, and if, a master selects one of these koans (or some other of his choosing), the student concentrates for hours, days, months, or longer on his koan until nothing else exists for him. When, finally, he breaks the chain of logic that has been holding him to the common world, "student and *koan* are as one, [and] there is neither examined nor examiner" (Stryk 1968, 367). This moment is described as the "Great Doubt." At this point, the master may upset the student's equilibrium in a seemingly obtuse, yet well prepared move: he may ask a simple question, make an absurd statement, or even strike the student (one student loses a finger in a famous case) in order to force the student over the edge of rational, logical thinking. If all goes well, the "Great Death" of the student's ego will lead to enlightenment, or satori.

The pain and potential violence involved in this "awakening" process may prompt us to ask, as we did with Taoism, whether the benefits of Zen outweigh the troubles: is this merely a negativist mysticism bent on an abstracted annihilation of life and action?

A Zen devotee would answer with an emphatic no. Yes there is a negative phase in which doubt and cynicism about the values and morality (and even reality) of language, concepts, and actions—in effect, the everyday world—must be entertained and these values eventually rejected; but ultimately, "this transcending is not attained by merely negating the soul or the will, but by throwing light upon its nature, by realizing it as it is in itself" (Suzuki 1949, 159). Or, in terms of Western philosophical concepts (which must, of course, be viewed with some suspicion),

> there is a higher epistemological perspective achievable through the process of personal self-cultivation [zazen] and this higher epistemological perspective is correlative with the ontological status of reality. Unless one achieves a higher epistemological perspective, true reality does not appear. (Nagatomo 1992, 75)

Thus Nagarjuna's devaluation of conceptualization is not at heart nihilistic, but rather is a movement toward a different, or "higher," perspective, and this process approaches "emptiness" *(Sunyata),* as doubt over the efficacy of the common dualistic mode of thinking leads one to the empty/plenary world-as-it-is.[12] The detachment of satori is not the absence of life and soul; rather, it is the perfection of life. "Absence means freedom from duality and all defilements" (Stryk 1968, 339)—the release from preconception—and thus the freedom to live each moment fully. And this goal of a life free from suffering is anything but an abstract concept for an impractical mystic:

> The common notion that mystics are dreamers and star-gazers ought to be corrected, as it has no foundation in facts. Indeed, psychologically there is a most intimate and profound relationship between a practical turn of mind and a certain type of mysticism; the relationship is not merely conceptual or metaphysical. If mysticism is true its truth must be a practical one, verifying itself in every act of ours. . . . (Suzuki 1949, 319)

It is in the *act* of living that Zen is expressed, not in any abstract formulas or reflections.

This concern with every act leads to our last—and very important—observation: Zen writing, Zen stories, and Zen itself are all rooted in the moment. Abstraction and conceptualization are nearly nonexistent in Zen, at least in a naive or uncomplicated manner. Dogma or codification are considered suspect in the extreme and are rejected outright. Thus, any stories that are told, poetry, *koans*, and comments from master to student are either concerned with concrete realities,[13] or with exemplifying the contingent nature of dualistic thinking, not with setting up a systematic religion or philosophy of "Zen." Zen paints a picture of normal everyday life—but from the vantage of the master. What we get are glimpses of the "real" world from the Zen "point of view."

> Taking all in all, Zen is emphatically a matter of personal experience; if anything can be called radically empirical, it is Zen. No amount of reading, no amount of teaching, and no amount of contemplation will ever make one a Zen master. Life itself must be grasped in the midst of its flow; to stop it for examination and analysis is to kill it, leaving its cold corpse to be embraced. (Suzuki 1949, 362)

This empiricism and concreteness reveals the importance and depth of the connection between Beckett's writing and Zen. Although the aspect of Zen with which Beckett is most commonly connected is its description of the continuous, cyclical suffering of the world's inhabitants, I believe that his implicit rejection of the logical and the narratively cohesive, as well as the value he places on terseness and brevity and the sense of imminence and immediacy his plays evoke connect both the form and the underlying intent of his work in profound ways with the tenets of Zen. In *Not I*, for example, in which Mouth (a lighted pair of lips some eight feet above stage level) recounts the story of a woman who moves from silence to incessant speech, the recursive narrative, which depends more on a form of accretion than exposition for meaning, generates through Mouth's words an imminent, compelling picture of an ego in the throes of the Great Doubt. In denying any explicit reference to herself, Mouth strengthens yet problematizes the continuity of her ego-consciousness: her refrain, "who? . . . no! . . . she!" (217) forces to the front the insupportability of the concept of the "I," and at the same time reveals the strength of this concept. Mouth's suffering is exposed by the play as the direct effect of her inability to release the "I" from the conceptual duality of presence-absence.

From the ancient (though still profoundly influential) religio-philosophy of Zen, let us now turn our attention to what must seem the opposite end of the spectrum: an outgrowth of Western empiricism, the physical science and mathematics of dynamic systems—or Chaos—theory. The vast gulf in temporal and cultural milieus notwithstanding, there is an amazing amount of common ground between Zen and Chaos theory. Chaos theory, as I will indicate, is a system that incorporates much of the same re-visioning of the universe, as well as much of the same cultural reenfranchisement of a

where $T_1 > T_2$, and thus ΔS is positive (entropy grows). If, for example, an engine does some work (like move a car), it not only provides the useful energy necessary to push the car, it also generates a great deal of heat that is dissipated into the world at large and is therefore unretrievable. This essentially means that the universe can travel only one way. We can never "rewind the film" to repair the piece of porcelain we just shattered by dropping it on the floor (consider how a film is obviously playing in reverse if on it we see hundreds of pieces of porcelain spontaneously combine into a plate. See Hayles 1990, chapter 2 [esp. pp. 38ff.], for a more complete discussion of the broader socio-scientific environment in which this law was postulated.)

Eventually, this change in attitude—combined with the brilliance of Einstein, Heisenberg, Planck and others—led to formulation of the theories of relativity and quantum mechanics. It is notable that while to a large extent the theory of relativity has been considered the capstone of classical physics, quantum mechanics, which evolved quickly in the 1920s, is generally recognized as a massive break with the classical paradigm. According to quantum mechanics, the distinction between particles and fields (or waves) is not an absolute one, as all fields produce momentum and all particles have energetic wavelengths associated with them.[15] As a result of this, the two quantities that must be known for physics to function—position in space and velocity—cannot be known with infinite precision at the same time. Basically, this is what the famous Heisenberg uncertainty principle—$m\Delta v\Delta x \gtrapprox h$—shows: the uncertainty in the momentum ($m\Delta v$) times the uncertainty in the position (Δx) of a particle is nearly equivalent to, but never less than h, a very small number called Planck's constant. However, the tiny value of Planck's constant ($4.14 \times 10^{-15}\ eV \bullet s$) assures us that, on the level of everyday events, we will never notice this absolute uncertainty. For example, if we know the velocity of a 45 gram golf ball traveling at 75 m/s to 1%, the resultant uncertainty of the ball's position will be on the order of 10^{-32} meters, which is about 10^{17} times smaller than the nucleus of an atom. Thus, it was not until extremely accurate measurements of very small objects were possible that quantum mechanics became relevant and these uncertainties were noticed. On the other hand, our modern world is absolutely dependent on the intricacies of quantum mechanics: the computer, the tool that practically defines our work and culture today, is built on the solid-state transistor, whose development was the direct result of quantum theory's postulation of the statistical behavior of electrons in semiconductive media.

Though not generally considered of consequence to the everyday world, the new understanding of the universe generated by the twin theories of relativity and quantum mechanics clearly necessitated a paradigm shift from classical to modern physics (and from "premodern" to "modern" sociological attitudes). First, no matter how large the so-called Laplacian brain, the universe cannot be understood fully for all time; and second, as a result of the uncertainty principle the experimenter is an integral part of the experiment performed. The latter observation is a consequence of physical interaction: when a physicist attempts to locate the position, say, of a particle, she necessarily imparts energy to that particle (either through light focused on the particle or by some other means of measurement), and this energy *unpredictably* changes the velocity of that particle. The result is that the method, and even the psychological intent, of the observer—the stochastic elements of the experiment—are integrally related to the experiment itself. Therefore there can be no abstracted, disinterested observer, as in the classical paradigm.[16] Furthermore, according to the first of the observations above (and to a large extent because of the necessary involvement of the experimenter in the experiment) the universe in its entirety is *in essence* unpredictable. The ramifications of this claim are akin to the Nietzschean aphorism, "God is dead," as the possibility of an omniscient, rational, overarching god who understands and controls all elements of the universe (the Laplacian brain), is necessarily rejected.[17] Thus, moving in tandem with a cultural world grown suddenly fearful of its own horrible abilities (via the Great War), and fearing a complete lack of cosmic direction, quantum mechanics undermined any deistic understanding of the universe. At the same time, however, it opened the world to an exciting freedom and possibility that could not fully exist in the older socio-scientific order.

The stage was set for the next half-century, as scientists and philosophers wrestled with the profound implications of a new vision of the universe. At the same time, there was a continual counterargument that the random fluctuations of electrons, while profound in theory, have little to do with the statistical behavior of large objects, or even large groups of small objects. Quantum mechanics and electrodynamics was considered the province of abstract mathematicians, scientists, and philosophers, not the domain of the everyday world.

After the further disillusionment and fragmentation caused by World War Two, even the idea of a well-ordered realm of the "real," macroscopic world began to seem more a construct than a reality, and, over the next decades, artists and thinkers started playing with the boundaries of narrative cohesion and absolutism (in essence, of closure of the universe). At the same time, stunning advances in the digital computer allowed more and more massive calculations and sets of numbers to become accessible: calculations that would take hundreds of hours with pencil and paper could be performed in seconds by computers. Via the convergence of these sociotechnical streams, by the 1970s, the stage was set for thinkers to "discover" in the real, macroscopic world, the same chaotic uncertainty found in the world of the atom.

The original empirical evidence and impetus for what would come to be known as Chaos theory came from the unlikely area of meteorology in the early 1960s. Edward Lorenz, a meteorologist with a background in theoretical mathematics and an interest in using the primitive computers of the day to model the changing nature of the weather, discovered that tiny changes in the conditions he put into his computerized weather machine could create vast differences in the outcome of the "weather" in future days.[18] This seemed to go against reason, as classical physics and even quantum mechanics had taught that small fluctuations in initial conditions (the conditions of the universe "now") would be damped out over time, so that, on the large scales of macroscopic behavior—like weather systems—there would arise no appreciable differences between two nearly identical systems. What Lorenz's simple series of computerized formulas indicated, however, was that these supposedly inconsequential variations in fact *did* make a difference in large-scale behavior. Lorenz also realized that this fact—that minute fluctuations lead to large variations over time—meant that one would never be able to predict a complex (or nonlinear) system like the weather in deterministic fashion. As with quantum mechanics, a repudiation of the efficacy of the Laplacian brain was in the offing; yet here, the inability of this "brain" to predict accurately the future state of the universe from initial conditions was not simply one of theoretical, small-scale import: what Lorenz had uncovered was that, even on the macroscopic scale of the quotidian, we can never hope to predict deterministically or even with any degree of accuracy the movement of the universal machine. The inability to determine the precise outcome of a complex system means that nonlinear systems inherently defy singular solutions. A famous example of this in the meteorological world is the "butterfly effect": if we had weather stations planted over every cubic meter of the earth that all took measurements simultaneously, we could still never predict the weather around the world indefinitely from that time forward: the motion of the air from the wings of a butterfly that went undetected by these weather stations could change the weather from sunshine to rain in New York City a month later.

What, we might ask, if we could put weather stations over the earth in infinitely small spaces so that everything was covered? Would it not then be possible to predict the weather indefinitely? This is where the results of quantum mechanics become significant: no matter how small and accurate our measuring devices, there is *fundamentally* a level of accuracy (given by the Heisenberg uncertainty principle) that we will never be able to achieve. Thus, no matter how powerful and numerous our measuring devices, and no matter how smart the brain interpreting these measurements, it is *absolutely* impossible to predict the large-scale behavior of the universe in the future. As earth-shaking as this discovery was, it was not heralded for several years, as no serious scientists or mathematicians gave much heed to the workings of weather forecasters. It was not until the mid-1970s, through the work of such people as Benoit B. Mandelbrot (on the empirical side) and Feigenbaum (on the more theoretical side) that the study of Chaos gained a significant reputation in the scientific community.

If, then, the science of Chaos necessitates a paradigm shift in the sciences (and other fields) today, what exactly is the domain of this new field? To begin with, we should note the linguistic subtleties of the term *Chaos theory.* First, as a convention in this work, the *science* of Chaos is distinguished from the normal usage of chaos by the capitalization of the word; hopefully, this will reduce the confusion between the two terms, the first of which is a carefully defined field, the second of which is an ancient Greek term with a lot of history—and therefore connotative baggage—associated with it. Second, while in this work the aura of connotations around the term *chaos* (and *Chaos*) make it highly useful, it is precisely to be rid of the chaotic connotations that scientists who work in the field now rarely refer to their work as the study of Chaos. For most scientists these days, this new field is termed *dynamic systems theory,* which indicates that the science has to do with nonstatic, nonlinear systems of equations or natural phenomena.

While this semantic caveat may not seem important, it does indicate a decisive break with the classical mode of thinking on the problems of motion and dynamics. In a Newtonian system, while most systems are understood as dynamic in the sense that they are in motion, the equations describing them are supposed to be solvable to a unique, static solution describing a motion that alters in a consistent, well-behaved pattern over time. Events and equations that do not match this format were/are considered aberrations of little significance. For dynamic systems theory, on the other hand, the evolution of a set of equations or phenomena is understood *usually* to consist of the systems that Newtonian mechanics assumes are aberrations. In other words, in this new way of modeling the universe, the motion of particles cannot be reduced to equations yielding easy algebraic or analytical solutions. The patterns of movement of these particles vary in a fundamentally unpredictable, dynamic manner over time. As an example of the difference of perspective, classical physics would concentrate on a smoothly flowing river (a laminar flow) that behaves in very predictable ways that can be described by solvable equations. Dynamic systems (or

Chaos) theory, on the other hand, would concentrate on the turbulence of a river rapids where water is being splashed, jarred and whirled in violent, unpredictable ways that cannot be described by easily solvable equations. In the first instance, a floating leaf would continue along a fairly straight path; in the second, the leaf would be tossed about so much that predicting where it would be a minute later would be a guessing game. What this all means is that individually we *cannot* predict what will happen to objects (or numbers in an equation). At the same time, however, we can describe the time-dependent behavior of the system as a whole.

One of the best ways to see the difference between the classical paradigm and the newer paradigm of dynamic systems theory is to work with one of the most important spatial modeling tools in physics, that of phase space. Phase space is a malleable abstracted space—something like a thin sheet of rubber that can be pulled, bent, and stretched—that contains not only the everyday dimensions of height, length and width, but the associated vectors of motion in each of these three directions. The motion of a particle in real space is determined by how it "rolls" along the curved sheet of phase space. However, for a completely uncoupled three-dimensional system, there are six associated dimensions in phase space, which is obviously rather difficult to picture![19] What use is this abstracted space? In essence, phase space maps the two most important elements of physics—position and motion (note for example the Heisenberg uncertainty principle)—together in one space.[20] Using this mapping, it is possible to visualize the characteristics of an object's motion graphically via a pattern on a piece of paper, on a computer screen, or in one's mind.

Let us look at two examples of phase space diagrams—one the diagram of the all-important pendulum, on which Newtonian mechanics is based, the other the diagram of the Lorenz "butterfly attractor," probably the most famous phase space diagram ever drawn. The first of these figures exemplifies the classical view of the universe as well behaved and algebraically solvable, while the second evinces the ordered chaos of dynamic systems theory. First, the Newtonian pendulum.[21] If we let go of a *frictionless* pendulum from a small distance off-center, it will swing back and forth with the same period indefinitely. In two-dimensional phase space, the figure this pendulum traces out is a simple circle (see figure 1).

As the pendulum swings downward from its highest point, where x is its maximum value and v is zero (intersecting the x axis), it gathers speed in a well-defined manner until v reaches its maximum speed and x is zero, or the pendulum is straight down (intersecting the v axis). At this point, the speed again begins to drop (as the pendulum swings out and rises) and the displacement, or x value, rises; then the pattern begins again (figures 2–4).

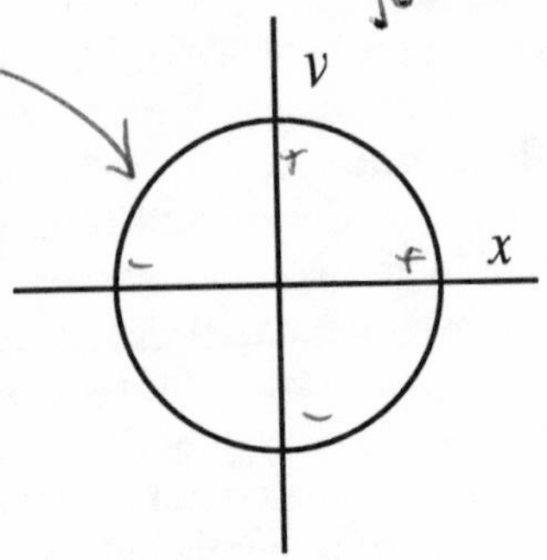

Fig. 1. Phase-space diagram of the two dimensional attractor of a pendulum in constant motion.

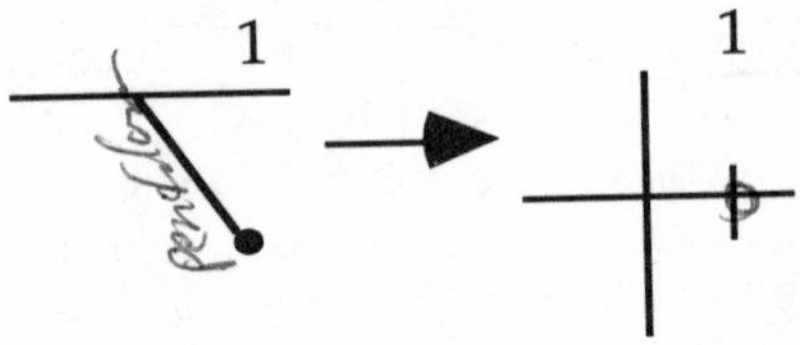

Fig. 2. The motion of the pendulum begins, the point in phase space intersecting the *x* axis.

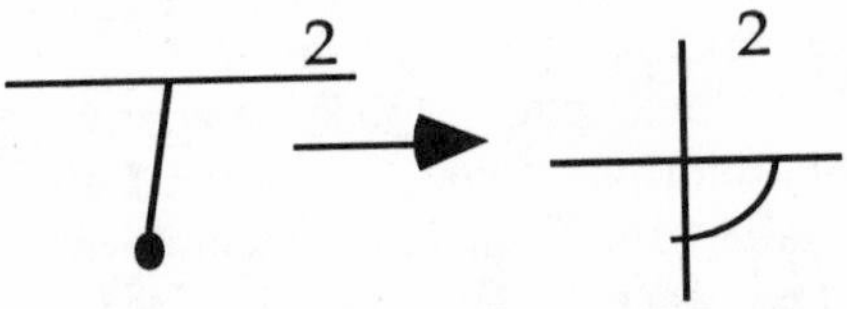

Fig. 3. The pendulum has swung down to its lowest point, the speed is greatest, and the displacement is near zero; in phase space, one quarter of the circle has been traced out.

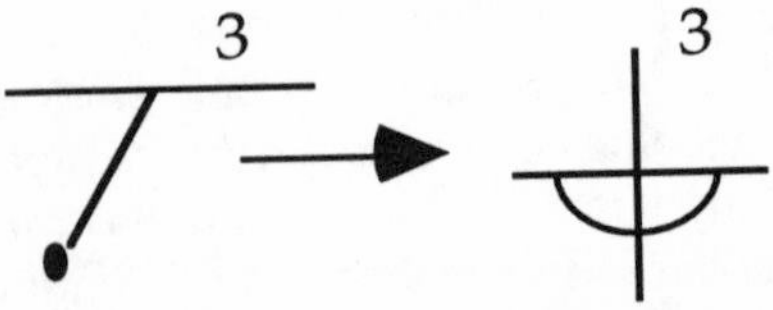

Fig. 4. The pendulum and its phase-space diagram have now completed half their motion; speed is again zero and displacement is maximum, though on the opposite side.

Thus, the pendulum circles indefinitely in a closed loop, the physical system repeating every time the circle closes on itself. We now have perfect closure and a well-defined pattern in phase space, indicating well-behaved motion in real space.

If, instead, we take a "real" pendulum with friction acting on it, the motion of the pendulum in phase space will be a spiral into the center, where both *x* and *y* are zero—indicating no motion (see figure 5).

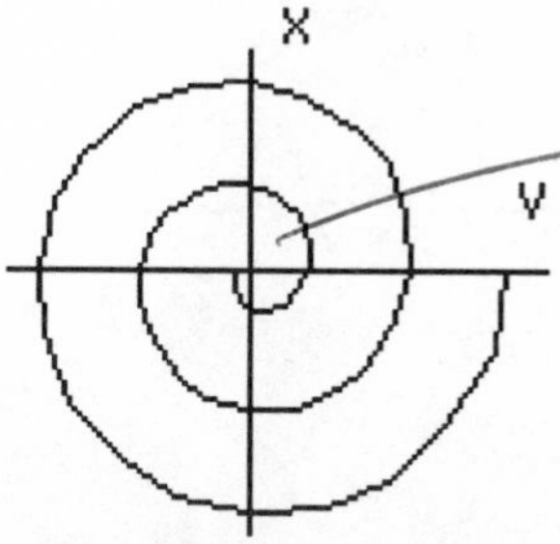

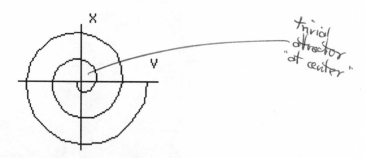

Fig. 5. The spiraling phase-space motion of a damped pendulum; the spiral is *not* the attractor—the attractor is the point at the center of the *x* and *v* axes. This is known as a "point," or trivial attractor.

The phase space circle for the pendulum in the first case and the point in the second case are called attractors; they "attract" the motion of the particle (in phase space) to them. What this means is that any minor fluctuation or disturbance to the pendulum (such as a draft) may momentarily cause the motion to move away from the perfect circle (or point); but this "extra" motion will soon be damped out, and the motion of the pendulum will return to the pattern of the attractor.

How does what Lorenz discovered in the equations of motion of his weather simulator differ from the attractors traced out by the Newtonian pendulum? Let us begin with the famous Lorenz, or butterfly, attractor. This is a three-dimensional attractor (as opposed to the two-dimensional attractor circle of the Newtonian pendulum); thus, since we have only a piece of two-dimensional paper on which to draw, all we can draw is the "shadow" of the attractor on paper (we must therefore imagine from figure 6 what the actual attractor looks like).[22]

From even this crude drawing of the attractor, we can see the two spirals that form the "wings" of the butterfly; more important, we can see how complex and finely detailed, yet ordered and bounded, the attractor seems to be. What is not readily noticeable from this projection is that, in three

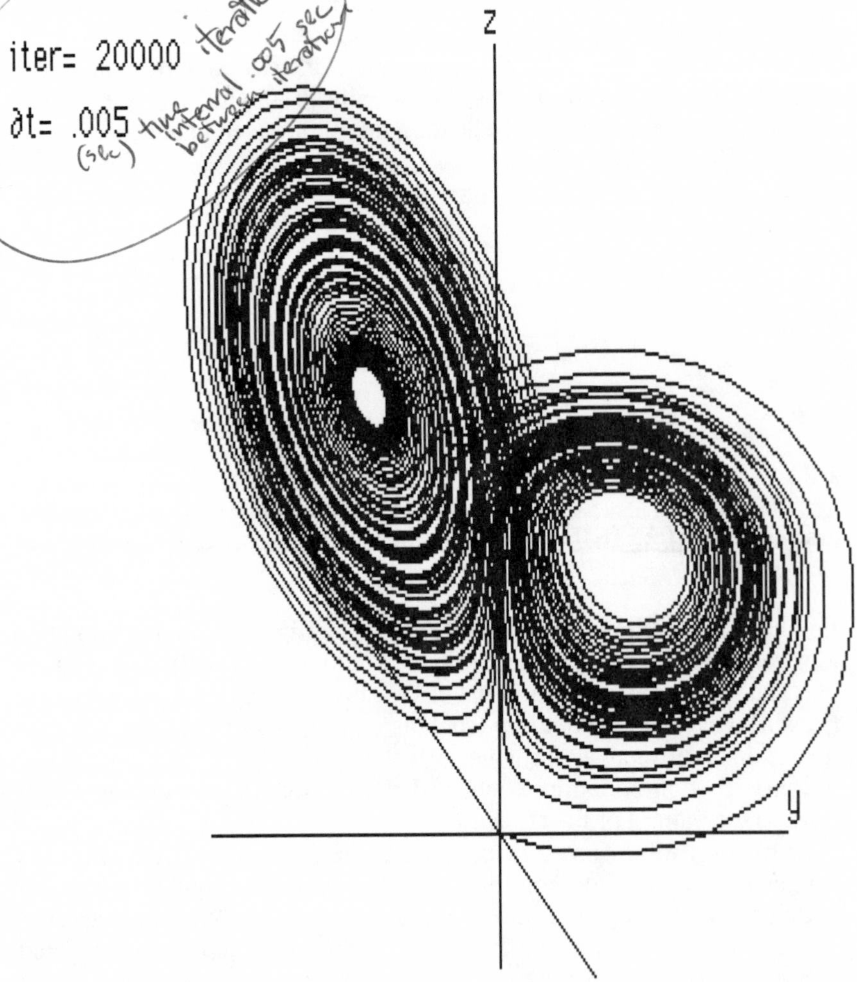

Fig. 6. The strange attractor Lorenz discovered. Note that the two spiral arms are in three-dimensional space, at approximately a right angle to each other.

dimensions, the lines traced out by this attractor *never* intersect. This means that no matter how long the equations of motion are left to run, they will never circle back upon themselves and begin a cycle over again. While the points may become infinitely close to each other (causing the points in the projection to appear to merge), they will never overlap; yet at the same time, the figure is clearly bounded with an obvious intuitive "form" (the butterfly-like wings).

In systems like this Chaotic Lorenzian weather system, behavior, not analytical solutions, is describable. This is an important element in the new "vision" of dynamic systems theory: as opposed to the classical paradigm, and in conjunction with quantum dynamics, we have no way of predicting what will occur to individual elements of a system; we can only describe the behavior of the system as a whole. The "pool ball" atoms of the Newtonian universe gave way to the unpredictable motion of atomic particle/waves of quantum mechanics, but this did not affect our macroscopic world. Now, with Chaos theory, even the readily visible macroscopic elements of a system—for example, water in a river rapids—are found to be *fundamentally* unpredictable. Yet—and this is just as important—the behavior of the system as a whole is completely, deterministically, predictable. Although we cannot predict with any accuracy where our leaf on a rapids will turn up downstream, we can describe the motion of the water as a whole; therefore we can with absolute certainty give the range of positions in which the leaf may turn up. Thus the paradox: Chaos theory is the science of deterministic unpredictability.

This class of attractor, which has been studied in greater and greater range and detail as computers continue to improve, is generally known as "strange" because the phase-space figures have at one and the same time the boundedness of a classical attractor and the never-ending nonclosure and complex behavior of insoluble systems. Investigation of these attractors has been of great significance because they indicate the ordered nature of seemingly chaotic systems—*and* because the attractors explain why, for example, Lorenz's equations eventually produce such different results from such similar initial conditions. As the points along the attractor are infinitesimally far apart, *any* variation of the initial point at which we begin (including quantum fluctuations) will create potentially vast differences in the later behavior of the system. Thus the apparently chaotic behavior: in Lorenz's chaotic weather machine (or a turbulent river), if we place two particles arbitrarily close together (that is, so close that we cannot tell that they are not at the same spot), they can and will end up in very different places sometime later. Mathematically, this behavior is explained by the stretching and folding of phase space until the "dough" of space is infinitely thin and folded; therefore two points that start out next to each other on this dough will, after being stretched and folded many times, end up in apparently random positions relative to each other, even though the action of folding and stretching can be simple and deterministic.[23]

The "deterministically unpredictable" nature of Chaos theory is, however, only half the story. There is a very important branch of Chaos theory, pioneered by Ilya Prigogine and recently taken up by others, which is more concerned with the striking fact that Chaotic or highly complex systems (those far from equilibrium), can and often do produce order. Although this branch is related to the "order in Chaos" branch discussed above, its concentration is different: whereas the branch we have been discussing focuses on the type of order that exists within a Chaotic system (and the chaos lurking within ordered systems), the Prigogine branch focuses more on the fact that actual (everyday) order can arise in a complex system. Because of the complex interaction of order and disorder in systems "at the edge of chaos," this branch has in recent years assumed the name, "complexity theory." The rich interaction of a multitude of elements in these disordered systems (which range from the stock market to the origins of life) allow "the system as a whole to undergo *spontaneous self-organization*" (Waldrop 1992, 11).

The importance of this developing aspect of Chaos theory cannot be overstated, since it indicates that, for example, from the chaos of the Big Bang, it was almost inevitable that ordered systems such as our planet and solar system would develop. The regenerative force of this theory, allowing ordered states to arise from highly entropic ones, will be of great import to our discussion of *Endgame* (and other plays), as it complicates the nineteenth-century vision of a universe winding down (via the second law of thermodynamics) to which Hamm seems attached.[24]

In addition to this very important aspect of Chaos theory, there are two other elements we must discuss in order to fully appreciate the new vision of the world presented by this science. First, we need to elaborate which types of systems tend toward Chaotic behavior (more precisely, which special systems do *not*); and second, how and why Chaotic systems pack a great deal of information (as defined by information theory) into a tiny space.

The first of these we have already touched on in addressing the differences between the Newtonian model of the universe and the newer, Quantum/Chaos model. Let us use the all-important (in physics, at least) pendulum as an example. In the Newtonian paradigm, the swing of the pendulum is well ordered and algebraically solvable; the nonlinear elements of the system (if, for example, we release the pendulum from too high or drive it too hard) are not taken into account, as they are considered a minor aberration to the well-behaved system. On the other hand, Chaos theory claims that the "minor aberration" to the well-behaved system is, in fact, the system's normal mode of behavior, the predictable behavior of the Newtonian pendulum being only a special case of the unpredictable behavior of the *complete* pendulum system. In the classical example, the pendulum gently set in motion rocks steadily back and forth, keeping time like a metronome. In the second case, the "overdriven" pendulum rockets violently about, then comes to almost complete stillness, then moves in wide, unpredictable arcs. In both cases the swing of a pendulum is being described; yet, what is significant about the swing (the linear or the nonlinear part of it) has shifted. To be more specific, the formula for the force-dependent motion of a simple harmonic oscillator (the Newtonian pendulum) is $F(x) = -kx$. This is a linear equation, as the force on the bob is equal to its position, x (to the first power). More generally, however, the formulaic representation of a real pendulum has one or more terms that are *not* linear: $F(x) \approx -kx + \mu x^3$. The first term is the same, but the second (where μ is normally a very small number) relates the force acting on the bob to x to the third power—a nonlinear term—so when x is small, the term μx^3 essentially disappears and we are left with the linear equation of the simple harmonic oscillator.[25] The nonlinear domain of Chaos theory is breached, however, when this second term becomes large (either because μ is of significant size or because x is great), making the equation far more complex to solve and causing the motion of the particle to become unpredictable. The difference here between Chaos theory and the classical paradigm is not that either has added something new to the problem of the oscillator—even in the seventeenth century, it was well known that there were "correction terms" to the linear pendulum equation. What has changed is that the nonlinear term has been moved from the fringes of science, where it was basically ignored, to the center of the ring, as it were, where it is now considered the most important and interesting element of the equation. As with Zen, "The change is not in how the world actually is . . . but in how it is seen" (Hayles 1991, 8).

Part of the reason for this change is certainly the technology of the computer, which allows graphical, analytical solutions to be performed—something impossible before the computational power of these machines—but this change has also come about for sociological reasons, as the scientific community now finds it acceptable to describe the behavior of a system without needing to know its deterministic solution (something akin to the God-existentialism shift that took place during the late nineteenth and early twentieth centuries). For Beckett, as we will find, this change in vision is a crucial step in defining art of a new order.[26] As he said of the painter Bram Van Velde, and which applies equally well to his own work, "There is more than a difference of degree between being short, short of the world, short of self, and being without these esteemed commodities. The one is a predicament, the other not" (Beckett 1949, 102). In other words, the problems generated by the shortcomings of the old paradigm create a "predicament" for those living under its sway. Making a clean break to another mode of seeing, however—being "without" the baggage of the old system— frees one by removing the source of the problem.

One of the methods Beckett, Zen, and Chaos theory share in precipitating this shift in vision is the process of iteration. For Zen, the practice of zazen is one of endless repetition in search of the breaking point of the ego-consciousness. In Beckett's plays, as later chapters will clarify, a circling back over similar events and words helps break down narrative closure and linear explication of plot, allowing a new view of the world to creep in at the edges. These plays then function like Chaotic water in a river, "moving back and forth in local eddies and swirls, sometimes against the macro flow of the piece, following now one stream, now another . . ." (Hancock, forthcoming, 3). For Chaos theory as a whole, this metaphor is appropriate, as the behavior of a system can be described without an algebraic solution to it via the "swirls" and "eddies" of iterative feedback loops.

Put simply, the behavior of a time-dependent system (like that of a river) can be described by iterating the system through many cycles, which are some small time, ∂t, apart. If, then, we start some system at position x_0 and velocity v_0, and proceed to calculate the position and velocity after time ∂t, we have done one iteration. Next, we take the *output* velocity and position ($x_{\partial t}$ and $v_{\partial t}$) and put them back into the same equation, calculate the equation after another time ∂t and generate our next position and velocity ($x_{2\partial t}$ and $v_{2\partial t}$). Continuing this feedback loop, where the output of the last calculation acts as the input for the next one, we can "draw" the behavior of the system for an indefinite period of time. The practical limitations of this method are that, if the calculations for each iteration are at all complex, and if we must do many iterations to get a good sense of the behavior of the system, the time necessary to generate a picture of the system's behavior can quickly grow very large. Thus the computer, which can perform millions of calculations per second, is absolutely essential to the iterative feedback calculations performed in the work of Chaos theory. For example, the picture of the Lorenz attractor above is generated by this method of feedback iterations, and required 20,000 iterations (with time interval ∂t of 0.005 seconds) of a fairly complex series of calculations. By hand, generating this picture would be little short of impossible, but with a home computer it took just a few seconds' time. It is the effect of feeding the result of one iteration into the starting value of the next calculation, in conjunction with the nonlinearity of the equation itself, that forces the small fluctuations in initial conditions to become macroscopic differences as the system evolves.

As a kind of iconic representation of the nonlinear, nonclosed, self-similar nature of Chaos theory, the Mandelbrot set has become nearly equated to Chaos theory in many people's minds. The Mandelbrot set (named for Benoit Mandelbrot, who also coined the terms *Chaos theory* and *fractal geometry*), has come to characterize the extraordinary richness of dynamic systems theory for both the layman and the specialist, and yet the set is strikingly simple in its description (and is thus easy to reproduce). To find the Mandelbrot set, we merely iterate the equation, $z \to z^2 - c$ (where z is a complex number and c a complex constant)[27] for many values of c, and find out if the equation "explodes," or goes to infinity. If it does, it is not in the set, and if it remains bounded, it is part of the Mandelbrot set. From this extremely simple formula, if we iterate all values enough times (a simple, but number-intensive undertaking), we will see the picture in photo 3 (inset).[28]

This symmetrical, blimplike shape has what looks like lobes and tendrils coming off it, which, if we look more closely, contain within themselves yet more interesting and complex forms (see photos 4–8).

Thus, from iterative feedback of this simple formula comes an amazingly complex and finely detailed group of images from a set that literally can never be pictured fully: no matter how small the scale or how many iterations we perform, there will always be points within the ∂c of our calculations, and we will never know *with certainty* whether, given enough iterations, the points at the boundaries of the set would eventually race off to infinity. Thus, no matter how powerful our computers or how finely we look at the set, it will always contain new surprises and figures—yet many of the same patterns reappear over and over again on a smaller and smaller scale. This similarity of form over scales (though the image never *actually* repeats, no matter how closely we look) means both that it has a constant fractal dimension and that it generates maximal information.

The first of these terms, *constant fractal dimension*, indicates that the "roughness" of the object is consistent over all scales, meaning that from the smallest to the largest scale the Mandelbrot set repeats itself in terms of complexity and look, all the while never merely duplicating itself at any level. The roughness of a figure like the Mandelbrot set can be given a "fractional" dimension (hence the term *fractal*), which, in this case, lies between the integers 1 (a line) and 2 (a plane). As the old paradigm of Euclidean geometry (which acknowledges only such integer dimensions as a two-dimensional plane) teaches, a fractional dimension is simply not possible, yet describing a figure like the Mandelbrot set in terms of fractals is much simpler and more meaningful than attempting to describe it in terms of Euclidean geometry.

To clarify the differences between these two systems, let us use Mandelbrot's own example of the coastline of England. If asked to measure the English coastline, we would assume from Euclidean geometry that the size of our measuring stick makes no real difference to the number we will get when we measure the coast (aside from the greater accuracy of the smaller stick). If, however, we proceed with the thought-experiment, we see that, if we start by using a measuring stick one kilometer long, we might find that the coastline measures 30,000 kilometers; if we next use a meter stick, we might remeasure the coast as being 40,000 kilometers—this the result of all the small coves and outcroppings we missed with the longer measuring stick. Then, if we use a stick one centimeter long and uncover yet more bumps and crannies, we might find the coast to be more than 55,000 kilometers long. If we continue measuring, using smaller and smaller rulers, we might eventually measure individual grains of sand, molecules, and atoms; thus the length of the English coast will grow continually as our measurements work at a smaller and smaller scale. This sounds like chaos: a coastline with ever-increasing length! Yet, what is consistent with the coastline, just as with the Mandelbrot set, is its degree of "bumpiness." Without regard to what size ruler we use to measure the coastline, it will always repeat its angular ins and outs to the same degree, with each scale looking much like every other. Thus the coastline, the Mandelbrot set, and (according to Chaos theory) rivers, mountains, and a vast number of other things in the world are what are called "self-similar" figures; they repeat the same *type* of image (without ever repeating exactly) over a multitude of different scales, from micro- to macroscopic. At the same time, the self-similarity of these objects on vastly differing scales indicates how tiny fluctuations can lead to large variances later on: as the scales are "coupled" by a consistent, fixed-point symmetry, small initial changes (which are significant on a small scale—and this scale looks like its larger cousins) proceed rapidly up the level of scales until they are of macroscopic importance.

The second aspect of the Mandelbrot set noted above—that it generates maximal information—is connected with what is known as information theory. Briefly, this is a science, developed in the 1940s and 1950s, one of whose main tenets is that information and meaning are independent, separable entities in a message. In other words, the random series of letters, "dfsoiujernoihv," contains more information than the word "tree." You might object that "tree" obviously contains more information than "dfsoiujernoihv," but according to information theory this is not true. Whereas "tree" contains much more meaning (at least to an English-speaking reader), it is highly predictable in its structure. For example, if I wrote "tre_ ," you would have a good chance of filling in the blank with an *e,* whereas if I wrote out the sequence "dfsoiujernoih_ ," you would have no idea what comes next); and, therefore, "tree" contains much less *information* than "dfsoiujernoihv," which is constantly surprising in its randomness (unless, that is, it is repeated three times!). What this separation means for the Mandelbrot set (and for Chaos theory and fractals, in general) is that a simple formula like $z \to z^2 - c$ contains maximum information within it, as it is self-similar but never repetitive. Chaotic systems, then, maximize systemic information, generating much richer patterns than can possibly be contained in any uniquely solvable Newtonian system. An important distinction information theory also brings to the fore is that of "useless" information. A "word" like *eroicxfoijeido,* while containing maximal information, contains little useful information. To adjust this theory to encompass useful information, early workers made a distinction between useful and useless information: "True, gibberish is maximum information. But since it is not desired, it does not really count as information. Hence the maximum amount of information is conveyed by a message that is partly surprising and partly anticipated" (Hayles 1990, 55). Thus, for example, a work of literary art contains maximal good or useful information, as it uses the anticipated elements of language, but in new and surprising ways.[29]

The complex, unpredictable, yet self-similar nature of fractals that helps define Chaos theory is also of extrascientific importance: in many postmodernist and absurdist writings, for example, the value of predictability is secondary to the excitement of generating more information through unpredictability, the ordering of these works moving from the narrative (or linear) to the tangential scalar (nonlinear). Nowhere is this connection clearer than in the unique, pioneering work of Samuel Beckett. His plays reject the classical paradigm of narrative closure, moving instead toward a structure (or, better yet, a pattern) based on principles associated with Chaos theory. The iterative loops of action and self-similar text and performance his plays contain place his work squarely in the realm of Chaos theory. For example, *That Time*, a play in which a "listener" hears "his own [voice] coming to him from both sides and above" (228), is "just another of those old tales to keep the void from pouring in" (230), cycling through and around A, B, and C's self-similar speech patterns while, at the same time, permuting the order in which each person speaks. The play builds meaning from the iteration of this information-rich interaction of nonlinear speech events that repeat over scales both large and small. "That time," then, is the pattern lying in the interstices of A, B, and C's speeches, which becomes meaningful only in the act of listening.

To indicate the important ways in which Chaos theory, Zen, and Beckett's plays dovetail and illuminate each other, let us begin with what is seemingly a minor point of semantic coincidence: Zen and Chaos theory's use of the term *bifurcation.* It is striking (in actuality it was what first brought the two together in my mind) that both those who write on Zen Buddhism and those who work with Chaos theory employ a term so rarely used, one that is also important in reference to the divided pairs who people Beckett's stage. When, for example, Kasulis writes about Nagarjuna's critique of causality, he states: "Since all four possible answers [for causal relationships] yield absurdities, the bifurcation between cause and effect is itself suspect" (Kasulis 1981, 21). The language of Chaos theory is replete with references to bifurcation: in general, the solutions to equations bifurcate as a system goes from linear to nonlinear, Chaotic behavior.

One of the most famous examples of bifurcation in Chaos theory is the iterative solution of the "logistic," or population equation,

$$x_n = rx_{n-1}(1 - x_{n-1})$$

where x is less than 1. When r, the rate of growth, is small, iteration of the equation settles to one solution, but as r grows, the equation first bifurcates, and then bifurcates again and so on on its way to Chaotic behavior (see figure 7).

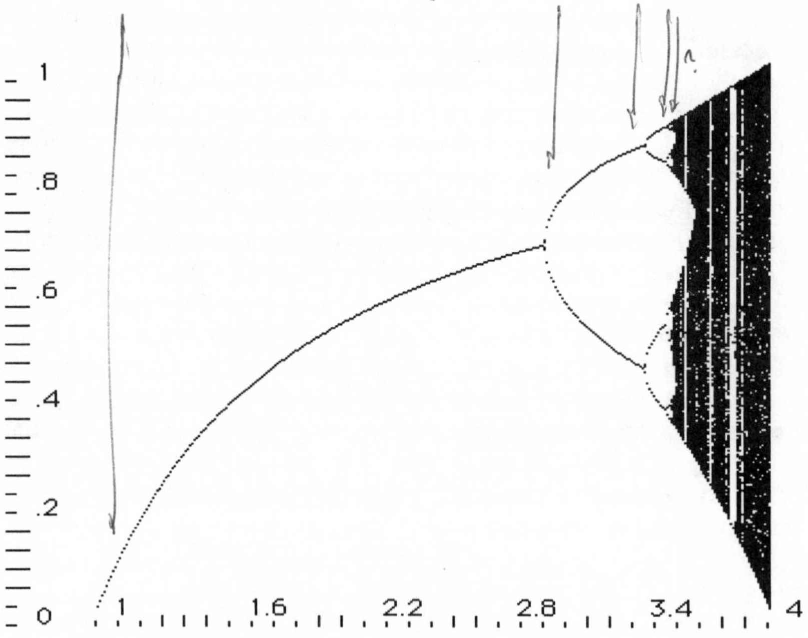

Fig. 7. Bifurcation of the logistic equation, $x \rightarrow rx(1-x)$

Gleick writes of this systematic movement toward Chaos, "These bifurcations would come faster and faster—4, 8, 16, 32 . . .—and suddenly break off. Beyond a certain point, the 'point of accumulation,' periodicity gives way to chaos . . ." (1987, 73).

Although this coincidence of language may not seem terribly significant, it is, in fact, an important clue to how each system of thought apprehends the world. Each sees bifurcation—a schismatic dualism—as an important element in the behavior of the universe. Although at first it certainly seems that the two take opposite tacks on the subject, with Zen being highly suspicious of dualistic thinking and Chaos theory lauding it as an ordered descent into chaotic behavior, this is not entirely true (a fact that will have to wait a moment to be verified, as we need to discuss some other issues first).

Beyond this conjunction of terminology, there is a general sociological confluence of the modern sciences with Eastern mysticism. As evinced by recent popular books like *The Dancing Wu-Li Masters* and *The Tao of Physics*, there is a tendency in the collective psyche of Westerners to associate modern physics, especially quantum dynamics, with a specifically Eastern frame of reference. This recent trend has identified the radically relativistic (that is, lacking any absolute) vision of the universe postulated by relativity, quantum dynamics, and (implicitly, at least) Chaos theory with that of Taoism and Zen. The highly cynical attitude that Taoism and especially Zen maintain toward the common bipolar values of the world is similar to the healthy skepticism with which we now view the classical, Newtonian paradigm: both claim that the world is not as simple as—or, in a different light, it is far simpler than—we have thought. In information theory, for example, the relative context of an event determines its existential value: "In Shannon's equations, the informational probability of an element can be calculated only with reference to the ensemble from which it is drawn, that is, not absolutely but through a series of differences" (Hayles 1990, 178). Conscious determinism gives way to chance and statistics; monism gives way to moral relativity, yet the entrapping paradigm of antagonistic dualism gives way to a more encompassing, less judgmental vision of the world.

In her introduction to *Chaos and Order*, Hayles explicates the differing world-views of the East and West through their distinct relation to the term *chaos* (or, in Chinese, *Hun-dun*, an onomatopoetic word suggesting "whirling water" [1991, 3]). Whereas the Western tradition has always viewed chaos as a negative state to be conquered and controlled by the forces of order, the Chinese tradition suggests that chaos is a valuable element of the world one that can be destroyed by too much desire for order:

why ?? ?

> That chaos has been negatively valued in the Western tradition may be partly due . . . to the predominance of binary logic in the West. If order is good, chaos is bad because it is *conceptualized* as the opposite of order. By contrast, in the four-valued logic characteristic of Taoist thought, not-order [without-order] is also a possibility, distinct from and valued differently than anti-order. The science of chaos draws Western assumptions about chaos into question by revealing possibilities that were suppressed when chaos was considered merely as order's opposite. It marks the validation within the Western tradition of a view of chaos that constructs it as not-order. In chaos theory chaos may either lead to order, as it does with self-organizing systems, or in yin/yang fashion it may have deep structures of order encoded within it. In either case, its relation to order is more complex than traditional Western oppositions have allowed. (1991, 3; my emphasis)

Here, the Zen/Taoist contention that disorder, or chaos, deserves an important, positive place in the scheme of things is linked directly with the findings of Chaos theory: chaos (or Chaos) is not the opposite of order; rather it is "order's precursor and partner" (Hayles 1991, 14). Chaos for this science becomes something akin to the chaotic Void of Eastern tradition, giving life to "self-organizing systems," and walking the fine line between non-differentiation (the Ur-Tao, or original face) and deep structures of order from which the "ten thousand things" of life arise.

In this complex interaction between order and disorder, we again find a direct link with the *Weltanschauung* expressed in Beckett's drama: the plays are not a movement away from order to its opposite; they are, instead, an investigation of the richly complex, chaotic realm of life at the boundaries of order—life in the "real" world. Thus, in Zen, Chaos theory, and Beckett's drama alike, Chaos, or the undifferentiating world of enlightenment, or the plenary void of a character like Godot, acquires a more positive aspect as progenitor of the ordered, conceptualized systems we commonly see as the world. In Beckett's case, in fact, it is the struggle between the order-and-concept-driven person and the Chaotic world around him or her that forms the major dramatic thrust. In his plays, as well as in Zen and Chaos theory, it is life "at the edge" of the order-disorder paradigm that is being studied.

This refocusing toward what are traditionally considered boundary or fringe systems, in fact, forms another important link between Chaos theory, Zen, and Beckett. All three (as we have seen with Chaos theory and Zen, and will discover with Beckett) move what is traditionally at the fringe into the center. In other words, they proclaim that what we consider "normal" or central to life or science is, in fact, only a small part of a deeper structure that actually lies in the center. For Zen, this de-marginalization occurs as the polar, dualistic "reality" of life becomes only a secondary, even illusory element of the undifferentiated universe that constitutes reality. David Loy says of this, "All philosophy is an attempt to understand our experience, but here the critical issue is the type of experience that we accept as *fundamental*, as opposed to the type of experience that needs to be 'explained.' The Western epistemologist usually accepts as his data our familiar dualistic experience, dismissing other types . . . as philosophically insignificant aberrations" (1988, 8; my emphasis), while Eastern thinkers value nonduality over what they consider illusory dualism.

In Chaos theory, the deterministic model of the (macroscopic) universe, for centuries and eons held to be the way of the "real" world gives way to a locally undeterministic system—a system, however, that contains deep structures or patterns of order in its seeming chaos. As opposed to quantum dynamics, which proclaims an indeterminacy but relegates it to the fringes of the knowable, Chaos theory claims that the order of indeterminacy extends to the center of the everyday world in which we live: "chaotic systems need not be esoteric or rare. Indeed they are more common in nature than ordered systems. But they were not *perceived* to be so until a paradigm shift occurred that placed them at the center rather than the margin of inquiry" (Hayles 1991, 9–10). Here, as in Zen, chaos is not the polar opposite of order; it is instead a medium in which order (and disorder) can be found. In other words, order contains chaos which contains order: the two are eternally intermingled in a "without-dualistic" manner.

For Beckett, as well, we find that the dramatic setting, the existential problems the characters face, and especially the final tableaux of the plays all indicate in immediate fashion the trouble of trying to live in a conceptual world, and at the same time the existence—first at the edge of consciousness, then growing in centrality—of this other, undifferentiated world. Chronologically, Beckett's plays reveal more and more clearly the untenable nature of the bipolar world and the necessity and centrality of this supposedly fringe mode of existence. Like the Self-infused arrow approaching an always diminishing target, or like the always almost but never quite finished pile of grain in Zeno's paradox[30]—which is often quoted in *Endgame* and is implicitly important to all the playwright's work—Beckett's drama destabilizes causality and connection, as well as the desire for these supposedly central elements of stage and life.

In light of the destabilization of the old, commonplace paradigm and the revisioning of the fringes that both Zen and Chaos theory allow, two other important schools of critical thought spring to mind and are worth an aside here, as well as further exploration later: feminism and deconstruction theory. Though here and later I will not make any attempt to be thorough even in representing the breadth of implications of or differences between these systems (as that would be the subject of another work entirely), the radical destabilization of our ordered, patriarchal world, which is fundamental to representative deconstructive and feminist works, runs so close in places to what we have explored in Zen and Chaos theory that it would be difficult to ignore the overlap.

If we limit ourselves to one strand of feminist thought—that represented by Winnett, deLauretis, and others—we find there a compelling argument for revisioning the common (or patriarchal) paradigm in light of women's pleasure and vision. In exposing the essentially masculine patterns of narrative coherence that form the common paradigm of Western plots, Winnett states,

> We have been taught to read in drag and must begin to question seriously the determinants that govern the mechanics of our narratives, the notion of history as a sense-making operation, and the enormous investment the patriarchy has in maintaining them. (1990, 516)

Seen in this manner,

> narrative strategies . . . [are] not universal or a-temporal but historically and semiotically specific—I mean specific with regard to the history of cultural forms, media, genres, and spectatorship or context of reception. . . . Thus, to our contemporary eyes, even the texts of classical narrative cinema display, as feminist critics have repeatedly shown, the very gaps and paradoxes that the operation of narrative is meant to cover up. . . . (deLauretis 1987, 108–9)

As opposed to this, feminism proposes an alternate vision of narrative "pleasure": ". . . I want to explore the different narrative logic—and the very different possibilities of pleasure—that emerge when issues such as incipience, repetition, and closure are reconceived in terms of *an* experience (not *the* experience) of the female body" (Winnett 1990, 509). In parallel fashion to Zen, Chaos theory, and Beckett's drama, these writers first expose the conventional nature of the common paradigm, then propose an alternate vision in which the same elements of fiction (or reality) are understood in terms of a fringe element—that of women. The central, masculine paradigm of literature is unseated by the traditionally marginalized vision of feminism.

In similar fashion, Derridean deconstruction destabilizes the traditional solidity of language itself:

> Barthes pointed out that the text is a tissue of quotations, not a line of words releasing the single "theological" meaning of an author-god but a multidimensional space in which a variety of writings blend and/or clash. . . . [And] Derrida shows that the meaning of such a line of words can

> never be completely fulfilled or totalized, hence the text never attains self-presence; the continual circulation of signifiers signifies that meaning has no firm foundation or epistemological ground. (Loy 1992, 235)

This existential philosophy of language, like the science of Chaos theory, owes a debt to information theory, as both depend on a distinction between the information carried in a message and the meaning conveyed; and both attempt to generate (or expose) maximal useful information at the expense of cohesive meaning.[31] In deconstruction, the centralized relationship between signifier and referent is destabilized by the marginalized force of the quasi-potential "trace," an interloping third element that exposes the necessary slippage between sign and meaning. However, "When the center is empty—or has been emptied by discourse that claims to be marginal—there is no meaningful distinction between margin and center in terms of the power they exercise" (Hayles 1990, 195); thus language is re-viewed as multiple—even "multivalent," to borrow from Bakhtin. Here, too, what has been regarded under the old paradigm as a set of minor, fringe aberrations—small errors in transferring meaning from sign to referent—is moved to a central role, replacing a deterministic system with one that is chaotic but potentially richer in the resultant "play" of language.

If we return to a portion of Hayles's extended quote above, it is apparent that she not only indicates a movement of these systems from the fringe to the center of our world, she also brings up the important point that Chaos theory—and transitively Zen and Beckett's work—creates a new vision of the world:

> The science of chaos draws Western assumptions about chaos into question by revealing possibilities that were suppressed when chaos was considered merely as order's opposite. It marks the validation within the Western tradition of a view of chaos that constructs it as not-order. (1991, 3)

Neither Zen, nor Chaos theory, nor Beckett claim that they are creating anything new in the actual world, simply that they are providing a new (simpler, more accurate) way of seeing the things already all around us. For Zen, the world of enlightenment is simply the world of suffering and disease seen in a different light: "since nothing is self-existent [absolute], *Nirvana*, too, is *Sunya*" (Loy 1992, 246). It is only the vision, not the world, that is altered for those achieving satori. In Chaos theory, too, it is not the world that is changed, it is our modeling or understanding of it: "The change is not in how the world actually is . . . but in how it is seen" (Hayles 1991, 8). Here again, it is our understanding of the world that lies at the heart of the paradigm shift: we have not discovered any new phenomena, we have come up with a new, more encompassing way to understand what we already encounter. In Beckett's plays, characters and audience both are forced from the "old style" of understanding theater and existence to search for some new mode of comprehension. Like the tube of toothpaste that Winnie bemoans in *Happy Days*, our old vision of the theatrical world is "running out."

On another level, we can also see how, in similar fashion, the koan is emblematic (though by no means exhaustive) of Zen's "without-mind" take on the universe, while the iterative feedback loop of equations like $z \rightarrow z^2 + c$ symbolizes Chaos theory. Each of these is a catalyst for the novice or newcomer, something indicating the vital "other" vision of the world on which we can hang while trying to unravel the deeper workings of each system. For Beckett, the emblem of his new vision of the world is almost certainly the play *Waiting for Godot*, the most influential and iconic of all his works for the general public. The "classical" paradigm of realism, the assumedly central and "true" vision of the world through theater, is replaced by a new vision of theater and life in which Zeno's paradox of causality takes center stage. In a fashion analogous to those of Zen and Chaos theory, *Godot*, emblematic of Beckett's plays, makes no claim to re-creating theater; it is simply a new way of seeing—or, better yet, "being" theatrical. Both actors and audience must adjust their views about what constitutes theater, as narrative and action give way to existential wandering, a theatrical vision that is actually closer—or more central—to our lives. As Stanton B. Garner says of Beckett's plays as a whole, they are a response to the "marginalization" of the theatrical in theater through a more complete concentration on the essential physicality of theater itself: ". . . Beckett's work represents an evolving and increasingly complex response to a set of essentially phenomenological questions concerning subjectivity, embodiedness, and perception" (1993, 447). This observation, though couched in phenomenological terms, indicates the visceral break Beckett's plays, starting with *Waiting for Godot*, make with the classical, narrative-driven paradigm.[32]

3

Waiting in *Godot:* The Distance between Arrow and Target

> Ritual is the husk of true faith, the beginning of chaos.
>
> —*Tao Te Ching*

> "What must I do, then?" I asked thoughtfully.
> "You must learn to wait properly."
> "And how does one learn that? . . ."
> "Wait until it is time."
>
> —Eugen Herrigel

Certainly *Waiting for Godot* is a stylistically groundbreaking piece, as well as a deeply ambivalent and ambiguous look into the human condition, which, though under the microscope of criticism for a half-century, has not been exhausted, either intellectually or dramatically. Thus, both structurally and metaphysically, the play encourages further assessment. In addition, as Beckett's most accessible (or at least most available) work, it is for many an entry point into Beckett's oeuvre, and even for the "theater of the absurd" as a whole. As Wolfgang Iser puts it, *Godot* (and, by association, Beckett's theater as a whole) is of fundamental importance to the second half of the twentieth century, allowing us "to judge how art is to be experienced in the modern world" (1981, 140).

Given such broad importance, both aesthetically and socially, *Waiting for Godot* must be emblematic of some kind of paradigm shift in the theater: like Stravinski's *Sacre du Printemps*, which, though not the first piece of "modern" music, became associated with, and for many equivalent to, music's break with the romantic paradigm, Beckett's play somehow encapsulates and reflects a shift away from the norm of narrative theater. Contained within *Godot* are the elements of a new theater—a new way of seeing stage and life—which are played out in different manner and scale in his later drama, but which always revolve around the same issues set forth in this play. "*Waiting for Godot*, with its excision of traditional plot, can . . . be seen as the first in a series of [Beckett's] plays that strip away inessential elements of drama but keep the essentials of theatrical form" (Hutchings 1991, 27). Thus, in the metaphorical relation to *Zen in the Art of Archery* (laid out in the previous chapter), *Waiting for Godot* is effectively an introduction to the "tools of the trade": the bow, arrow, and target which are essential to the journey, through archery, to a new vision of the world. The Zen approach to archery utilizes the same tools as the sport (or method of war) that is archery, but these tools are reused, even redefined, in the context of Zen. Therefore, the first step in Zen archery is to put aside the "old way" of using these tools. Likewise, *Godot* uses, rejects, and reestablishes the tools of the old style of theater—plot, motivation, staging, lights, etc.—allowing a new theatrical vision to emerge. Beckett's play, then, is the first—and, consequently, last as well, beginning containing the end—step toward a new paradigm.

What, specifically, is this paradigm shift? Zen and Chaos theory, which both destabilize the old system of thought (or vision) and establish a new way of seeing the universe, are perfect tools to help uncover more precisely what Beckett has done in this and subsequent plays. In the binocular view provided by the intersection of these two systems, new layers and patterns in Beckett's work become clear.

Beckett has indicated an excellent starting point for an exploration in terms of this binocular view in "The perfect title of a literary work" (Calderwood 1986, 363): the key to the play is found in its title—waiting. Obviously, waiting is a central issue for the characters: for Vladimir and Estragon, one might even say that waiting for Godot is their "job," or, at least, their vocation, and even for Pozzo and Lucky, who spend their time on the move, the time it takes for them to go from one place to another is essentially one of waiting (this is truer in the first act, in which Pozzo and Lucky have "somewhere" to go). Yet waiting is a difficult concept both to define and to demonstrate: to wait is to "not" do something else.

> So waiting, which implies the absence of the waited-for, is itself mysteriously absent. Moreover, waiting is a self-erasing nonactivity, since it negates the transient activities we engage in while waiting. . . . Although [other] . . . activities are undeniably occurring, they are rendered parenthetical to what we are "really" doing—i.e., waiting. (Calderwood 1986, 366)

Waiting, then, is a nonaction that negates any actions which occur while under its sway. Waiting, we might say, is the antithesis and precursor of a dramatic action: if characters wait, they do so for something (a person, a thing, even a state such as death) which, by convention, will arrive. It is this act of arriving that is the dramatic action justifying the play.[1] *Godot*, though, flips this convention on its head, centralizing the traditionally marginal role of waiting, and consigning to obscurity and indeterminacy the "pivotal action" of arriving. Thus, *Waiting for Godot* is, as its title suggests, a play that modifies traditional dramatic tools by infinitely deferring the "action" of the play.

How, then, can we explore such a central yet "mysteriously absent" thing as waiting? Zen Buddhism can help in this matter, for in Zen, the self-negating action of waiting is also of fundamental importance. More specifically, Zen abjures waiting, as it negates the present: "waiting (more generally, any expectation) has been repeatedly identified as the most problematic tendency in meditative practice [through which enlightenment is achieved]" (Loy 1992, 228). In Buddhist meditation, a sense of expectation or waiting for something to happen is a very common, almost obligatory, stumbling block, as every young disciple desires, and therefore *waits* for enlightenment. So perhaps Estragon's statement, "Nothing happens, nobody comes, nobody goes, it's awful!" (27), is, on some level, the complaint of a novitiate in meditative practice. Estragon, like the struggling novice, is waiting for *something* to happen (what that would be, neither may know). And Estragon is by no means alone in his sense of waiting and frustration: Vladimir regularly reminds the forgetful Estragon that their purpose in standing near the tree at dusk is to wait for Godot. On one level, at least, Godot is "the promise that is always *awaited* and not fulfilled, the expectation that brings two men to the board night after night [highlighting, of course, the metatheatricality of the play]" (Cohn 1973, 132; my emphasis). The two feel forced to stay near the tree, expecting some vague reward for their ritual observance (and afraid of the consequences of their noncompliance). They are unhappy where they are but are not "strong enough to do otherwise" (Burkman 1986, 50). The pair's inability to cease waiting, therefore, closes off and negates other possibilities: to wait is to collapse—violently—the "multiplicity" of present time and space (see Nealon 1988, 524–25) into the single "action" of waiting that negates even itself.

Their agony of waiting thus forces Didi and Gogo into a temporal dilemma as well as a spatial one (as the two problems obviously are bound up in one another): waiting is not merely existing in a place, like the single-treed intersection, but being there during a certain time interval. Near the beginning of the play, Vladimir and Estragon get into an argument over the time (the date) when they are to meet Godot:

ESTRAGON: You're sure it was this evening?
VLADIMIR: What?
ESTRAGON: That we were to wait.
VLADIMIR: He said Saturday. (*Pause.*) I think.

ESTRAGON: You think.
VLADIMIR: I must have made a note of it. (*He fumbles in his pockets, bursting with miscellaneous rubbish.*)
ESTRAGON: (*very insidious*). But what Saturday? And is it Saturday? Is it not rather Sunday? (*Pause.*) Or Monday? (*Pause.*) Or Friday?
VLADIMIR: (*looking wildly about him, as though the date was inscribed in the landscape*). It's not possible!

(Beckett 1954, 10–11)

This uncertainty is, of course, a wonderfully comic moment; but it also touches on the center of insecurity in the characters—especially Vladimir here—for waiting is, almost by definition, an uncertain period during which time the waiting party experiences the mystery of the future in the form of a question: Will the person or thing I am waiting for arrive after all? If the wait is short and the party is reliable, this insecurity is minimal; but if, as in the play, the wait is one of many evenings and the party awaited likely may not arrive, the act of waiting becomes tedious at best, and can even give rise to fear and/or anger, depending on the relationship between those involved. *Waiting for Godot* thus corresponds to an uncomfortable real-world experience but heightens it through the static nature of the set and lighting, punctuated by the instantaneous descent of night at the end of each act.

We can see how much suffering this dragging sense of time causes the characters, from Vladimir's joyous reaction to Lucky and Pozzo's arrival in act 2: "We are no longer alone, waiting for the night, waiting for Godot, waiting for . . . waiting. All evening we have struggled, unassisted. Now it's over. It's already to-morrow" (50). His happiness turns out to be premature, but Vladimir's lines make clear how painful the duty or bondage of waiting for Godot (or night, or death, whichever comes first) really is. For Zen, this nonact of waiting "creates" time: "insofar as we hope to overcome our [present] *lack*, we are thrust into the future, toward that awaited moment when self-presence will be gained; as Jacques Derrida implies, belief in progress, in the future itself, is a version of it [a compensation for this *lack*]" (Loy 1992, 245). Setting aside for future chapters Derrida's involvement in the issue of temporal determinacy, we can see from this quote that hope or expectation springs from a sense of lack, emptiness, or insecurity.[2] This insecurity then forces us to conceptualize a projected future "time" and to reconstruct memories, thus creating a past. By way of contrast, in the highly phenomenological state of enlightenment, the baggage of past and future are released, and the awakened person lives fully in each moment.

What proves significant for *Godot* is not whether this view of time—that all time is the present, if lived properly—is correct, or even whether Beckett himself agreed with it, but that the play itself tends toward this phenomenological approach.[3] Although the characters fight to maintain the everyday sense of time that Winnie, in *Happy Days*, will term "the old style" (days of the week, dusk and night, etc.), the play physically arrests time by holding light levels at an "evening" setting, then speeds it up by a quick fade to night, complete with a five-second moonrise. Furthermore, when each character, in turn, attempts to put the pieces of his memory together into a continuous past, he is refuted by the other characters. First, Estragon attempts to confirm past and present with Vladimir:

> ESTRAGON: We came here yesterday.
> VLADIMIR: Ah no, there you're mistaken.
> ESTRAGON: What did we do yesterday?
> VLADIMIR: What did we do yesterday?
> ESTRAGON: Yes.
> VLADIMIR: Why . . . (*Angrily.*) Nothing is certain when you're about.
> (Beckett 1954, 10)

Obviously Vladimir is little help in Estragon's quest for narrative cohesion. Later, when Vladimir confronts first Pozzo and then the messenger boy about their recollections of past events, he is, in turn, treated in the same manner:

> VLADIMIR: I've seen you before, haven't I?
> BOY: I don't know, Sir.
> VLADIMIR: You don't know me?
> BOY: No Sir.
> VLADIMIR: It wasn't you came yesterday?
> BOY: No Sir.
> (33)

This is all well and fine, we may think watching the first act. After all, Estragon and Vladimir may be mistaken (how would we know?). But when, in the second act, Estragon, Pozzo, and the boy fail to remember the events we witnessed only minutes before, we are certainly inclined to join in Vladimir's frustration:

> VLADIMIR: You don't remember any fact, any circumstance?
> ESTRAGON: *(weary)*. Don't torment me, Didi.
> VLADIMIR: The sun. The moon. Do you not remember?
> . . . .
> VLADIMIR: And Pozzo? And Lucky?
> ESTRAGON: Pozzo?
> VLADIMIR: The bones.
> ESTRAGON: They were like fishbones.

VLADIMIR: It was Pozzo gave them to you.
ESTRAGON: I don't know.

(42–43)

These lines—which employ a role reversal from the exchange, above, between the two in the first act (and can thereby also cause consternation for the half-remembering audience)—demonstrate the intensifying difficulty the characters and we are having "keeping tabs" on time itself.

The continuity of time and space that Didi, Gogo, Lucky, Pozzo and we search for is withheld by circumstance: faulty memory, staging, repetition, and metatheatrical elements—which introduce an extradiegetic level to the question of time and continuity—destabilize any attempts to create a coherent past, present, and future.[4] Time thus becomes an almost palpable element within the play: obtuse things happen (or don't happen), memories flag, and (non)events are repeated, all dragging time to the forefront as audience and characters *wait* for the "day" to be finished. Is the play, then, a rendering of the "awful" physicality of time? Is waiting through an endless cycle of repetitions, perhaps only for death in the end, all there is? The tendency in early critical response is to claim that this is, indeed, the end of the issue: Ruby Cohn finishes one of her more extensive examinations of the play as follows: "'Our cries' compose its dialogue, orchestrated by Beckett, and understood in many languages" (1973, 139).

If, however, we utilize Zen to examine the problem of time in *Godot*, we find that the characters' apparently insoluble dilemma of waiting and suffering is perhaps only apparent. Nagarjuna (discussed in chapter 1) produces an insightful reductio ad absurdum of the causal way we normally conceive of time. Kasulis summarizes the argument thus:

> Nagarjuna's point is that although many philosophical theories deal with the breakdown of time into past, present, and future, the relationship among these three terms is paradoxical. Each of the three terms is meaningful only in relation to the meanings of the other two. Yet, by the very definition of the terms, their referents (the past, the present, the future) never exist simultaneously. Therefore, the assumption that the terms *past*, *present*, and *future* refer to an objective reality outside language is absurd. Stated differently, if these terms refer to nonlinguistic bits of reality . . . , there can be no possible connection among those bits (since they never exist simultaneously)—and without those interconnections the terms themselves are meaningless. The conclusion is that it is absurd to think of the past, present, and future as having any extralinguistic reality. (1981, 19)

Referring back to Loy's claim that our conception of time is generated by a sense of ego-insecurity, or lack, we can see that "normal," causal time and language are bound together and linked inextricably with the craving "I," or Self, which needs consistency to secure its existence. But this craving, in turn, engenders the hope-(non)fulfillment cycle of desiring and waiting that comprises the karmic world of *dukkha*, or suffering. In other words, it is craving for *some*thing to happen that creates the sense of waiting, creating the sense of time, creating the suffering in *Waiting for Godot*.

The characters in the play, through a language arising from insecurity/desire—the insecurity of and desire for existence in some permanent form—cannot exist within the world the play presents as "reality." Why not? Because they attempt to view their world in terms of past, present, and future, in terms of days and hours, of appointments made and kept, of dusk and night. "Vladimir and Estragon cannot leave the place they are in or think beyond the limits of a static, objective metasystem because of the rigid, violent limits placed on both their actions and their thought by the modernist metadiscourse represented by Godot.[5] Their minds are slaves to Godot in the same way Lucky's body is a slave to Pozzo" (Nealon 1988, 525–26). However, any attempt at a Kantian/modernist conceptual grid is consistently thwarted by the play (and the characters themselves), and it is the failure of those on stage, as well as those in the audience, to break the cycle of expectation that causes suffering.

Waiting thus occurs in the play on a moment-to-moment scale as well as on the larger scale of Didi and Gogo's nightly wait for Godot to arrive: characters, particularly Vladimir and Pozzo (in the first act at least), expect past events to be the same as those occurring at the moment. They expect certain events to repeat in the future, from waiting for Godot the following day to Gogo's waiting—once he remembers—for Pozzo to give him more chicken bones. However, this type of "experience is *retrospective* in that we try to understand experience through previously learned [memorized] categories. . . . Our common understanding of experience is therefore a *reconstruction,* in that it imposes categories that were not present in that experience when it originally occurred" (Kasulis 1981, 60). Memory functions as a grid of expectation placed on true reality and serves as a key element in the characters' sufferings. Thus it is potentially a positive, rather than a negative, attribute of these characters that they remember as poorly as they do. According to Zen—and even according to the rules of the play itself—it would be best if no one remembered the past or projected the future; then, of course, there would be no waiting for Godot. Toward this goal of self-forgetfulness, Estragon, early and often, leads the way in his own stumbling manner:

> Estragon, who seems least aware of what he is doing, where he is, and why, is at the outset really the farthest along of the four. . . . While Vladimir tends to intellectualize and ponder metaphysical questions, Estragon seems

> to intuit the nature of their predicament more profoundly, even though he may seem, like many a wise fool before him, to be merely slow-witted. (Burkman 1986, 39)

Intuiting, rather than reflecting, Estragon unwittingly tends toward the Zen goal of "fully present" living.

As the play's always-deferred structure necessitates, this problem of memory extends beyond the characters. For the audience as well, memory is a disservice when attending *Godot*. The common paradigm of causality is drastically diminished, if not completely overturned in the play; and our concurrence with, say, Vladimir's memory of actions and events in the first act produces nothing but frustration for us, too. Beyond this, a comparison of the second act with the first, as well as of this play with more traditional ones (employing our own memory of the past), engenders surprise, even anger, at the plotless circularity of the play. "How," we claim, "can this be a play, or even a representation of some reality?"

Yet, what is equally obvious is that the play is ultimately about reality—ours: "The seed of *Godot* is Luke's account of the crucifixion, as summarized by St. Augustine: 'Do not despair: one of the thieves was saved. Do not presume: one of the thieves was damned.' The two thieves are Didi and Gogo; the two thieves are Pozzo and Lucky; the two thieves are you and me" (Cohn 1973, 130). The world of *Godot* centers around the ambiguous pairing of seemingly arbitrary opposites, cycling around the same events with the same people, apparently getting nowhere fast—it seems, in other words, *chaotic*.

In Newtonian physics, as with "realistic" narrative-driven plays, the world is theoretically infinitely discernible and repeatable. Given careful constraints on an experiment or expert writers and actors, the experiment/play supposedly can be repeated ad infinitum, producing essentially the same results. The import of this repeatability is that the present is merely a fractional moment in an infinite past and future which, given enough data and a "Laplacian" brain, we could determine completely:[6] memory is secure and control over the "real" world is at least hypothetically possible. While quantum physics disturbed the order of the Newtonian paradigm, this disturbance was, for the most part, relegated to the fringes of knowledge and the universe.[7] It was only with the advent of Chaos theory that a fuller, macroscopic, and potentially more positive, appreciation of quantum theory's uncertainty principle developed.

In Lorenz's and Mandelbrot's early experimental forays into the field of Chaos theory, computers grinding out series of nonlinear calculations[8] produced numbers that seemed random, or chaotic, but which actually contained order (of a sort) behind and beneath the randomness. Lorenz, for example, discovered that, given tiny variations in initial circumstances, vastly different results could evolve from his simple nonlinear weather equations. Significantly, these differences occur over a period of virtual "time": iterative calculations that approximate the "feedback" of real systems wherein the output of one event or calculation is input for another. In other words, even if our initial numbers are very close to each other, iteration of a nonlinear equation can cause the two results to grow apart wildly. Thus, time and repetition are crucial elements in the development of Chaotic behavior.

At the same time that results of individual starting points grow more and more chaotic, there is a systemic patterning across scales. The paradigm shift of Chaos theory then entails re-presenting the results of iterations geometrically or graphically, as opposed to analytically,[9] thus revealing the underlying sets and strange attractors that "define" Chaotic systems. And, as we have seen, while some iterations of equations following a strange attractor may produce very similar results (and some very disparate ones), by definition there will never be any cyclical repetition of the results of one of these systems; consequently, two similar initial conditions will never fall into line with each other to complete the cycle of repetition. What occurs, then, is that if we stop the computer calculations at any arbitrary point in "time" (the equivalent of a single day in our computer world), we have no good idea where that result will appear. But we can always be certain that the result will fall somewhere in the set of points defined by the strange attractor. Individual events (or actions) are essentially random, as we cannot predict with any certainty where they will occur; but these events, taken as a whole, form a complex (or strange) pattern which both attracts and defines the chaotic behavior itself. As with Zen, what occurs here is essentially a shift toward a phenomenological perspective: "Such a shift entails profound reconceptualizations; the essentially analytic space of Euclidean geometry, Cartesian philosophy, or Newtonian physics is very different, for instance, from lived, or inhabited, spatiality, with its perceptual contours and structures of orientation" (Garner 1993, 448). Reversing the analogy, this phenomenological shift means, in fact, that Chaos theory re-creates the "real," experienced world more closely than classical physics and mathematics.

In *Waiting for Godot*, therefore, to claim that the actions and staging of the play are chaotic and devoid of connection and order is analogous to taking a close-up view of the few, unpredictable points falling at random on a strange attractor when we arbitrarily stop the flow of equations at a given moment. If, on the other hand, we view the play from the holistic perspective of "stage-space," we may be able to see emerge the pattern of a nonclosed attractor.[10] The pairings of characters on stage are related but not identical (with Didi and Gogo often virtually indistinguishable, even interchangeable, as in their exchange about time, yet widely varied in perspicacity and attitude; and Pozzo and Lucky in the classically ambiguous master-slave relationship). The acts repeat but not exactly.[11] The stage is nearly the same, yet the tree springs leaves during the intermission. On a moment-to-moment basis, actions and words are replayed, but each time with a difference. Thus, on scales large and small, causality and cohesion are banished from the world of *Godot*. An example of this small, moment-to-moment iteration is the nearly exact repetition between Vladimir and Estragon of question and answer to the most important problem of suffering: Estragon, frustrated in his attempts to take his boot off, finally asks for help, leading to Vladimir's question:

> VLADIMIR: It hurts?
> ESTRAGON: *(angrily)*. Hurts! He wants to know if it hurts!
> VLADIMIR: *(angrily)*. No one ever suffers but you. I don't count. I'd like to hear what you'd say if you had what I have.
> ESTRAGON: It hurts?
> VLADIMIR: *(angrily)*. Hurts! He wants to know if it hurts!
> (Beckett 1954, 7)

In this brief exchange, words, and even mood, are repeated exactly; the repetition, however, is not equivalent, as the speakers are interchanged. While this may not seem an important caveat, the point is that even this deceptively similar iteration is saturated with difference. Thus, while *Godot* bends back upon itself many times on large and small scale, it is never *closed*—it never repeats exactly, a situation *Godot* eschews, since exact repetition would allow us to extrapolate a deterministic future and past for the characters and thereby create closure for the play. Instead, the events are pulled, or attracted, back within some bounds and into some sort of pattern, at the same time that at each moment events are unpredictable. While the world of Beckett's play is chaotic, it is chaotic in the more limited, technical sense we have previously defined as the orderly disorder of Chaos.

If we now examine how this evaluation of time and order in *Godot* relates to the Zen interpretation discussed above, we come to a difficult impasse: whereas Zen relegates absolutes and permanence to the realm of illusion, claiming that all is, in fact, flux, Chaos theory seems to take the opposite approach of claiming that what appears changeable from moment to moment is, in fact, part of a larger, absolute pattern that encompasses the little pieces we usually take to represent reality. Fortunately, Loy has done an in-depth examination of this issue of all-absolute versus all-flux (1988, 215–24), showing that this apparent contradistinction is, in actuality, merely

1. A riverlike detail from the Mandelbrot set. The picture was generated using a program written by Alessandro Levi Montalcini.

2. This image was generated from photo 1 using the program Metacreations Bryce2, which “extrudes” 2-D pictures into realistic 3-D landscapes.

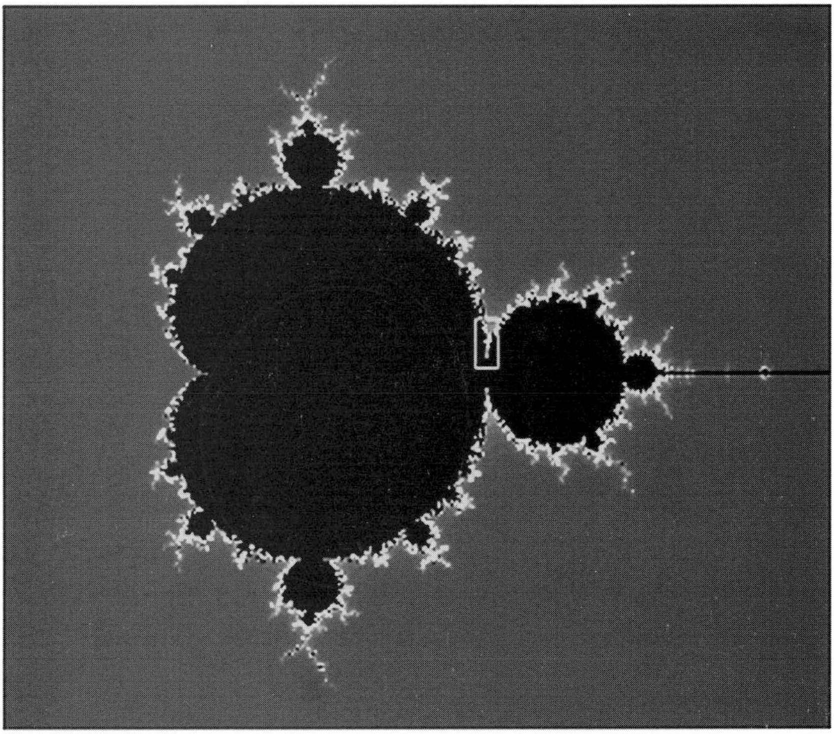

3. The "full" Mandelbrot set. The rectangle (as with the other rectangles below) indicates the location of the area shown in photo 4. The dimensions of this picture are: x (the real axis) goes from -1 to 2, y (the imaginary axis) goes from -1.5 to 1.5. The number of iterations of the $z \rightarrow z^2 - c$ equation for each point is 65. In this and some of the other figures below, I have cropped the picture, so these dimensions are only approximate.

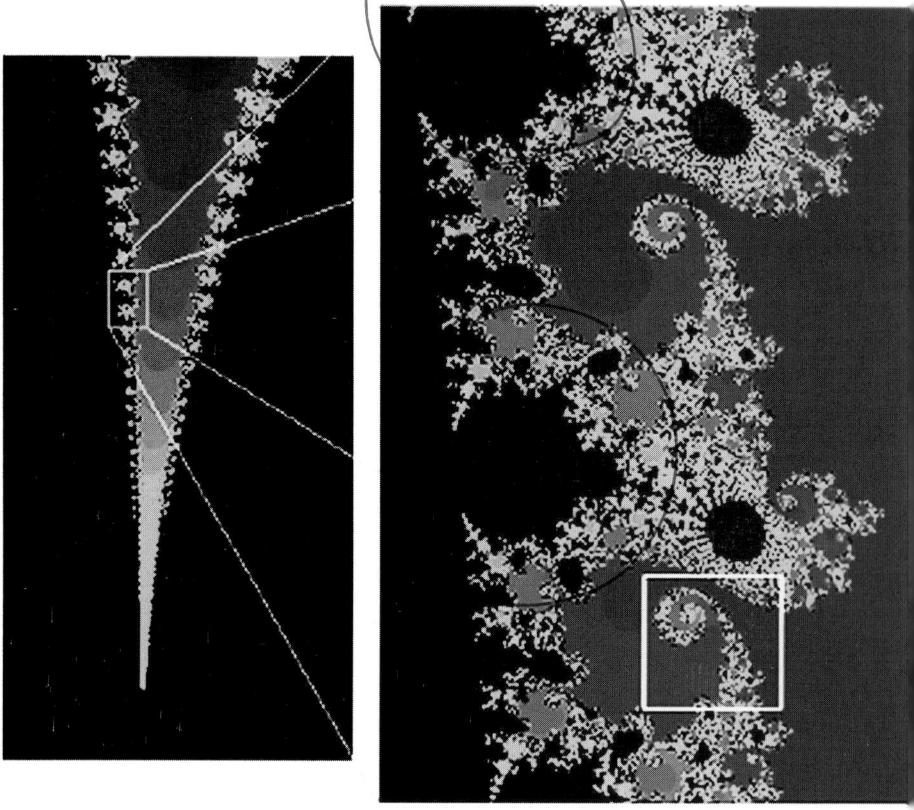

4. Progressive enlargements of a small portion of the Mandelbrot set. Note the "sprout," left center of the right-hand image, which looks similar to the whole set. The dimensions of the picture on the left are: $0.7 < x < 0.8$, $0 < y < 0.1$; iterations per point are 150. On the right, $0.745 < x < 0.752$; iterations are 400.

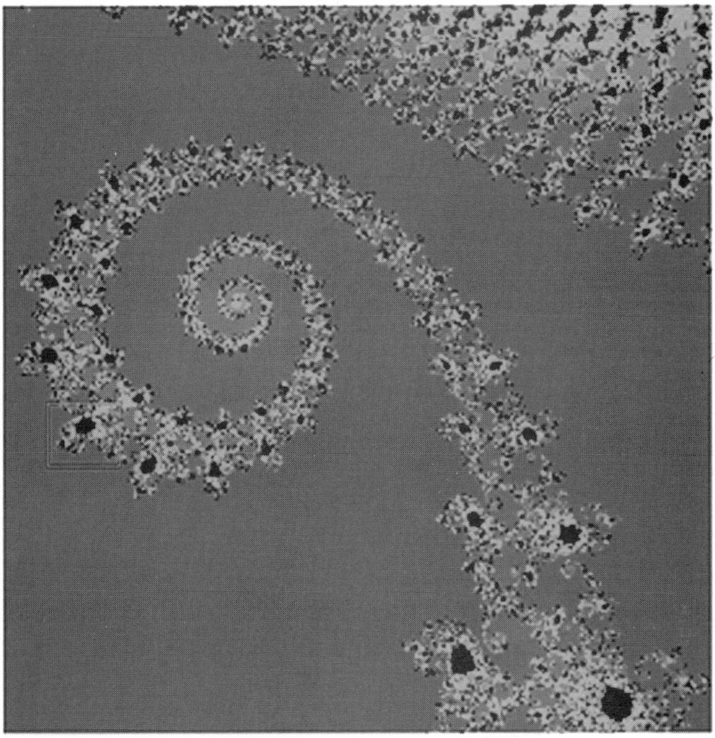

5. The spiral from above, enlarged. Here $0.74779 < x < 0.74884$, $0.07105 < y < 0.07210$; iterations are 500.

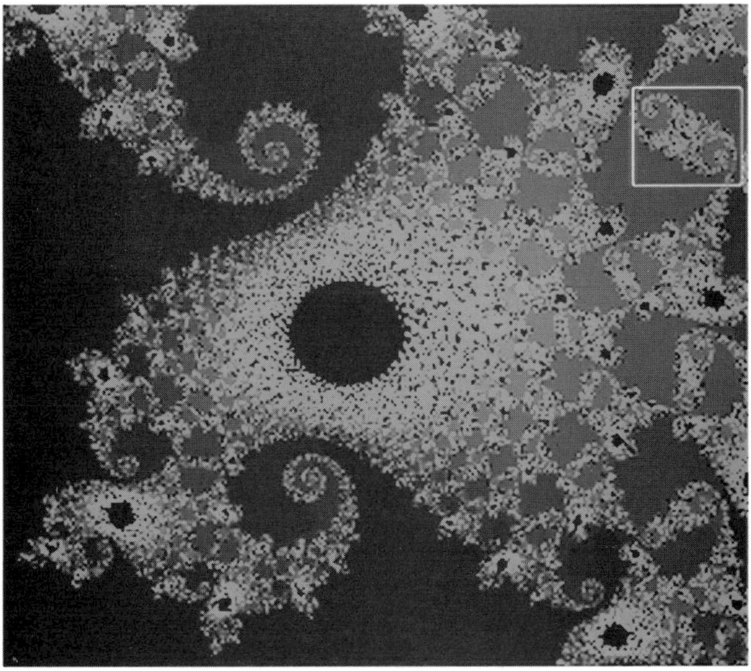

6. An unusual-looking piece of photo 5, enlarged. Here, $0.7478635 < x < 0.7479685$, $0.0714385 < y < 0.0715435$; iterations are 750.

7. The portion indicated in photo 6 is enlarged, revealing even more beauty and detail. Here, $0.7478653 < x < 0.7478810$, $0.0714595 < y < 0.714752$; iterations are 1,000.

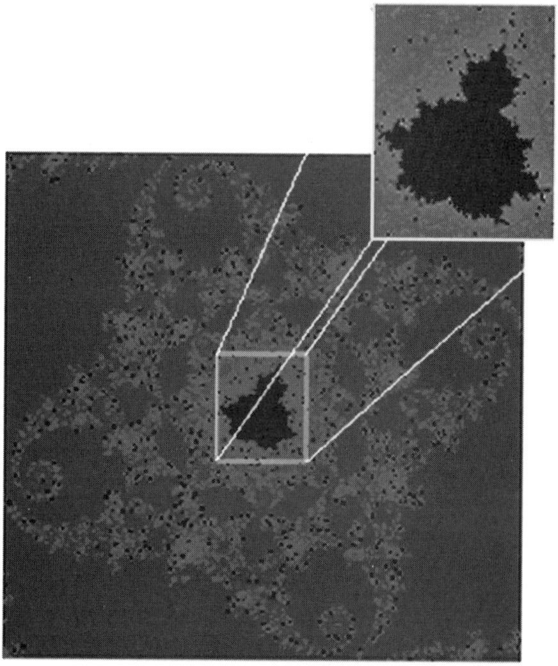

8. An expansion of the central portion of photo 7, revealing, deep within the Mandelbrot set, a small subset that looks like the original figure (as the inset expansion clearly shows). In the large figure, $0.7479585 < x < 0.7479613$, $0.0715212 < y < 0.0715240$; iterations are 1,500. In the small inset figure, iterations are 2,500 per point.

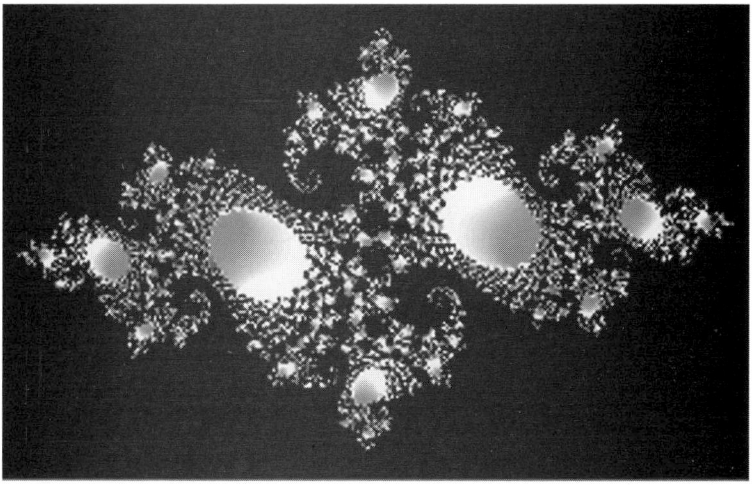

9. A Julia set generated from a point at the boundary of the Mandelbrot set. The exact value of c at which this figure and the one below it is generated is: $c = 0.743036$, $ic = 0.113467$.

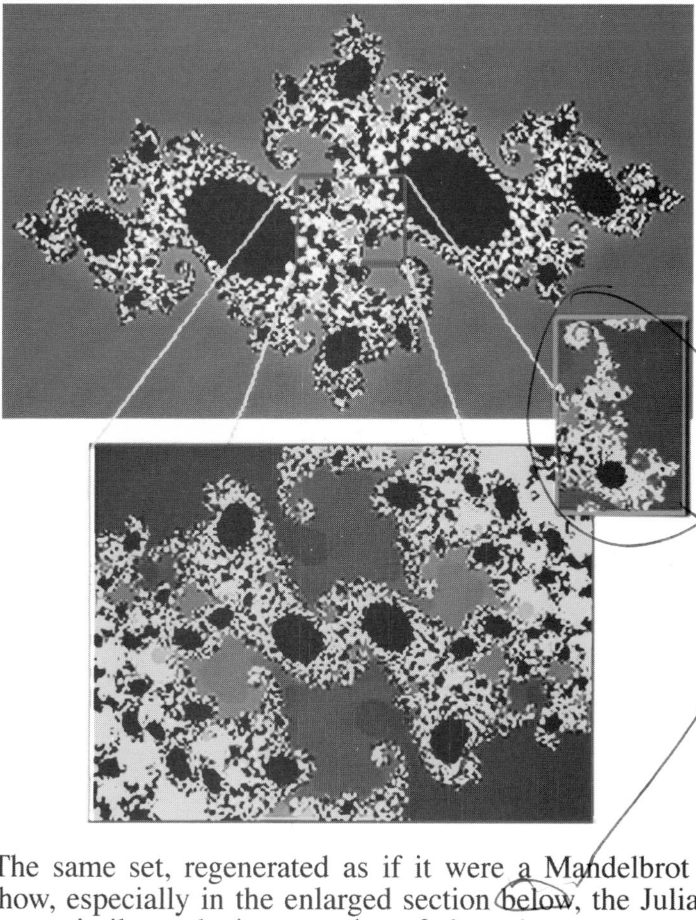

10. The same set, regenerated as if it were a Mandelbrot set. Note how, especially in the enlarged section below, the Julia set looks very similar to the inset portion of photo 4.

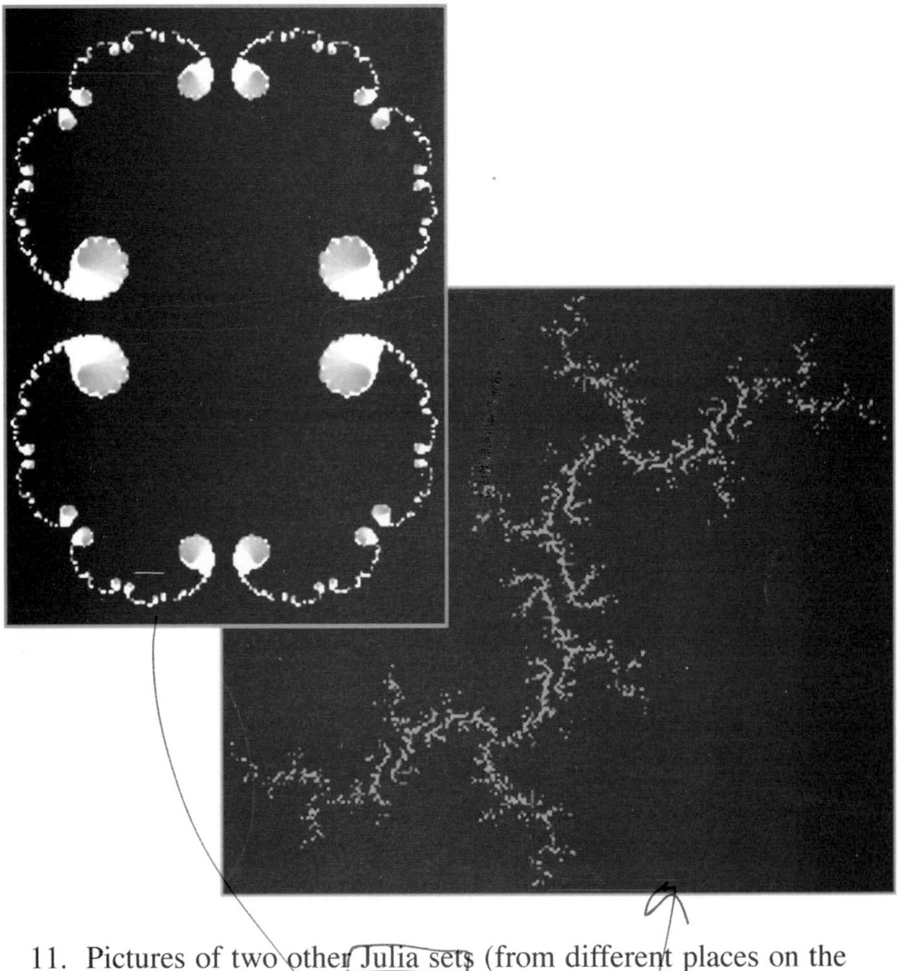

11. Pictures of two other Julia sets (from different places on the Mandelbrot set), hinting at the vast range of appearances the Julia sets can assume. The exact value of c around which the figure on the left is generated is: $c = -0.28$, $ic = 0$. For the figure on the right, $c = 0$, $ic = 0.82$.

two sides of the same coin. In general, Loy utilizes the spatial metaphor of a rock dividing a river (a metaphor that calls to mind the central image of *Ohio Impromptu*'s internal narrative): we can either look at the rock as a stationary object (an absolute) which defines the flowing river and thereby negates the flow of water, or we can see the (permanent) rock as an illusory construction of past and future, thereby negating the permanence of the rock.[12]

Although these two alternatives seem at considerable variance, it is important to note that "neither . . . affirms the rock in relation to the current. Both deny the self-existence of the rock as . . . counterposed to something objective" (Loy 1988, 218). The difference between subject and object (or experiencer and experienced) is discarded as illusory; so the difference between the true-flux and true-absolute positions is nonexistent. It is only our construction of time into the categories of past, present, and future that gives rise to the apparently objective difference between rock and river. Stated differently, nirvana or enlightenment (or phase space) is not a static state "outside time" as we usually conceive it (the act of conceiving here being the first wrong move), but is simply another way of seeing the flow and change that is time itself. It is not any abstract entity, but our perspective, that has changed.

When, during the rare moments in which the characters in *Godot* forget their appointments, their needs, and their desires—when, in other words, they simply exist in and of the stage moment—they are carried away with the current of time. The need for causality evaporates, and they are a small piece of eternity: "If everything is carried along together in the current, then phenomenologically there is no current at all" (Loy 1988, 218), and permanent flux is attained. One of the moments when the characters come nearest this state occurs when Vladimir realizes that there is another perspective on his world: "At me too someone is looking, of me too someone is saying, He is sleeping, he knows nothing, let him sleep on" (Beckett 1954, 58). Like the Buddha who awoke from his sleep of life, Vladimir momentarily senses that his normal way of comprehending the universe may not be the only one, or even the best one. Although he flees from this insight in panic, Vladimir evidently understands for an instant that his normal perspective on reality is, in essence, dreamlike. In *Waiting for Godot*, these moments are rare and at best implicit, but we will see how Beckett's plays delve into the matter with progressively more "presence."

The problem for *Godot* is that the "sleep" of these characters is filled with dreams of causality and time. By following the common paradigm of postulating time as an external container for actions and objects, which it must be if "things" are *supposed* to have any real (extratemporal) existence, and events are *supposed* to happen at a given moment, an illusory doubling arises:

> *in order for time to be a container, something must be contained within it: objects. And for objects to be 'in' time, they must in themselves be nontemporal—i.e., self-existing.* In this way, a delusive bifurcation occurs between time and 'things' generally, as a result of which each gains a spurious reality. (Loy 1988, 220)

What happens is that wanting and waiting create an apparent disjunction, or rift, between time and space, and Self and self (subject and object), and therefore a doubling occurs that is necessary for conceptual comparison—a doubling which, in Beckett's dramatic world, takes on physical characteristics, as the characters often appear in pairs. Although necessary for logical, causal thought, assigning any reality to this delusive bifurcation is, according to Zen, the source of all suffering. This doubling, which in Beckett's plays manifests itself physically as well as mentally, is an artifact of the old, causal paradigm and as such must be regarded with great suspicion.

If we look for a moment beyond the confines of *Waiting for Godot*, we observe what many critics have studied in depth: Beckett's work is consistently peopled with doubled pairs of characters.[13] From the pairs of pairs in *Godot* and *Endgame* to the pairing of character and voice in such plays as *Footfalls* and *Rockaby*, there is a remarkable constancy to his use of paired characters.[14] A review of the literature indicates a wide range of interpretations of this pairing, from echoes of early mythological characters and ritual to the splitting of one person's psyche. Often, in fact, the mere existence of these doubled characters is taken to be an indication of a need for reintegration (or "re-membering"). It may seem, then, that "nothing is left to tell" about the subject. From the perspective(s) of Zen and Chaos theory, however, we see that the split between characters is only apparent, a vestige of the causal paradigm: it is only the causal, *waiting* frame of mind that creates this bifurcation.

In *Godot*, this "old style" framework is emphasized, though in a negative light: characters, to the best of their abilities, use their intellect to understand and therefore control the world. By doing so, they either discourse on or directly attempt several of the most important philosophical and religious solutions the West has used in attempting to alleviate the problem of existence-as-suffering. In general, the metaphysical solutions attempted by the characters in *Godot* devalue the phenomenal and reify the intellectual capacity to understand and solve problems of the human condition. One result of this antagonistic relationship is the split that takes place between physical and mental "bodies": even in Christianity, the most consistent influence on Western culture in the last two millennia, the body is considered "bad" (e.g., "the flesh is weak"), whereas the mind can potentially apprehend God. By denying the partnership of body and mind, however, a delusive and costly desire to control the "outside" (nature—or the body) arises, a desire that drives science, industry, and morality in our society. A perfect example of this frame of reference is Pozzo in the first act. Pozzo feels that he owns the land—"my land"—on which Didi and Gogo are waiting; he considers his slave, Lucky, a "pig" that he can order around, and he feels he is able to move about freely from one place to another. He is, of course, proven wrong in all accounts in the second act, but when we first see him, Pozzo is mired in the certainty that intellect (of a bourgeois sort) and power can control fate and nature.

In the end, it is this overemphasis on the conceptual that engenders the world of suffering in *Godot*—and therefore its doubling: the intellectual world necessitates relational thinking, and this thinking requires a distant, distinctly doubled object upon which to think.

> Experience . . . teaches us that everything, every relationship in our samsaric world, is a relative one, that there is nothing that exists with absolutely no reference to anything else; there are no absolutes, and if there were, we would not be able to understand them any more than we can understand an absolute like mathematical infinity, beginningless Time or the First Cause. Such comprehension is beyond intellect since to understand anything with the intellect there must be a relationship. (Foster 1989, 251)

For the meager intellects of Vladimir, Estragon, Pozzo, and Lucky (although Lucky's intellect may not be as impoverished as that of the others) to operate, there must be a relationship of "things" in which they can operate; after all, Beckett's contemporaneous project, *The Unnamable*, pushes the limits of intellect in a vacuum, exhausting the powers of the mind *sans* relationship. And in *Godot*, as in most other Beckett plays, the perceived necessity for cognitive thought is manifested in physical form: the pairs of characters think their thoughts to each other. There is no soliloquy or aside in the play; the players simply talk their thoughts to each other. When, for example, Gogo tries on the pair of boots (which he does not recognize as his own) left on stage between acts, the following exchange occurs:

> ESTRAGON: *(vehemently)*. No no, no laces, no laces!
> VLADIMIR: You'll be sorry. Let's try the other (As before.) Well?
> ESTRAGON: *(grudgingly)*. It fits too.
> VLADIMIR: They don't hurt you?
> ESTRAGON: Not yet.
> VLADIMIR: Then you can keep them.
> ESTRAGON: They're too big.
> VLADIMIR: Perhaps you'll have socks some day.
> . . . .

ESTRAGON: I suppose I might as well sit down.
He looks for a place to sit down, then goes and sits down on the mound.
VLADIMIR: That's where you were sitting yesterday evening.
ESTRAGON: If I could only sleep.
VLADIMIR: Yesterday you slept.
ESTRAGON: I'll try.

(Beckett 1954, 44–45)

Although this exchange does not constitute a crucial moment in the play, it does show the extent to which Didi and Gogo vocalize their thoughts: for Estragon, the act of sitting must be voiced first, and Vladimir elicits vocal confirmation of his opinions about the shoes and his memory of "yesterday," though he gets no confirmation of the latter. Although there are many silences in the play, potentiating some private thinking, these silences tend either to involve physical comedy (e.g., the hat scene) or to be complete breaks in the fabric of character thought itself. Notably, the command Pozzo uses to precipitate Lucky's one massive outburst is the imperative, "Think!," at which point, Lucky, like an automaton,[15] begins discoursing in a sometimes humorous, often disturbing, "transreasonable" (Nealon 1988, 524) parody of philosophical jargon. Lucky is not commanded to vocalize his thoughts (to "speak"); nonetheless, he talks out loud, a result everyone on stage seems to expect.

Thus, in *Godot*, as in other plays we will examine, the pairing of characters has the important function of giving character thought a physically bifurcated relational context in which to operate; and thus we can consider the pairs as, in a sense, reflections or mirrors of each other, though the logical follow-up question of which one is being reflected lies outside our immediate scope.[16] Didi and Gogo, and Pozzo and Lucky, are not reflections *of* each other; they exist in a context that reflects, or doubles, them. This point is more clearly made by reverting to the metaphor of language: for Westerners, language is a construct made between two subject/objects (people)—for a country like Japan, on the other hand, language is that which exists prior to the subject/objects which inhabit it.

> In English, for example, we speak of language as a bridge spanning the gap between *I* and *you*. The isolated *a* and *b* together create an *R* so that communication can take place. In Japan, however, the event is viewed quite differently: the *R* is primary. The *R* is the given out of which *a* and *b* take their shape. . . . Thus the conscious bifurcation between I and you is diminished. (Kasulis 1981, 7)

Applying this metaphor, Didi and Gogo, and Lucky and Pozzo, are independent people, *a* and *b*, given the standard Western interpretation of language and interrelationships. Given a Japanese interpretation, however, they are aspects of a relational event that precedes and encompasses them.

This ontologically unitary perspective is further intensified if we use the specific relational context of Zen—that of No-thing, or *Mu*—in which the context is a "without-context." Whereas the Japanese linguistic context minimizes the difference between *a* and *b*, the Zen context of *Mu* collapses that distinction completely: "As Mumon advises, one must *be Mu*, not think about it" (Kasulis 1981, 11). Traditional thought, even if minimizing the difference between *a* and b, can never be rid of the distinction; just as conceptual, categorical thought must be essentially relational. In the without-context of without-thought, however, this distinction can and does collapse into nothingness, and we realize that those who we assumed were two (Vladimir-Estragon, Pozzo-Lucky, stage-audience) are, in fact, paradoxically, unitary. There is no change in what *is* (happening) on stage, merely a shift in our "sight." This re-vision of the play has profound implications, both for our viewing of the play and for our understanding of its ultimate project. Behind the lack of purpose or plot in the play, we now see the without-purpose it implicates; behind the bifurcation of characters, we glimpse the oneness from which they spring; behind the order we see the chaos, and behind the chaos we perceive a new order.

Interestingly, the only other complete work to deal with Beckett and Zen, Foster's *Beckett and Zen*, is subtitled, "A Study of *Dilemma* in the Novels of Samuel Beckett." *Dilemma,* of course, literally means "two propositions," or a bifurcation of concepts. As the subtitle suggests, and as has been perceived by an overwhelming number of Beckett's respondents, exposition of dilemma, perhaps that of existence itself, is at the core of Beckett's work: fiction, drama, and poetry. To be specific, in Beckett's work, a logical impasse is reached, best described as the "Can't go on. I'll go on" dilemma, which leaves characters, audience, and author alike skewered on the horns of the existential dilemma. When we examine his plays in light of the twin dilemmas of expression and existence, we realize that Beckett's project is not to answer the questions he evokes in his plays—as, for example, traditional narrative plays would do—but to present insolubility itself. "It is not the resolution of situations that Beckett wishes to convey but the nature of what he described to Driver as the '*chaos*'" (Foster 1989, 45; my emphasis). Though he does not use the term *chaos* in the technical sense we have been using it—that is, Chaos theory—the term is nonetheless provocative. The sense of the word as used by Beckett seems most likely to be something like "the nature of the world as it really is." Existence is physically split into pairs of characters and acts in *Godot*, destabilizing any cohesive sense of identity or closure, and order becomes not just inconsequential but counterproductive to an apprehension of the "chaos" of reality.

When Paul Foster attempts to conceptualize Beckett's existential dilemma, however, I believe he arrives at the wrong conclusion: "The root dilemma in Beckett is the desire to express, checked by the impossibility of expression" (Foster 1989, 34). This seems an accurate description of the "Can't go on. I'll go on" statement that ends *The Unnamable;* but is it? In his conversations with George Duthuit, Beckett, speaking of the painter Tal Coat, reveals more explicitly "his" dilemma: there is "nothing to express, nothing with which to express, nothing from which to express, no power to express, no desire to express together with the obligation to express" (1949, 98). The term Beckett uses—*obligation*—indicates a more Zen reading of this problem: the base dilemma is the desire *not* to express, checked by the impossibility of nonexpression. Thought and language as expression are not desired; they are aspects of life from which it is impossible to escape, at least within the common Western paradigm: every time we conceptualize a situation, every time we use language, every time we think at all, we are expressing at some level a re-presentation (Schopenhauer's *Vorstellung*) of the world. In Beckett's work, nothing would be better than to escape this driving necessity, but the existential dilemma eludes explicit solution. From an ordered perspective, the logical necessity of expression precludes any possible nonexpression. Thus the characters in *Godot* (and his oeuvre as a whole) feel compelled to go, whether verbally—"can't go on. I'll go on"—or physically—"let's go. *They do not move*"—even while they find it impossible to continue.

If, however, we rework this dilemma of expression and existence in terms of Chaotic without-order, then the implicit "solution" of an a priori collapsing of apparent distinction becomes possible. In Chaos theory, the bridge between the easily soluble, basically linear behavior of a nonlinear equation with small nonlinear coefficients and the advent of chaotic behavior (as the nonlinear component becomes significant) is often a bifurcation, or splitting of the solution to the problem. Thus, what had had a single solution and will have a chaotic (non)solution at some point has two (and then more) solutions. This intermediary stage—one in which chaotic and ordered behavior mix with greater frequency and complexity—implies that in the "real" world, chaos and order mix with great regularity and richness, when, in fact, it is only our careful screening of the world, through re-presentation, that has led us to overlook this fact. Thus, for Zen and Chaos theory alike, bifurcation is an important bridge in the perspective shift from everyday categorical metaphysics to a new, more appropriate view of the world.

Beyond acting as a simple reaffirmation of Zen, however, Chaos theory reveals something of great importance on this point: James Yorke's early mathematical treatise on chaotic behavior proved, as the title proclaims,

"Period Three Implies Chaos."[17] This proof means that any (one-dimensional) formula or natural system that could or would produce three solutions at once for a given coefficient value *has* to produce Chaotic behavior as well. The profound implications for the natural sciences notwithstanding, this finding directs us to look into *Godot* further to see if, in a work meant to convey "chaos," there is a "period three" that destabilizes the apparently fixed pairings, enabling a potential solution to the existential dilemma in which characters and play seem stranded.

We have already examined the pairings of characters in *Godot*, but these seem to be self-contained pairs (Didi-Gogo, Pozzo-Lucky) that interact in ways which tend to make each pair one half of a larger pair of opposites; for example, Vladimir and Estragon might be considered the stillness aspect of the larger pair, while Lucky and Pozzo embody a constant need for motion. While Zen has indicated that these pairings, or splits, may exist only because of our perspective, there is no mention (yet) of the importance of a third party. If, however, we quickly gloss the history of Western culture, we see that the three-party relationship has exemplified instability and change in everything from the Roman triumvirate to Freud's philosophy of mind. Additionally, the three-party relationship is one of the most heavily used tropes in literature throughout the West's written history: the dramatic quality of this unstable grouping draws artists to it again and again. Thus, what Chaos theory has "uncovered" in the natural world seems to have been anticipated by mankind's literary and historical tradition.

Where in Beckett's play is this third character? The obvious answer lies in the title—the third party, the one who sets this play in motion (or at least gives it a reason for occurring) is Godot him/itself. This character, the object of some degree of desire—the desire to wait at least—and fear, destabilizes the relationship between the characters we see on stage and allows us to see these characters operate under dramatic tension, although the tension here cannot be classified as realistic by any means. What is interesting for *Godot*, and for Beckett's theater as a whole, is that the third character "on stage" is only implicit; it has no external, objectively verifiable existence outside the play. In *A Streetcar Named Desire*, to name a single counterexample, the primary triangular relationship is that among Blanche, Stella, and Stanley, Stanley being approximate to Godot in the sense that he is a less clearly defined character around and through which the two sisters struggle. In *Streetcar*, however, Stanley is obviously a verifiable object for the audience's gaze. We can make our own judgments about his character and thus evaluate the other characters in terms of our understanding of him (as well as the other way around). In *Godot*, however, this is not the case. We are completely reliant on the stage characters to provide information about this most important third "character"; and, as the characters we do see are not willing (or able) to define Mr. Godot, we are left with only a vague notion of who or what Godot is.

Because of the indeterminacy of Godot, both characters and audience are forced into a mysterious world in which there is no privileged, objective, "outside" metaphysics to explain what occurs. And this leads back to Zen, which claims that, as we are all floating with the current down the river of change, we cannot see reality from some external quasi-objective vantage point. Thus Godot, because he/it apparently lacks existence in any verifiable manner, destabilizes both the relationships between characters and events on stage and that between the audience and play. Because of "his" active disruption of cohesion and closure, Godot brings to light the possibility of a unifying vision of the divided world of the play.

Yet the potential this "Godot factor" allows for a reduction of the bifurcations in *Waiting for Godot* leads to an apparent problem between our two critical tools: the Zen vision of the world is concerned primarily about breaking down the apparent division between subject(s) and object(s), valorizing the reality of a unitary reading. The vision of Chaos theory, on the other hand, apparently lauds the opposite—doubling and tripling are to be valued as harbingers of the real world. Once again, the two seem to be at odds with each other; but, again, this division is only apparent, the intersection actually allowing a richer reading of each. Upon closer examination of the famous bifurcation diagram, the "logistic equation" diagram (seen briefly in figure 7), we find that the simple, one-dimensional second-order equation, $x \rightarrow rx(x - 1)$for small values of r, stabilizes to a straight line (effectively acting as a linear equation). At a specific value of r, however, the equation bifurcates, then each of these lines bifurcates, and so on, until a chaotic mess appears (see figures 8 and 9).[18]

If we compare this diagram to a chapter from the *Tao Te Ching*,[19] an amazing convergence appears:

> The Tao gives birth to One.
> One gives birth to Two.
> Two gives birth to Three.
> Three gives birth to all things.
>
> (Lao Tzu 1988, 42)

Remarkably, this passage almost seems a description of a diagram first produced more than two thousand years later. The Tao, the plenary void, becomes visible when it becomes One (the single line). Yet, to be visible, any one thing must of necessity have something else to compare it with; and, thus, the Two is born (the bifurcating line). The two are apparently stable, but when two things are perceived, the act of perception creates a third, destabilizing the situation and giving rise to the apparently infinite

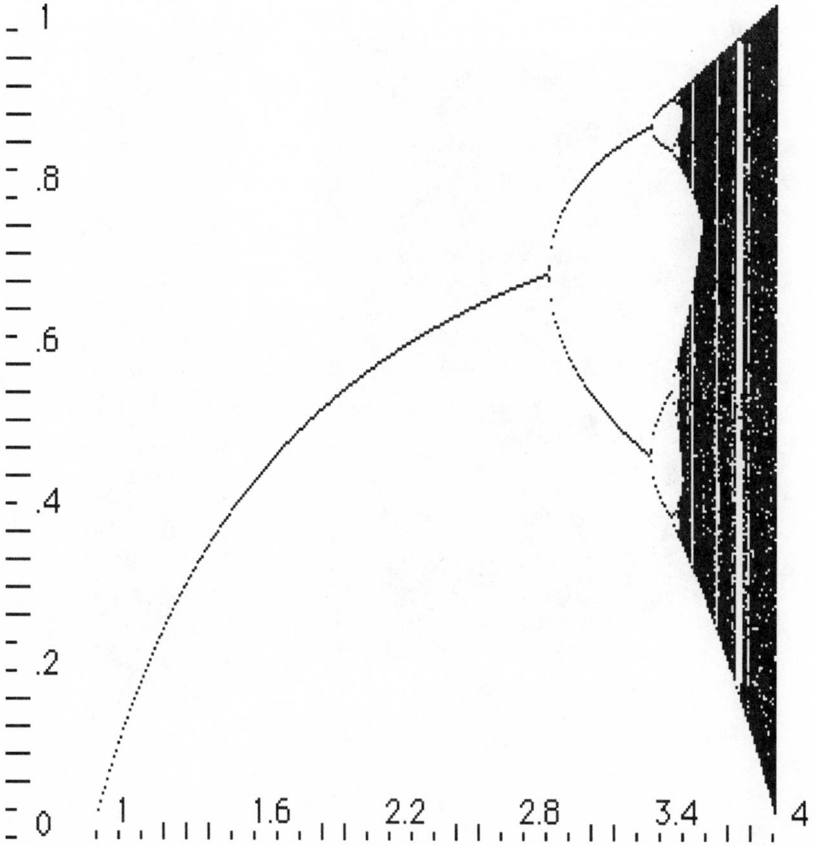

Fig. 8. Bifurcation and ordered descent of the logistic equation $x \rightarrow rx(x-1)$ into chaotic behavior

world of the everyday. Thus, Three creates the Chaos of reality. Here, reality is truly in the eye of the beholder, because a metaphysical re-presentation that sees only the "ten thousand" things cannot perceive the unitary Tao (or *Mu*) behind them, and, at least for the conceptual world, to describe the ineffable, unitary Tao is impossible. "A completely unique object, if such a thing were imaginable, could not be described" (Hayles 1990, 31).[20] Instead, we must understand that this Ur-Tao, which cannot be written about

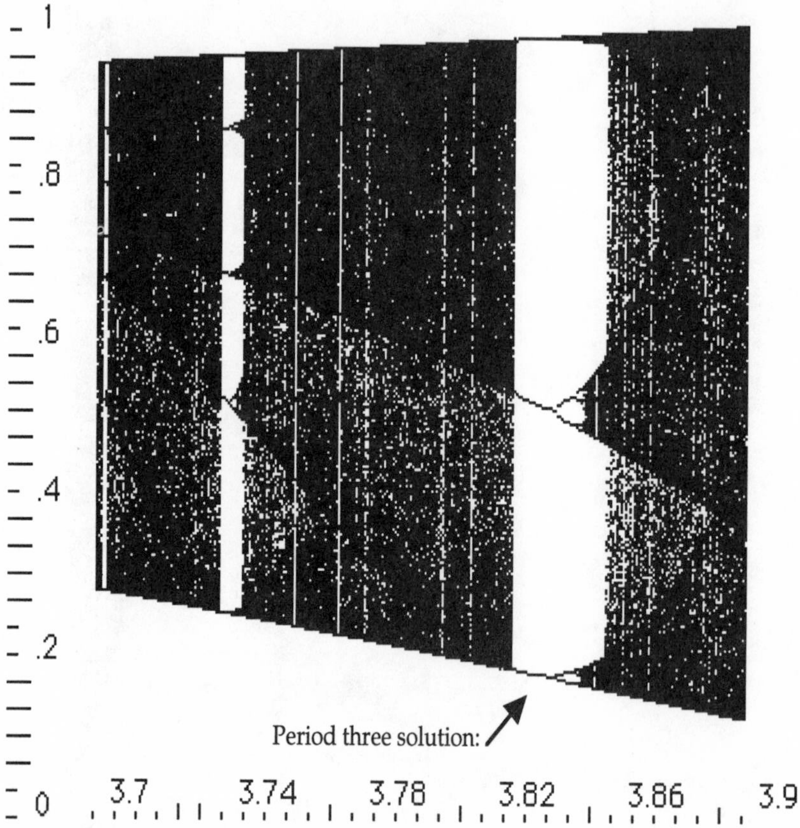

Fig. 9. Expansion of a small section of the population diagram showing the amazingly intricate interplay between chaotic and ordered behavior, as well as the sudden appearance and orderly descent back into chaotic behavior of a "period three" solution where the arrow indicates

or described, is "*both* absolute and relative" (Kasulis 1981, 35), its characteristics changing like water flowing to fit different containers.

In Chaos theory as well, this seemingly paradoxical situation obtains: "Chaotic systems are both deterministic and unpredictable" (Hayles 1990, 14), the absolutism of the deterministic interacting with the relativity of the unpredictable. Thus, the ambiguous Mr. Godot is, like the Tao, at the intersection between the ineffable and the linguistically relative, therefore existing within and giving birth to the iteration of the random assortment of characters and situations, and at the same time outside of this world. He/it is a void that contains and produces the vast complexity of the system of *Waiting for Godot*. The four characters on stage, then, are involved in "an initiation rite that leads them to experience the void [which is Godot] as sacred" (Burkman 1986, 35).

Coming to understand that the implicit Godot is a void that is constructive rather than destructive is also tied into what has come to be known as information theory. As we have seen, this model separates information per se from meaning, and thus posits "static" or "noise"—the unpredictable part of a message—as the *informationally* richer portion of the message. Therefore, "The more chaotic a system is, the more information it produces" (Hayles 1990, 8).[21] The interplay of the orderly with the implicit and the unpredictable thus produces a richly informational message. With its mixture of repetition and unpredictable behavior, *Waiting for Godot* is a rich play precisely because of its unpredictable noise, a noise which, according to both Chaos and information theory, allows it "to reorganize at a higher level of complexity" (Hayles 1990, 57).

A beautifully concise example of the complex noise extant in this play is Lucky's outburst near the end of act 1, "a language game . . . which can be seen as a transgression and disruption of the limits of the ultimate metagame—Western metaphysics, the language game of truth" (Nealon 1988, 523). In Lucky's speech, in a nutshell, is a Chaotic system of language, revolving around a nonclosed strange attractor, producing a sublime mixture of unpredictability and recursive scaling symmetry. In tantalizing fashion, the speech begins by considering a conditional proposition: "Given the existence . . . of a personal God . . . outside time . . ." (Beckett 1954, 28). The speech begins, therefore, by postulating an absolute (and therefore ineffable), yet describable, being that exists on the same plane of intersection as bifurcating Chaos, the Tao, and Godot. This introductory remark (d)evolves into a web of scholastic citations, subordinate clauses, classical allusions, memento mori, and a compendium of sports activities—and even this list falls well short of what has been read as a dirge for Western civilization, and even an indication of the decay of the universe.[22] All of these elements function as noise in the speech, eventually drowning out any possible thread of continuous, closed-ended meaning and leaving the audiences, both on stage and off, reeling from the sheer volume of information being spewed at us. Yet this volume is, according to information theory, a positive element of the speech, the chaotic mode of presentation maximizing the speech's value. Furthermore, the chaos of the presentation is, in actuality, Chaotic in the technical sense: the speech is not completely random gibberish, but a carefully constructed set of evolving revolutions of material presented.

A necessarily incomplete catalogue of the evolving kinds of "noise" we encounter in the speech reveals the underlying importance of this element in it. It also indicates, in miniature, the importance of noise to the workings of the play itself. To begin with, there is the Latin noise of the repeated "quaquaquaqua," which helps give the early stages of the speech a scholarly, philosophical tone. Then Lucky begins to use alliterative noise in phrases like "divine apathia divine athambia divine aphasia," the primacy of meaning being displaced by the sound of the words—though, of course, the humorous "divine aphasia," or lack of speech, also requires a reorganization of thought at a higher level of complexity. This tendency toward the (apparent) primacy of sound over meaning continues intermittently (but with a definite increase in frequency) throughout the speech. Also, as quickly becomes apparent, the scholarly citation of sources for ideas is a humorous form of noise in Lucky's speech. We might think Puncher and Wattmann are valid sources, but by the time we get to Messieurs Fartov and Belcher, it is apparent that Beckett is poking fun at the use of citations. Along with this joke at academia's expense is the noisy use of academic jargon like "hereinafter . . . the labors of . . . in short . . . in brief . . . etc." The physical half of life is also brought into the fray—a litany of sports, both real and imagined, popping up here and there throughout. Among all these forms of noise, however, the most insidious and self-reflexive is Beckett's re-visioning of allusion as noise: from references to William Shakespeare—"Miranda" alluding to *The Tempest*, "the labors lost of Steinweg" implying *Love's Labors Lost*, and the repetitive contemplation of "the skull the skull the skull" conjuring up thoughts of *Hamlet*—to the extremely funny quotation of Churchill—"on sea on land and in the air"—Beckett reduces Freud/Bloom's "anxiety of influence" to an array of random references that deconstruct rather than accrue narrative meaning.[23]

Even Lucky's original train of thought, the conditional, "Given the existence as uttered forth in the public works of Puncher and Wattmann of a personal God . . ." (28)—a train of thought both he and we strain desperately to string together into a coherent narrative whole—turns out to be just that much more noise, since the thought remains forever "unfinished" as Vladimir removes Lucky's thinking hat. Thus, although the compendium of noise in Lucky's speech may seem to the audience like an irritating interference blocking the "real" message Lucky is trying to communicate, it is, rather, the noise that assumes complete dominance in the speech. By the end, the interplay of sense and non-sense proves to be the real message of the Lucky's words.

If we can only see Lucky's monologue from the vantage point of Chaos theory and Zen, we perceive a new, more complex and natural order behind the messy surface. Rather than forcing the speech to fit the bounds of the conceptual dialectic, sense/non-sense, Zen and Chaos theory indicate that we should move beyond these categories, apprehending the speech as an information-rich interplay of the probable and the surprising. Though concentrating on the idea of postmodernism and language, Jeffrey Nealon addresses precisely this issue of altering our vision of Lucky's speech:

> This thinking on the other side of the limit is precisely what Lucky's speech consists of. It is, however, not *non-sense*. Simple non-sense would still be thought dictated by the dialectic of reason; it would involve a simple crossing over to the other side of the dialectic—doing or saying the *un*-reasonable thing—leaving the limits intact. Lucky's think is not *unreasonable*, it is . . . *transreasonable*: it does not simply offer us the other side of the dialectic of reason, but moves at and beyond the margins of the dialectic, beyond the limitations that have been placed on language. In Lucky's speech, Beckett exposes and transgresses these limits, mixing bits of grammatical sense (inside the limit) and transgrammatical non-sense (outside the limit) to the point where the limit itself is effaced, opening up the field of what can be thought. (1988, 524)

The quotidian dialectic conceptual paradigm is effectively shorted out by the complex interplay of sense and non-sense. If, however, we are able to move beyond the categorical imperative, we see this speech instead as a "peaceful" (Nealon 1988, 524) movement away from conceptual reason to the nonclosed, plenary without-context of prereflective information.

As opposed to large sections of *Watt* and the sucking stone incident in *Molloy*, for example, this speech, like the play itself, does not permute its "noisy" words and events with algebraic regularity; rather, it cycles them in nonrepeating, but self-similar, fashion. Across different scales, patterns of noise recur with the same pattern—though on all levels, the next occurrence is not precisely predictable. To see this more clearly, I have "mapped" occurrences of two important phrases in Lucky's speech—"for reasons unknown" and "unfinished." If we compare the patterning of these occurrences against the self-similar, fractionally dimensional "Cantor dust," we see important similarities (see figures 10–12).[24]

It is obvious that, while the recurrences of these phrases in Lucky's speech do not repeat with quite as much regularity as the Cantor dust, they do recur in similar patterns across various scales.[25] This point is remarkable on its own, as it indicates that Lucky's speech (and perhaps language itself—but that is beyond the scope of this work) is modeled on a quasi-mathematical, self-similar structure. For our present purposes, the import of this graphical comparison is that Chaos theory opens up a new way of

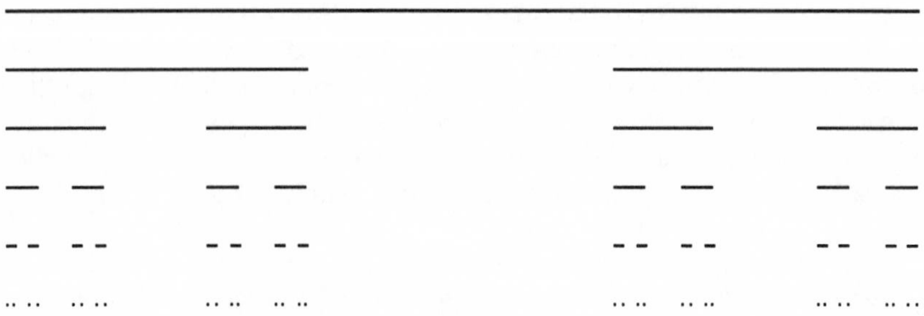

Figure 10. First five levels of what will become the Cantor dust. In the last line, the spacing takes on a distinct long-short-long patterning.

interpreting the speech itself. Instead of struggling to piece together meaning and a narrative thread, we can instead see the patterning of the interplay of order and noise as valuable, even beautiful in its own right. This observation reinforces the similarity of vision between Chaos theory, Zen, and *Godot*, as all demonstrate (either explicitly or implicitly) that the concrete reality of the Chaotic moment is more valuable and truer to life (even more beautiful) than the conceptual grid we construct as, and force on, reality. Thus, the speech functions at once as a severe criticism of our common notions about existence and metaphysics, and as example of an alternative manner in which to interact with reality.

What we perceive, from our causal frame of reference, as noise, is not, then, really noise, but an a priori reality that is distorted by the noisy mask of regularity we normally place over it, calling that linguistic/conceptual construct "reality" instead. The complex multivalency of reality we normally try to sweep under the rug of our minds, calling it a set of unimportant, unsolvably complex fringe aberrations, is not, given this change in view, complex, nor is it a fringe aberration. The random multiplicity of this supposedly fringe world is only apparent, the underlying structures in actuality remarkably few and simple—if we just stop trying to construct a narrative of meaning by finding causal links between the individual points of "being-time" (Loy 1988, 222) in reality.

This last point brings us back to the assertion made earlier: the pairings of characters in *Waiting for Godot* are, on some level, collapsed into a singular state. If the complex attempt to order our vision of everyday life clouds the simpler patterning that lies beneath and before it, then the doubling of characters on stage in *Godot* is a physical manifestation of the ordered randomness of Chaotic systems and without-thinking of Zen Buddhism. The fluctuating relationships of Didi and Gogo, of Pozzo and Lucky,

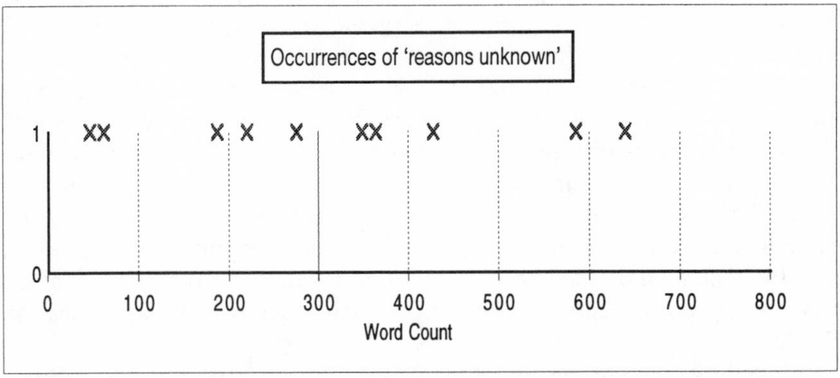

Fig. 11. Position of phrase, "reasons unknown" in Lucky's speech—note the long-short-long patterning.

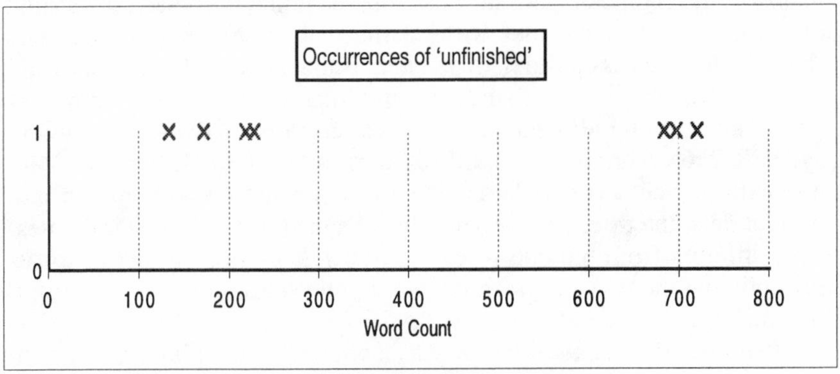

Fig. 12. Position of word, "unfinished" in Lucky's speech—note again the Cantor dustlike patterning of long-short-long.

and in self-similar scaling fashion, of the Didi-Gogo pair and the Pozzo-Lucky pair, seen from this light, are a dynamic relational "event" existing sufficiently at each moment they and we participate in the play's world. Indeed, we as audience become part of another pairing scale, interacting in a dynamic pattern with the characters on stage, and thus we also (as we must in this system) take part in the moment-to-moment relational collapse, living, in acting terms, "in the moment" without regard to conceptual structures and absolute divisions. As Loy puts it, "If there are no nontemporal objects [which exist outside of the changing moment], then the present does not gain its value or meaning by being related to past or future: each event or being-time is complete in itself" (1988, 222). Like the well-trained athlete, "Hinging total awareness on the pivotal moment we call the present" (Kasulis 1981, 58), we forget the conceptual duality of us-them, me-you, time past and time present, and so forth, concentrating only on the self-sufficient moment of "being-time" at hand. With only a set of acausal points of time existing wholly in and of themselves, yet revolving around the "plenary void" of the attractor that defines their limits, the play itself becomes the legendary rubied net, each ruby—or element of the play—reflecting all the others *at that moment*.[26] Thus, the apparently complex multiplicity generated by the interplay of order and disorder that occurs in the play—and even at specific performances—participates in the wholeness of *Godot* itself.

Recalling the importance of the parable of the two thieves, we can now add significantly to the statement. Indeed, the two thieves are important to the play and to us: they are Didi and Gogo, Pozzo and Lucky, "you and me," but they are one more thing as well: they are the *same*. The dynamic collapse of the characters tells us that, from the point(s) of view of Zen and Chaos theory, the saved thief *is* the damned thief. As Nagarjuna states, "That which, taken as causal or dependent, is the process of being born and passing on [i.e. the world of suffering and impermanence], is, taken non-causally and beyond all dependence, declared to be *Nirvana*" (quoted in Loy 1988, 246). As nothing is "self-existent" or absolute (Loy 1988, 246), the real difference between damnation and salvation is merely one of perspective; thus, the thief who apparently is handed damnation is not, in essence, different from the one who is saved. The pair of thieves is apparently split, but the two are in reality simply two sides of the same existential coin.

What does this mean to the play as a whole? If the thieves/we are indeed the same from the perspectives of Zen and Chaos theory, then Pozzo's lament,

> one day we were born, one day we shall die, the same day, the same second, is that not enough for you? *(Calmer.)* They give birth astride of a grave, the light gleams an instant, then it's night once more
>
> (Beckett 1954, 57)

is as much a cry of victory over the temporal world of becoming-and-passing-away as it is a lament over our bondage to it. If the process of birth, suffering, and death is equivalent to the state of nirvana, then it is only(!) a matter of shifting his/our understanding of reality away from a logical narrative process view to one of self-sufficient moments cycling around central themes in a nonclosed but bounded pattern for us to apprehend the play as the fully realized gleaming instant between creation and night.

Both because of the importance of Pozzo's statement to *Waiting for Godot*—and, indeed, to Beckett's work as a whole—and because of the remarkable affinity between this new view of Pozzo's statement and the following quotation, it is worth citing at length Loy's presentation on the Zen perspective toward this most important issue of life and death:

> Because life and death, like spring and summer, are not *in* time, they are in themselves timeless. *If there is no one nontemporal* [i.e., with an eternal soul] *who is born and dies*, then there is only birth and death [flux itself]. But if there are only the events of birth and death, with no one "in" them, *then there is no real birth and death* [as no "one" is being born or dying]. Alternatively, we may say that there is birth-and-death in every moment, with the arising and passing away of each thought and act. . . . Dogen: "Just understand birth-and-death itself is *Nirvana*. . . . Only then can you be free from birth-and-death." (1988, 222; Dogen quotation from the "Shoji," or Birth and Death, fascicle of his *Shobogenzo*)

The clear indication here is that, if we rid ourselves of the false distinction between the saved thief and the damned one—false because each of these men is a collection of a-causal points in the flux of existence, not an absolute, independent being outside time—then the moments of birth and death collapse into identity at the same time that their ultimately illusory nature is revealed. There is, in essence, no birth or death, as there is "no-thing" to be born or to die. Here again, the importance of the quasi-present Godot becomes apparent: through Godot's destabilizing influence, the characters on stage—even we and the characters—are stripped of their apparent temporal and physical differences, and instead are apprehended within the unity of a dynamic relational without-context.

Godot him/itself, living in the twilight of presence between existence and nonbeing, must then be like the archer's bow which at once allows arrow and target to interact and undermines any static difference between the arrow and the target. Godot is the ever-changing glue that holds the dynamics of each moment together. Thus, by destabilizing the relationships on (and off) stage, he/it actually acts as No-thing, the Zen relational "without-context" that determines the mode of interaction between Zen initiate and environment. At each moment, Godot *is already* whatever the characters "need" him to be.[27] Thus, while the characters wait for salvation from Godot, he/it implicitly provides this salvation (and, at the same time, damnation) at every moment. It is only an inability to awaken to the true nature of each moment by discarding the sleep of memory (their/our "sense of absolute presence . . . dependent on memory and anticipation" [Connor 1988, 119]) that keeps the characters waiting. "Was I sleeping while the others suffered? Am I sleeping now? To-morrow, when I wake, or think I do, what shall I say of to-day?" (Beckett 1954, 58). Like the Buddha recalling the unenlightened state, Vladimir realizes that he may, in effect, be sleeping, dreaming of a world filled with causality and absolute objects. If the characters could awaken from their sleep and break the ontological need for a single metaphysical system (their concept of Godot), they would see that their world is, in fact, the multivalent, dynamic state of nirvana.

The indeterminate state between the two paradigms in which the characters in *Waiting for Godot* find themselves caught as the play progresses brings us the final moment of the play, a moment recycled from the first act by the attractor behind the play, and a moment that will recur over and over again throughout Beckett's dramatic canon:

> VLADIMIR: Well? Shall we go?
> ESTRAGON: Yes, let's go.
>
> *They do not move.*
>
> *Curtain.*
>
> (60)

This final, frozen tableau is reminiscent of a moment Zen practitioners know as the "Great Doubt" (in Hakuin's terms)—the moment which necessarily arises before the causal ego-consciousness can be displaced and enlightenment can occur. Forced by circumstance and desire, a Zen student will sit in zazen until,

> No longer sitting to be enlightened, one merely sits to sit. Feeling almost dead in any case, no longer protecting any part of the self, the disciple sits with abandonment, totally unconcerned with the consequences. At this point, the Great Doubt may arise: a still-point of terrible tension in which one gives oneself up to the feeling of nowhere to go. (Kasulis 1981, 113–14)

In this moment, full of the dramatic tension we see at the end of *Waiting for Godot*, the student fully realizes the abyss of "letting go" that lies before her and freezes in ecstasy and fear.[28] One of Hakuin's descriptions of the internal workings of this state is as follows:

> Night and day I did not sleep! I forgot both to eat and rest. Suddenly a great doubt manifested itself before me. It was as though I were frozen solid in the midst of an ice sheet extending tens of thousands of miles. A purity filled my breast and I could neither go forward nor retreat. (Quoted in Kasulis 1981, 107)

The doubt, often generated by the study of an insoluble Zen koan, becomes so great that it is like a state of death, the student often ceasing movement, almost breathing itself, as she attempts finally to dislodge the causal ego's hold over her mind. "If you take up one *koan* and investigate it unceasingly your mind will die and your will will be destroyed. . . . It is as though a vast, empty abyss lay before you, with no place to set your hands and feet" (Hakuin; quoted in Kasulis 1981, 108). It appears that in the final moments of each act of *Godot*,[29] the all-consuming, koanlike non-act of waiting for Godot defeats all conceptual defenses, and a moment of "terrible tension" occurs, a "still-point" that is the Great Doubt, wherein volition and action cease to be effective and the "vast, empty abyss" of "nowhere to go" rushes in to fill the void. This is the moment of stasis in which all the potentialities of time and without-time—of being and without-being, of multivalency and unity, of chaos and determinism, of waiting and without-waiting—resonate in the gleaming instant before the death of the play's moment. In a space of half-seen truths, chaos and order, even birth and death, are two more pairs collapsing into dynamic unity.

In this final moment—at least in a potential space—Godot is made present: the hope and fear, the salvation and damnation of the characters and of the world are tied together through the relational context of the without-character of Godot into a self-sufficient moment of being-time. The pairs in the play, like arrow and target, are poised to enter a dynamic union through the tension of the drawn "bow" of this moment of Great Doubt. In an instant, enlightenment or death can come; but nothing moves. As the dynamic "still" of the world of *Godot* fades to night, all involved are invited to celebrate the arrival of the always-already present Godot, to stop waiting for some-thing to occur by participating in the Zen/Chaos vision of the unity of complexity in *Waiting for Godot*. On stage, however, Vladimir and Estragon wait.

4

End of Zeno's Game? Discarding Bow, Arrow, and Target

> Fractal processes associated with scaled, broadband spectra are "information rich." Periodic states, in contrast, reflect narrow-band spectra and are defined by monotonous, repetitive sequences, depleted of information content.
>
> —Ary Goldberger

> The drawing is thus a means to an end, and I cannot lose sight of this connection. The child knows nothing of this, but for me the two things cannot be disconnected.
>
> —Eugen Herrigel

To Hamm's anguished question in *Endgame*, "what's happening?," Clov's famous response is: "Something is taking its course" (Beckett 1958, 13). While this may be an evasion more than an answer to Hamm's question, it is interesting to look at Clov's response in light of our discussion of *Godot*, where the characters (at least, Vladimir and Estragon) end up poised between a need to wait for something to happen and liberation from this need. In *Endgame*, as in *Waiting for Godot*, the conventions of realistic theater are broken, as characters revolve in something like a diminishing spiral instead of evolving in narratively structured fashion. In *Endgame*, however, the main pair, Hamm and Clov, is closer in character and relationship to the Pozzo/Lucky pair in *Godot*: a flamboyant, blind master who abuses, yet is effectively bound to, his servant. *Endgame* is thus an ideal opportunity to examine the master-slave relationship so important to both plays but more foregrounded in this one. By focusing, then, on this different pairing, a difference arises between the two plays: in *Godot*, the main character pair, Vladimir and Estragon, are *waiting* for something to happen, while in *Endgame* something *is* happening—though neither Clov nor Hamm apparently has any good idea what it is.

The difference between the two plays may partly be explicated by returning for a moment to the archery metaphor. In *Godot*, the "old" way of using bow, arrow, and target (for example, narrative cohesion and explication) is destabilized as characters and staging show the difficulty of maintaining a discrete meaning or distance between the "objects"—bow, arrow, target; the character pairs, Godot, the play itself. At the same time, however, Vladimir and Estragon merely await the potential change in vision. Vladimir, at least, seems to understand that there is another way to understand existence, yet the two choose to continue waiting for the arrival of some conceptual closure to make sense of their nightly ritual. They are like an archer who, though knowing the arrow and target are in essence one, waits, hoping the arrow will strike its target. The old need for the conceptual closure of a distinct arrow striking a distinct target ensure that the archer must always wait for an illusory moment to arrive. In *Endgame*, the characters, effectively following Pozzo's revelation that existence is essence (as birth and death always and never take place), take the next step, seeing that conceptual baggage can only get in the way of letting the "something" happen. Thus they are closer to becoming like the archer who lets go of the notion of distinct entities—bow, arrow and target—and thus is freed to experience the dynamic interplay of these elements of self-sufficient "being-time."

Clov and Hamm, like Lucky and Pozzo, are more existentially active, experiencing the something that is taking place instead of waiting for it to come to them. All the same, the two are still not free: Clov waits for an excuse to leave (or kill) his master, and Hamm waits for "the end" of life and/or the world. That their waiting takes on a more active cast links the pairs of characters in *Godot* and *Endgame*; that the process of waiting becomes an excuse for—or, perhaps, necessitates—a creative, narrative attempt on Hamm's part imparts a unique twist to the character pair in *Endgame*. Whereas Didi and Gogo in *Godot* spend their time distracting themselves from the chaotic nonclosure of their world, in *Endgame*, Hamm especially is actively intolerant of the "noise" of his world, trying instead, through story or control, for an ordered universe of which he is master. From numerous instances in the play, we can construct something of Hamm's attitude toward others and the little room/world of which he is king: Hamm is (or, at least, has been) a powerful, thoughtless, even cruel master over his little corner of the universe, which by now has shrunk to the bounds of his great room. Apparently, however, the diminishing size of his domain is of less consequence to Hamm than that he control it: when he demands a tour of the room from Clov, Hamm urges his servant to push him "Right round the world!" (Beckett 1958, 25), and then to put him "Bang in the center!" (27) of this little world he has just toured.

At a closer look, however, even though Hamm seems in charge of his world, we easily see how helpless and small he is. He is unable to see or move, and in the end he is not content with his role as master of this "little bit of grit" in the void. Hamm needs Clov to provide food, toys, and "painkiller" for him, as if he were a small child. He also needs to know what is occurring outside his room, asking Clov to look on the "without" several times during the play. In addition, the seemingly powerful creator Hamm must have witnesses to his creation: he cannot tell his story without either his father or Clov listening to him recount the tale of his interview with the father of a young boy (who is commonly thought to be Clov). Somewhat like Prospero, to whom he makes reference,[1] Hamm's charge over those around him is great but necessarily fleeting. It is, perhaps, this knowledge of the coming end of power and life as much as innate predisposition that forces Hamm to need control and order so much—and which makes him desire his painkiller so much. There is no surprise that such a powerful, egotistical man does not easily relinquish his hold on the illusion of control and order he has maintained for some time. Yet the characters, including Hamm, and even the play itself resist closure and order: "The pervasive structure of negation [of referential meaning] and contradiction frustrates all partial investments of meaning and thereby fundamentally impedes every gesture of interpretation which strives for closure" (Schwab 1984, 195). This sounds very similar to what Zen and Chaos theory profess to be the "other" vision of existence: Chaos theory propounds the virtues of noise and nonclosure, while Zen Buddhism advocates a discarding of the ego in order that the person may live more fully and freely. The play, then, seems to push for the paradigm shift that Zen and Chaos theory embody: freedom to let "something" take its course without needing to categorically pin this "thing" down. Is a character like Hamm capable of letting go of his need for control and accepting this freer, nonclosed view of life?

A good place to start looking into the question of Hamm's desire for closure and identity through order is to look again at his need to circle the stage-space that he rules. Though it may not immediately leap to mind, stage closure is important to the play: Hamm wants his room, and his position in it, to be ordered and contained. As Clov pushes, Hamm exhorts him: "Right round the world! . . . Hug the walls, then back to the center again" (Beckett 1958, 25), indicating his need for a completed circuit around the edges of his domain, as well as his need to return to the exact position from which he started (according to his repeated instructions for Clov to place him dead center). In addition, as he is escorted around his room, Hamm must "Hug the walls" in order to know that he is safe within the confines of order, separated from the "other hell" outside (26).

At the same time, the security of the little world Hamm has created around him is essentially illusory—as Hamm himself instinctively knows.

Of the wall that surrounds and protects him from the chaos outside, Hamm notes: "Hollow bricks! . . . All that's hollow!" (26). Hamm's sudden comprehension of the minimal protection offered by the wall apparently has a significant effect on him, as he immediately and violently orders Clov to return to the center of the room. Clov, obviously conditioned by daily habit, complains, "We haven't done the round" of the room (26), but Hamm insists. Thus, fearing lack of protective "closure" from the space outside—as he is perhaps scared of how thin the division is between himself and the "without"—Hamm forgoes another form of spatial closure by not completing his circuit.

What is the consequence of this action? Little, it seems; but this stage movement clues us in to several crucial aspects of Hamm's character: his push for order, his shying away from the "mess" of creation, and his ultimate inability to achieve the order and closure he so desperately seeks on several fronts. First, as we have noted, Hamm drives himself and others (Clov, in this case) to produce complete, ordered events, for example, a circuit around his little world and back to its center. Second, Hamm is unable to face the dimly seen, dimly known "other hell" outside, preferring the familiar, hellish routine of his stale encapsulated cell. Third, the complete, ordered events Hamm desires do not take place as projected; in the case of his tour of the room, the perfection of a circle is broken short as Hamm returns from upstage. Additionally, when Hamm returns to center stage, he is not satisfied with his position, and perhaps cannot be. He spends some time requesting adjustments to his wheelchair, hoping to ensure his position at the exact center of his room/world. This repeated routine—as evinced by Clov's frustrated reaction to the whole scenario—indicates in Hamm a continual discomfort with his state, an inability to "center" himself properly, as it were. Thus, in Hamm (and those around him, through his influence) there are conflicting movements toward containment and dissolution, rigidity and creation, order and chaos—all connected through desire and fear.

In addition to a spatial element, Hamm's drive for closure takes on temporal dimensions—for example, through his circular "ritual" of the handkerchief. The first thing Hamm does (after Clov's lines, "Finished . . . nearly finished") is to remove the handkerchief covering his face, wipe himself with it, and repeat "Me . . . to play" (2). As he is just waking, this statement is interrupted by a yawn (a nice comic touch when combined with his next lines, "Can there be misery—*(he yawns)*—loftier than mine?"). Because of the obvious lack of intensity and revelation in this statement, we should see this moment as a ritual repetition, not a new event. Late in the play, we are treated to an inversion of this ritual, as Hamm, preparing to put the handkerchief back over his face, states again, "Me to play." Apparently he is now preparing for sleep, ending his day as he began it, in closed, circular fashion. Yet the expected end is not the one that occurs: Hamm is unable to finish in such a well-ordered way; instead, he launches into an extended monologue with no audience—a first for him. Unable simply to drift off to sleep, Hamm confronts his past and future, growing "very agitated" at the thought of "All those I might have helped" (68) and at being alone in his "old shelter" of a room. As opposed to the peace and stillness Hamm desires for himself, he babbles on "like the solitary child who turns himself into [many] children" (70). Finally, extremely fearful that he will not get a response (and therefore truly be alone), Hamm whistles for Clov, who does reappear. Thus, as with his trip "round the world," Hamm's fears (and even guilt) prevent him from executing a closed loop. This time, his perfectly, rigidly structured day falls apart as his fear of the torments of conscience and being alone supersede his wish to find closure.

"The dynamic . . . between a continual invitation to closure and renewed opening can be seen as one of the play's central strategic devices" (Schwab 1984, 196). Indeed, the dynamic is central to this study of Beckett's plays in relationship to Zen and Chaos theory. As we have seen, far from evaluating the conflict between closed order and open-ended chaos in polar terms, both Zen and Chaos theory claim that these opposites fall within the scope of their paradigms. For Zen, the rigidity, containment, and "order" sought after by Hamm's struggling ego is inextricably linked to the creative, chaotic dissolution that so threatens his sense of identity. If Hamm could only look at his existential suffering in a new way, he could see that the source of his suffering is not the hell "without" but the hell of conceptual division his mind puts him through: "Peace can only come when the impetus [to create words] is gone. . . . [F]or Hamm, impetus remains" (Maughlin 1987, 96). From the perspective of Chaos theory as well, the rigid, supposedly "positive" contradistinction between order and chaos of the classical paradigm is inaccurate, which makes the world far more complex than it need be. As with Hamm's room, there is no center of order and no distinct fringe of chaotic dissolution; instead, there is a dynamic mixture of the two everywhere. It is only by accepting that deterministic disorder is central to the function of the universe that a true understanding of what occurs can begin to take place.

Therefore, in light of both Zen and Chaos theory, Hamm's complex set of drives and needs must, as he experiences them, cause him pain: assumed to be opposites, the urge to create and at the same time maintain order, or to be a fully present person and also resist meaning—"We're not beginning to . . . to . . . mean something?" (Beckett 1958, 32)—must, of necessity, tear at him, dividing him against himself. Physically, these contradictions are projected onto the contrasting characteristics of those on stage,[2] Clov, for example, is unable to sit, while Hamm cannot rise, or the "metapairs" Nagg-Nell and Hamm-Clov are made up in contrasting colors.[3] Although Hamm appears central (both in terms of plot and of physical space), there is a fragmenting of character among those on stage, and Hamm exists on some levels as a "decentered self" (Iser 1981, 182). What this means is, of course, that he will never find the "center." Thus, although Hamm strives for control, there is no "psychic continuity" on stage so Hamm cannot even give himself "some coherent notion of personality" (Schwab 1984, 193). Hamm projects himself as protagonist of this *Endgame*, but there is, in essence, no single presence to fill this role.

Perhaps in order to resist this implacable sense of loss, Hamm desires not only to be protagonist of his "play," but author/god of his little world as well. Not only does Hamm "play"-act on stage, he also attempts to create (or at least convince himself that he does) those around him through orders and cajoling, as well as through his chronicle of events supposedly past. It is even conceivable that Hamm, on some level, has consciously "created" the fragmentary character of Clov.[4] In the great creative act of art and life into which Hamm thrusts himself—possibly in an attempt to stave off the chaos of his existence—the iterative routine of creation necessitates an admixture of order and chaos, of self-consciousness and sublime forgetfulness; elements which apparently do not sit well with their creator-god.

The most obvious of Hamm's creations is the narrative of a poor man who tries to get Hamm to take in his son—who might be the younger Clov—as servant. Telling his father (Nagg) to listen to his "audition," Hamm the actor/creator begins the next installment of his story by reflecting Clov's opening lines: "It's finished, we're finished. *(Pause.)* Nearly finished" (Beckett 1958, 50). Of course, the tale *is* nearly finished (though, similar to the play itself, there is no real need to know what has come before to understand the dynamics of the present moment). The end, however, does not come as expected; just at the climax of the story, as the father is "down on his knees" begging him to take his son in, Hamm leaves off, saying, "I'll soon have finished with this story" (53–54). From his anxious tone and next actions, it is evident that Hamm is worried about finishing this story. He feels, however, that if he continues, he will have to end it—he needs "other characters" in order to continue his tale but has no idea where to find them. It is this fear, in fact, that drives Hamm to the desperate measure of praying "to God"—presumably, for an answer to his problem. Thus, in the ritual of narration as well, it appears Hamm is driven toward conclusion and closure, perhaps out of necessity; but, at the same time, it is he who deviates from closing off this creative area. Here, this time in a creative act, Hamm sides with the mess of unfinished business over the clean boundaries of endings.

A quick reexamination of the three areas we have looked at—spatial, temporal, and narrative—shows that the "plot" of *Endgame*, at least for Hamm, is a movement toward the closure of ending resisted by some other element which prefers the unpredictability, anxiety, and even pain of the unknown. The set, the characters, the language, even the props (for instance, Hamm's painkiller) all indicate impending finality; but, at the same time, they all resist closure and ending—notably, this resistance can and does occur across as well as within the boundaries of each stage element, as, for example, rats and young boys keep cropping up off stage to destabilize the sterile end all those on stage profess they desire. Therefore, in order to get a good picture of the play, or even of one of the characters, we must view the piece in terms of a complex of spectacle, thought, and character (to steal from Aristotle), not in terms of fully developed, distinct atoms independent from one another. As with the study of Chaotic systems, it is more the "process than the substance" (Schwab 1984, 198) of the play that provides the most revealing and accurate picture.

What, then, is this "system" called *Endgame*? This is obviously not an easy question to answer, and many critics have attempted metaphorical solutions to the puzzle of the play. In his *The Shape of Chaos,* David H. Helsa presents some of the more accepted of these metaphors of and in *Endgame*: the play can be seen as a "game board" in its final stages (chess and/or cards),[5] "the interior of the skull of a man who is dying of dichotomy" (1971, 155),[6] the landscape of a creator whose ideas are running down, and the "throne room" of a king whose power is "absolute and meaningless" (152). Moving from the metaphorical to the physical, Helsa notes that the world of *Endgame* is one tending toward "maximum entropy" (155), wherein characters and stage alike are devolving toward the "cold death" prophesied by Lord Kelvin in the nineteenth century.[7] Certainly *Endgame* is, in a limited sense, a fable or parable of "the end"—of the games of life, the world, creativity, and so on—but it is also a story of the painfulness of this process, of the resistance Hamm and others put up, even of the potential transcendence of the closed-endedness of this game-of-death: if the conceptual bifurcation maintained by the play's metaphors is bridged, a generative reading of the play becomes possible. How is this possible? If the play itself tends toward the "maximum entropy" of death, where can the seeds of life be hiding? Analogous to T. S. Eliot's famous line, "In my End is my Beginning" *(Four Quartets),* Zen and Chaos theory maintain that the deconstructive (or perhaps reconstructive) kernel of antithesis lies in the center of its opposite—and both these polarities are merely branches of an a priori, prereflective unity which is visible if we change our understanding of the world.

How can this change in vision, which we have already followed in the case of *Godot,* help illuminate *Endgame*? To begin with, let us review Helsa's insight into the entropic dissolution of the world of *Endgame*. The world is winding down to a state where, as Clov puts it, everything will be "silent and still . . . each thing in its last place, under the last dust" (Beckett 1958, 57), apparently meaning that "things" will be arranged "in such a way that they will not interact with one another" (Helsa 1971, 155) and will therefore be unable to produce or create anything.[8] Well and good: this seems an adequate description of the state toward which *Endgame* moves. But let us look at Clov's entire speech: "I love *order*. It's my dream. A world where all would be silent and still and each thing in its last place, under the last dust [my emphasis]." Clov associates this state of maximum entropy with order, not disorder; thus, the "mess" of chaotic entropy is associated with a kind of order. Helsa notes the discrepancy:

> I realize, of course, that I have just used "entropy" as a synonym of "order," whereas in fact the term ought to be used of its opposite, "disorder" or "randomness." But in connection with Clov's speech it makes sense to use the term in this way. . . . (1971, 155)

Here the entropic order here is one of noninteraction, where things are organized so as not to associate with one another. Yet, in this sense, the system cannot be wholly entropic, as the relational context of all the pieces will be ordered or structured in some fashion; so the "last dust" can never settle down to a cold death. In other words, an ordered entropy cannot exist. Or can it? Perhaps Helsa was on the cusp of understanding the play in terms of Chaos theory (as the title of the work implies)—except that he wrote the book a few years before the tools were available to speak of "ordered entropy."

In a Chaotic system, order can appear spontaneously in a largely entropic state (à la Prigogine), producing "pockets" of well-behaved events or objects (like our solar system) in a chaotic medium.[9] Like the bifurcation diagram of the "population equation" (see figure 7, which shows the full diagram and indicates the large-scale orderly progression into Chaotic behavior), small areas of order can and do arise from the void of random Chaos. If we examine a tiny section of this diagram, we see how, amid an absolutely random mess, areas of order can appear that reflect, on a much smaller scale, the entire original diagram (figure 13).

Thus, from the "highly entropic" system of *Endgame*, there can arise a spontaneous order. Interestingly, as is indicated by the diagram, the opposite is also true: just after Clov's adulation of order, Hamm forces him to drop what he has picked up, thereby asserting once again the principle of

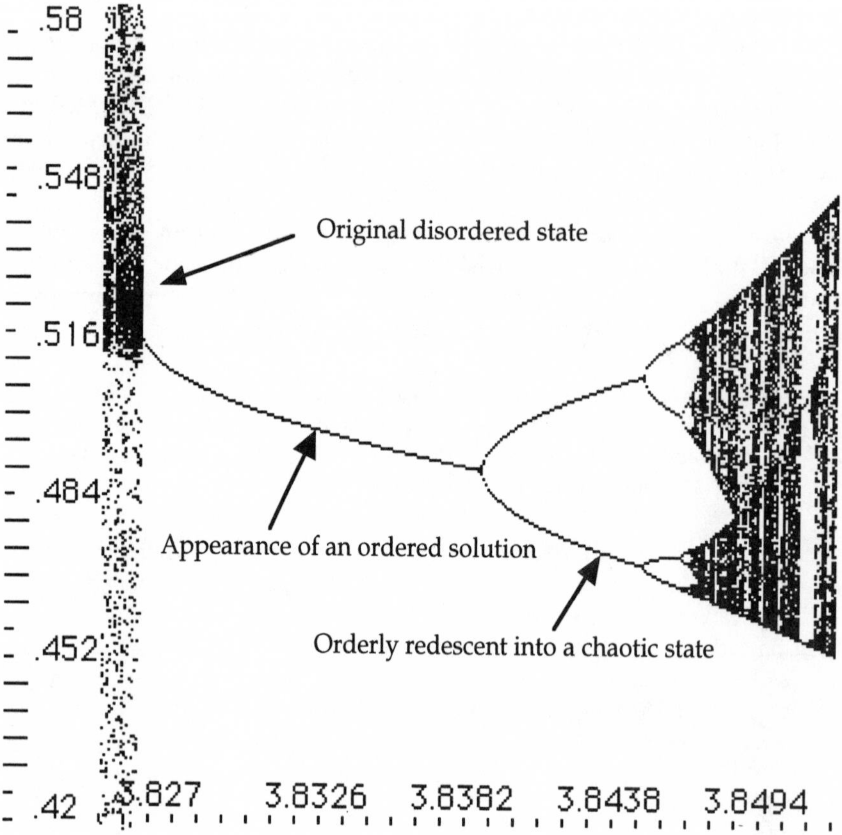

Fig. 13. An enlargement of a tiny section of the bifurcation diagram, seen in chapters 2 and 3. Note that this ordered section arises from chaos, left, and, in a well-behaved fashion, returns to it, right. Note also that this small selection reflects the diagram as a whole—but flipped upside down.

disorder and nonclosure. Clov's exchange with Hamm is indicative of the play's ambivalence toward either extreme:

HAMM *(exasperated):*
What in God's name do you think you are doing?
CLOV *(straightening up):*
I'm doing my best to create a little order.

HAMM:
Drop it!
(Clov drops the objects he has picked up.)
CLOV:
After all, there or elsewhere.

(Beckett 1958, 57)

Disorder, it appears, has won out. Just after this, however, Hamm proceeds to the next installment of his "chronicle," an attempt to stave off disorder or death with creative order. As with the bifurcation diagram, order and disorder compete here in miniature scale, each winning for a time in a game of chance. This complex mixture of order and disorder resists any simple "gesture of closure which would construe the play as the symbolic representation of a deteriorating world" (Schwab 1984, 192).

On a more universal scale as well, the world of *Endgame* demonstrates the rich interplay of order and disorder, a "buildup of uncertainty, the dispersion of sureness, and the loss of clarity as more words and attempts at action are added" as the play progresses (Maughlin 1987, 89–90). The world "without" is "extinguished," the sea is flat calm or "Lead," "The light is sunk," and the desert shows no signs of rain (Beckett 1958, 30–31). In other words, the outside world seems to have achieved the desired state of maximal entropy. Yet, order creeps in. Near the end of the play, an apparently young boy appears outside; more significantly, the "shelter" in which the play takes place is an ordered pocket in the "ashes" of the desolate system of *Endgame*'s world. Here, amid the desolation outside, is a small, improbable world in which tyrants wield power, people eat, tell stories and remember, and "centers" exist—almost. For, in this ordered pocket, chaos also lurks. Hamm's power is declining to uselessness, there is little food left, stories and memories run dry, and Hamm can no longer retrieve the supreme sign of order: the center of his room. The ultimate eradication of chaos, the center of a well-defined space, is no longer a valid option under the new paradigm where closed systems are not the norm, and chaos and order coexist. The mixture of chaos and order here perfectly fits the description of a Chaotic system, as, on both large and small scale, order and disorder intermingle in a world which, according to Chaos theory, is *not* devolving, but rather evolving into one of richer patterns and complexity. In *Endgame*, the centrality of monistic power and conceptual order, like Hamm himself, is on the wane; but the potential for a more vibrant, if unpredictable, existence is within the realm of possibility. If the characters can learn to accept the change from Winnie's "old style" to a new world in which roles, events, and objects are dynamic instead of static, they can reenergize their world through their new vision of it. Obviously this point needs further clarification, as an audience's first intuitive take on *Endgame* is most likely that the world is running down to a cold death. To look more closely at this energizing mix of chaos and order, let us first reexamine some of the closed-ended metaphors inscribed in the play.

The most important of the play's metaphors, at least according to the work's title, is that the piece is the last part of an "Old endgame, lost of old" (82). Certainly chess and cards are directly referred to by staging and/or characters,[10] and the idea of "playing" (with the double entendre of play-acting) is often referred to by Hamm and Clov—for example, "CLOV: Let's stop playing! HAMM: Never!" (77). From first appearances, the game metaphors indicate a "winding up" (as Clov puts it) of the world-as-game. The chess allusion—in terms of both stage and character language—is to the endgame, the final part of a chess match in which the outcome has often been determined long before and the players are merely playing out the final movements of a battle already decided. This is the situation to which Hamm refers when he "wearily" states: "Old endgame lost of old, play and lose and have done with losing" (82). In addition, the stage of *Endgame* is nearly empty. Only four (and then three) pieces remain—Hamm and Clov on the "red" side, and Nagg and Nell on the "white" side. For whatever reason, Hamm, kinglike in his throne and limited mobility, is in jeopardy, having only his pawn (or perhaps "cloven-hoofed" knight), Clov, left to protect him. On the other side are two white, immobile pieces, Nagg and Nell (perhaps, according to Helsa, captured earlier and thereby of little consequence [1971, 151])—antagonists with their own memories and desires. By the end, Nell has died (according to Clov), Nagg has disappeared permanently into his ashbin, and Clov is on the threshold of leaving. Hamm the king is finally, as far as he knows, completely alone and immobile.

Also, in terms of the card game metaphor, Hamm plays out a losing hand. He "discards" his toy dog, his gaff, his whistle—nearly all he has—leaving him with nothing but bluff. Poker-faced when Clov does not answer his command, Hamm finally comments: "Since that's the way we're playing it . . . let's play it that way . . . and speak no more about it . . . speak no more" (Beckett 1958, 84). As he had predicted for Clov, Hamm is now immobile in the "infinite emptiness" without "anyone with" him (36); the old king covers his face, lowers his arms, and "remains motionless." Apparently Hamm has lost in this final, winner-take-all hand.

Yet, even here things are not as closed and finalized as one might first suspect. If we examine the "brief tableaux" that begin and end this piece, an obvious similarity arises between the scene that opens the play and the one that closes it. In both, the setting is the same (except for the alarm clock, which usurps the backward-facing picture in the final tableau). In both, Clov is "Motionless by the door, his eyes fixed on Hamm" (1) (but clothed differently in each instance). In both, Hamm sits still, center stage (missing a sheet, however, at play's end). The scenes maintain enough similarity that, as in *Waiting for Godot*, we can easily envision the play circling back (almost) to its beginning to start over again. Although *Godot* has two acts in which we see at least part of this repetition, here we have to stretch the chain of events out over time on our own. Whereas *Endgame* requires more mental circumambulation, we still can see how this play follows *Godot* by conforming to the nonclosed "pattern" of a strange attractor. As with *Godot*, in *Endgame*, events on large and small scale circle back on themselves—almost: small, yet significant alterations in the texture of self-similar moments stave off any finality or closure, allowing instead a temporal and spatial range of surprises and "new information" projected out into the distant past and future. From repetitions that occur within the play itself—like Hamm and Clov's "What's happening?" routine that takes place in several variations during the course of the play—to repetitions that are discussed—"Why this routine, day after day?"—to repetitions that exist in the potential space of projected time—the iteration of the play itself—*Endgame* circles around its own unique strange attractor, points in the play coming arbitrarily close to each other but never connecting. Thus the play *must* evolve—even after the final curtain, and even after we leave the theatre, instead of "winding down" to stasis. In the open-ended space of the strange attractor, finality and ending can never be reached. Like Zeno's impossible heap of grains, the play can never "mount up to" a complete, closed-ended form.

If the chess game leads us to the new paradigm of Chaos theory, the metaphor of cards leads us back again to Zen Buddhism. When, near the end of the play, Hamm verbally and physically discards his belongings, there is no question that he does this out of desperation. He is throwing every last piece into the lost battle. Into the fray go his gaff (last hope for mobility), his toy dog (last companion), and his whistle (sign of his now useless power). Finally, referring once again to playing a lost hand, Hamm talks himself into silence: "let's play it that way . . . *(he unfolds [his handkerchief])* . . . and speak no more about it . . . *(he finishes unfolding)* . . . speak no more" (84). Here, at least for the character, must be a scene of finality and death, as Hamm reaches the end of his defenses against the death he perceives waiting for him.

If, however, we view this scene—and the play as a whole—from the vantage point of Zen Buddhism, we see that the explicit closure and finality shown here contain an implicit rebirth, or reawakening of sorts, as well. Historically, belongings are anathema to Zen followers, as they maintain mental and psychical attachment to the world of phenomena and suffering. As a result, Buddhist monks even today shave their heads, wear a standard loose-fitting robe, and carry only a few items (for instance, a plate and chopsticks) with them. The renunciation of worldly belongings, as well as of one's station in society, are required of every Zen novitiate. Obviously, for a person of relative wealth and position such as Hamm this move is all the more difficult, as one's identity and ease—and ostensibly one's survival as well—are tied up with these worldly goods.[11] Thus as Hamm discards his belongings like so many poor cards in a poker hand, he implicitly moves toward a state in which enlightenment can take place. That this state appears deathlike is evidence of the existential intensity of the dilemma Hamm faces: "Except for occasional feelings of uneasiness and despair, it is like death itself" (Hakuin; quoted in Suzuki 1949, 148). One seeking enlightenment—or, equally, seeking to escape the horrors of life as we experience it—becomes so wrapped up in the unraveling contradictions involved in dualistic thinking that she forgets everything else, even the fact of herself.

This quandary is, of course, the Great Doubt, "a state of perplexity which becomes so intense that it is experienced physically as well as mentally, and which functions to block conceptualizing" (Loy 1988, 206). Body and soul are consumed by the koan of duality (perhaps in one of its specific manifestations, like the question, "what is the sound of one hand clapping?" or, more appropriately in this instance, "What's happening?"); language, motion, and even thought itself fall away into silence and stillness. If one is successful in pursuing this Great Doubt, he will find that the "sense of duality is a delusion" and therefore that "nothing [more] needs to be attained" (Loy 1988, 206), since the only hindrance to enlightenment is the false sense of duality and causality in the world. In terms of the archery metaphor, Hamm, like the Zen/archery student, must discard bow, arrow, and target as distinct atomic units that can be manipulated and controlled. Instead, all elements of archery (and the universe) must be apprehended in toto at each moment of self-sufficient reality. Memory, ego-centered thought, and desire—and therefore suffering as well—are lifted from the successful novitiate, who is free to experience the fullness of each moment.[12]

Hamm's forceful decision to throw away his possessions and to remain silent and motionless indicates the potential for a freer, aconceptual understanding of life. But where does this final moment come from? Is Hamm more explicitly successful than the characters in *Godot* in proceeding to the next stage, that of enlightenment? If we examine the play as a whole, we find evidence that the staging and characters push Hamm, as well as the others, to a state that can be described in terms of the Great Doubt; we also find that Hamm is only potentially able to cross the barrier to enlightenment. Throughout the play, there is a definite move toward "lessness" (to steal a term of Beckett's own coinage)—a movement that continues into Beckett's later work. Items such as sugarplums, pap, and painkiller vanish from existence; characters either die or, in Clov's case, prepare for departure into the "other hell" outside; language thins, becomes useless, and fades to silence. Although, conversely, there is the iterative reenergizing of the play's open-ended revolutions, in a psychological sense at least, the world of *Endgame* seems one of diminishing returns.

Like any self-reifying consciousness, Hamm attempts escape from this ascetic, ego-killing routine. He tries to get a bicycle to escape by land and wants Clov to build a raft so "the currents will carry us away" (Beckett 1958, 34) on the sea—but there are no more bicycles, and Hamm fears the "sharks" outside his shelter. So Hamm turns to "story time" to help maintain his sense of self. Here it is not merely the creative act that helps: Hamm, as well, is the main player in his creation, a construction of power, ironic wit, and discernment:

> No, I've done that bit.
> *(Pause. Narrative tone.)*
> I calmly filled my pipe—the meerschaum, lit it with . . . let us say a vesta, drew a few puffs. Aah!
> . . . .
> I'm a busy man, you know, the final touches, before the festivities, you know what it is.
>
> (51)

In the end, however, the story also fails him. His self-conscious interruptions and alterations, like "No, I've done that bit," fragment his attempt at a cohesive narrative and his fictional characters eventually run out of things to do and say. Similarly, on stage, those around him rebel and leave him: Nell, either from "exhaustion . . . or wisdom" (Simon 1982, 505) presumably dies, while Nagg, upset that he is not rewarded for listening to Hamm's tale, "sinks back into his bin" (Beckett 1958, 56), and Clov, though not in fact leaving (at least not explicitly), ceases obeying Hamm, convincing Hamm that he has indeed left. Finally, nearly out of ways to stave off the stark reality of his contradictory, all-suffering world, Hamm attempts poetry, as well as one last attempt at his "chronicle." Though still imbued with self reification (as, for example, his comment about his poem: "Nicely put, that"), Hamm's last stabs at creation penetrate much more deeply into the true nature of his existence, indicating a level of perception and despair that finally thrusts him into silent confrontation with the "void" that has been lurking in the shadows of his cell. His poem, the haikulike sentence, "You cried for night; it falls: now cry in darkness" (83), indicates the dark expanse of loneliness and suffering that closes around him. The last installment of his story reiterates the Zen admonition that we should "live our lives as if every moment were our last," though altering the focus somewhat: "You want him to bloom while you are withering? Be there to solace your last million last moments?" (83).

Taken together, Hamm's two last "creations" indicate his incarceration on the horns of a koanlike dilemma of duality: "the end is coming, yet every moment is an end, which means that the end is always approaching—always here—which means that the end has always been here and that the end will always wait just ahead as well, which means that the end is never to be, which means. . . ." The bifurcation of "now" into past and future produces a paradoxical state with no solution: Hamm can never end his game because the game is always already ending. The dilemma of ending versus nonclosure, as well as its implicit solution, begins the play and is referred to several times throughout: Zeno's paradox of the "impossible heap" of grains. The moments of his life are like the grains of sand in Zeno's logical construction. Hamm and Clov both refer to this paradox and thus wait for the impossible to happen: for them to become a "heap," a life. Though logically impossible, the grains of sand—or the moments in a life—somehow, simply, *are* a sand heap:

> . . . Clov, you must *be there* better than that if you want them to let you go—one day. But I feel too old, and too far, to form new habits. Good, it'll never end, I'll never go.
> *(Pause.)*
> Then one day, suddenly, it ends, it changes. . . . I ask the words that remain. . . . They have nothing to say.
>
> (81; my emphasis)

Clov tries to find "presence" and identity ("being there") but cannot. All the same, a change happens; but what that change is, words and concepts are unable to explain.

The solution to both dilemmas, from the Zen standpoint, is quite simple. It is the illusion of causality which creates our assumption that there has to be connection between two "absolute" (or atemporal) grains of sand on the floor and some conceptual pile of sand which is there later—or between the always opening present moment and some closed "presence" or identity. The individual events that occur to the characters occupy wholly self-sufficient and independent "moment-times" which are *not* causally connected, nor do they "mount up to" any closed meaning, as they have nothing to do with each other. It is only our minds that connect what occurs "now" with something else that has or will occur at a different "moment-time": any "sense of absolute presence is itself dependent upon memory and anticipation" (Connor 1988, 119). Thus, it is the need for concepts and reflective categorization that creates the dilemma in the first place. As we have seen, for Zen, the causal dilemma is a false one:

> Firewood [for example] does not *become* ashes; there is the 'being-time' of firewood, then the 'being-time' of ashes. If there are no nontemporal objects, then the present does not gain its value or meaning by being related to past of future: each event or being-time is complete in itself. (Loy 1988, 222)

If this is true, then the "million last moments" are all moments of ending—and beginning. They are dynamically reconfiguring themselves on the fly as complete and independent events; it is up to us to "discard" our sense of causality (and therefore our ego-selves) in order to change our vision of the world from the bleak and painful dichotomy of polarized opposites to the simple, nonclosed patternings of nirvana.[13]

Is Hamm able to make this jump? The evidence suggests otherwise. Though, like Vladimir and Estragon in *Waiting for Godot*, Hamm and Clov arrive, in the final moment of stasis, at the potential for the Great Death, or enlightenment, they are no closer to actualizing the leap into the void that constitutes the ego's death than are Didi and Gogo. This failure becomes evident if we note that, as Hamm discards his possessions, he is symbolically throwing off the weight of his ego at the same time; yet when the end of the play arrives, Hamm retains his handkerchief, symbol of suffering (via the bloodstains), civilization, and social rectitude—all proclamations of a lasting sense of self and personal identity. In addition, Hamm's last statement (reflecting his waking moment) is to call attention to this last piece of Self: "Old stancher! *(Pause.)* You . . . remain" (84). In the original French, Hamm's statement is even more telling: "Vieux linge! *(Un temps.)* Toi—je te garde" (Beckett 1971, 216). In French, not only does the symbolic handkerchief remain, but Hamm claims he is "keeping" it. With such an attitude, Hamm can never cast off the last vestiges of his self-consciousness and escape his suffering. It is not without reason that the handkerchief covering Hamm's face at the end of the play is stained with blood, symbol of a suffering he inflicts on himself through his tenacious hold on conceptual dualism, or *dukkha*.

For Clov as well, the end cannot come, since his fortunes rest with Hamm: if Hamm is unable to escape his suffering self, Clov, in orbit with and around him, will never "be there" enough to be released from their union to follow his own path. Clov is dressed for the road and standing near the door by the end of the play; but like Didi and Gogo who "do not move," he is fixed in place, unable to part with his counterself. Staring fixedly at Hamm, Clov seems to wait for a sign from Hamm that he can depart, a sign which in all probability will never come. The pair, like their counterparts in *Godot,* remain poised at the end in a potential space, the promise of a better world lying just over the curve of the horizon, if they could only achieve the wonted paradigm shift, while the impetus to continue suffering remains a strong enough lure that the two will, in all likelihood, continue to iterate this pattern of self-energized suffering.

If we proceed cross-referencing *Endgame* with our examination of *Godot*, we might ask whether there is an implicit third party like Godot that imposes on the character pairs and destabilizes the play in similar fashion, allowing them at least the potential to achieve nirvana. Although there is no named character who might fulfill the same role, there is a presence which generates the same sort of longing and fear Godot does for the stage characters in the earlier play. This is the "other hell" outside—the "without." Place of starvation and destruction ("It's death out there"), Hamm, Clov, and the others are protected from this other world by the thinnest of walls, making the shelter's residents a mere speck of life in the vast void outside, "a little bit of grit in the middle of the steppe" (Beckett 1958, 36). At the same time, however, the "without" must be the place of hoped-for escape, whether it is Hamm's talk of escape via bicycle or raft, Clov's more nearly actualized exit, or Nell's escapist memories of Lake Como. Thus the world outside is one of danger, but, at the same time, one that holds the promise of release from present ills. Like Godot, this outside "hell" drives all the characters in the play—even the supposed prime mover, Hamm—destabilizing the stasis (or "dust") that weighs on those within Hamm's shelter. In the paradigm of Chaos theory, this third party (or element) enables and energizes the richer patternings of Chaotic behavior. Here, too, we see its power and potentially positive influence over the characters in the play. Obviously, though, anything with this much power over them must be viewed by the characters with ambivalence: if the flowing currents (which can take them away from their painful existence) contain sharks, then proceeding into this world can lead either to salvation or death; and, as this is essentially the Great Doubt which precedes the Great Death, we have already seen how the characters are at last paralyzed by the fear and hope revolving about the "without."

It seems significant that the term Beckett uses to refer to this potential world is the same as the prefix term we have been using to signify the a priori phenomenological state that precedes bifurcation into pairs, which, in turn, generates the apparent multiplicity of the world. The "without-thinking" state of Zen enlightenment is linked, linguistically at least, to the world beyond Hamm's skull-like shelter, reinforcing the connection between the "without" and the Great Death of the ego-consciousness. If the characters *were* able to move beyond the physical/psychical confines of their shelter, they would, by association, free themselves of their suffering, bipolar vision of the world.

One may argue that *Endgame*'s characters—all but Hamm, at least—

have in the past made the journey outside, as they themselves tell us. However, these memories, whether of boating in a lake or of "visiting paupers" in the nearby village, are of a dissociated past which has, at best, only a tangential relationship to the events happening at present. It is only the persistence of collective memory that maintains a connection between the world of "yesterday" and the present moment. In other words, if we are to assume that Nagg, Nell, and Clov have ventured out before, it was into a much different world that did not maintain the connotative mythological dimensions and ambivalence now carried by the "without." The memories that Nagg and Nell have of the outside world are as much an escapist misrepresentation of the "now" of the present moment as are Hamm's abortive fantasies of physical escape: during "stage-time," the outside world represents not a reality but an overdetermined potentiality through which lies death and/or new life.[14]

The overdetermination of this "without" can be made more specific: from the left window (from the audience's perspective), Clov spies the sea; from the right, a desert. From the two windows, though facing the same direction, Clov sees two mutually exclusive worlds, one of unending water, the other of parched land on which no rain can fall. The "without," then, comprises two opposing worlds, one of water and one of land, which nicely fit the polarities of the "old style," categorical paradigm. Paralleling Clov's vision of these two opposing worlds when he looks out the shelter's windows, Hamm's two fantasies of escape are based on two exclusive modes of travel—one, the bicycle, by land; the other, the raft, by sea. That neither Hamm nor Clov seem surprised that the two windows look out on such exclusive worlds indicates their willingness to live their lives in terms of this bifurcated world. Yet, as we have already seen in *Waiting for Godot* and will see in even starker delineation in Beckett's later drama, what seems at first glance a simple polarity becomes on further examination an intricate mixture of the two, a state more paradoxical, complex, and richer in implications than either of the two simple extremes could have been.

To begin at the end, when Clov looks over the "without" one last time for Hamm, he discovers to his shock, "Christ, she's under water! . . . How can that be? . . . It hasn't rained" (73). It turns out, of course, that Clov is looking out the wrong window—the window on the sea, instead of the desert—yet the ease with which the two can be confused is cemented by this incident. For an instant, Clov sees a desert drowned beneath the water, a mixture of the two polarities into a more complex and confusing (according to Clov's usual perception of the universe), but holistic, vision of the universe. For a moment (in Clov's mind, at least), water and earth are dynamically united, their mixed qualities shocking him and potentiating the enlightened awakening that eludes the characters. Clov, however, drops this potential by rationalizing his problem away. Discovering he was looking through the wrong window, Clov states: "Sometimes I wonder if I'm in my right senses. Then it passes off and I'm as intelligent as ever" (73). Reaffirming the priority of the conceptualizing world of logic and "intelligence," Clov effectively cuts off the consequence of his shocking discovery and falls back into the habit of viewing his world in fragments instead of pursuing the dangerous path of unity and complexity.

Earlier in the play, Nell—precursor to Winnie in *Happy Days*[15]—makes a more subtle, yet perhaps more successful, stab at realizing the underlying unity in the opposing elements of water and earth. In her brief moment on stage, Nell spends most of the time remembering with Nagg events past—notably the bicycle ride in the Ardennes, in which she and Nagg lost their legs, and a boat ride on Lake Como, where Nagg had first told her the tailor joke and where they had consequently capsized. In a past-looking parallel to Hamm's escapist fantasies, Nagg and Nell reiterate the duality of the "without," turning the memories over and over until both humor and tragedy have lost their separate hold, mixed together in a more complex fashion in the stories they retell: "it's like the funny story we have heard too often, we still find it funny, but we don't laugh any more" (19).[16] At the same time, Nell struggles toward a view of the world in which the two elements of water and earth are combined. This occurs in her memory of their boat trip on Lake Como: "It was deep, deep. And you could see down to the bottom. So white. So clean" (21).

At this point, Nagg launches into the extended and poorly told joke he had told that day (which, he claims, made Nell laugh so hard she capsized the boat). Fed up with the joke, Hamm finally screams "Silence" to quiet Nagg. Insensible to this exchange, Nell continues her train of thought: "You could see down to the bottom." Hamm, exasperated with the interference from the two, orders Clov to shut them up:

> HAMM:
> Clear away this muck! Chuck it into the sea!
> *(Clov goes to bins, halts.)*
> NELL:
> So white.
> HAMM:
> What? What's she blathering about?
> *(Clov stoops, takes Nell's hand, feels her pulse.)*
> NELL *(to Clov):*
> Desert!
> *(Clov lets go her hand, pushes her back in the bin, closes the lid.)*
> (23)

With this final exclamation, Nell is silenced for the duration of the play—or perhaps forever, as Clov later reports that she is dead. Yet, during the brief time she spends on stage, Nell manages to put together the divided pieces of the collective characters' world. She finally realizes what Clov will, by accident, nearly realize toward the end of the play: that the white sand deep at the bottom of the lake is in actuality the desert which supposedly exists separate from, and in opposition to, the sea which forms the other half of the "without." She is, then, "ahead of the other characters" (Simon 1982, 507) in terms of her ability to see the complex interaction of opposites. As if to reinforce the nature of Nell's discovery, just before her final exclamation, Hamm declares that he wants the two of them (like muck, or garbage) thrown into the sea. The juxtaposition of these two terms in such close quarters makes Nell's line of thought all the more clear to us, allowing us to understand that she has passed beyond the dualistic comparison of the two elements. Perhaps, instead of dying, it is Nell who, after discovering the unity of sea and sand, is the only one able to escape the iterative quest for closure to which the others seem wedded.

On a physical level, Nagg and Nell's accommodations again reflect the complex interplay of supposed opposites: lining the bottom their "garbage cage" is a layer of sand that used to be sawdust.

NAGG:
Has he changed your sawdust?
NELL:
It isn't sawdust.
(Pause. Wearily.)
Can you not be a little accurate, Nagg?
NAGG:
Your sand then. It's not important.
NELL:
It is important.
(Pause.)
NAGG:
It was sawdust once.
NELL:
Once!
NAGG:
And now it's sand.
(Pause.)
From the shore.
(Pause. Impatiently.)
Now it's sand he fetches from the shore.
NELL:
Now it's sand.

(Beckett 1958, 17)

Leading Nagg through the explanation, Nell maintains the importance of the change in their lining from wood chips to sand "from the shore"—a change in accommodations from the "simple" lining using an earthy element to that of beach sand, which connects water and earth in dynamic fashion.

The grains of sand, catalyst of Nell's insight and symbolic connection between earth and sea, also appear at the beginning of *Endgame*, when Clov refers to Zeno's paradox in the opening lines: "Grain upon grain, one by one, and one day, suddenly, there's a heap, a little heap, the impossible heap" (1). Thus, Zeno's paradox, whose consequences for *Endgame*'s characters and world we have already discussed at length earlier, has another function in the play: that of an elemental paradox between water and earth. Residents of the shore, the boundary layer between water and land, the grains of sand Zeno uses in his formulation of the paradox of causality also serve to show the more complex nature of the void constituting the "without" beyond Hamm's shelter. In the conversation between Nagg and Nell just quoted, explication of these two paradoxes exist side by side: the simple, "earthy" sawdust that "once" existed beneath them is now sand, a complex, ever-changing form existing on the boundary of land and sea. Disconnected past and present are the temporal grains of the sand that fill the bottom of their ash bins. The impossible heap of time, causality, and elements make up the lining on which the two live (and, by extension, on which the shelter itself, and thus all its inhabitants, live). Of course, as we have seen, the solution to these layered paradoxes is to throw out ("into the sea") notions of duality and relational causality, accepting the richer understanding of the world in terms of absolute relativity. It is this Great Death that Nell may finally experience as she disappears into her garbage bin, never to return.[17]

The other characters are not so lucky. In the end, they seem unable to make this leap, thus remaining alive on stage, locked in the paradoxical struggle between desire and necessity. Yet this is a play—and a very self-conscious one, at that (it is probably Beckett's most metatheatrical work)—so the characters, particularly Hamm and Clov, relate to the audience and to themselves not only as "real" people, but also as staged events.[18] This factor constructs the audience as part of the dynamics of the play to such a degree that the paradoxical nature of presence (or "reality") in/and theater itself is laid bare before us. Thus, the play, *as play,* also maintains a complex dynamic of closure and ambiguous open-endedness. In addition to the "normal" level of missing detail and confusion that exists in *Godot* and other of Beckett's plays, there is in *Endgame* a high degree of awareness in the characters that the audience exists, resulting in something of a turnabout between audience and characters. The most celebrated example of this metatheatricality is when Clov, turning the telescope he uses to view the "without" on the audience, states: "I see . . . a multitude . . . in transports . . . of joy. *(Pause.)* That's what I call a magnifier. . . . Well? Don't we laugh?" (29). Not only are Clov and Hamm aware of the audience, they even joke about its lukewarm reaction to the play itself. This and many other statements by the characters (such as Hamm's litany, "Me to play") indicate at least an intermittent knowledge that someone is "out there" watching them.

It is, of course, highly significant that Clov uses his telescope, a tool with which he sees the "without," to view the audience. "We" watching the play are thus allied to the "without," as he spies us with this device. Linked in darkness to the "sunk" light of the landscape outside the shelter, we are as alien to the stage world as was the old madman's apocalyptic vision of the world to the younger Hamm. Yet we are also privileged insiders allowed to watch the private goings-on of this group of characters. In the traditional voyeuristic mode of theater, we peer into others' lives, enjoying the vicarious drama of their existential problems, while, at the same time, being made aware of the artifice of this position as the characters notice our presence. We, as audience, must become conscious of the paradoxical role we play in this dramatic work. We are, at the same time, the chaos outside the play (for the mix of people who come together to witness theater is certainly a quasi-random group, an unknown factor in the play's evolution) and intimate participants in the performance witness. We are, at the same time, witnesses to a closed event (a play called *Endgame*) and the very factor which causes each iteration of the play to evolve differently, disallowing any real closure. Thus, the audience-stage relation is another level in which *Endgame* functions to destabilize any static distinctions between order and Chaos: audience and players reflect and refract one another in a manner that strives both for the closure of dramatic ending and resists this closure by uncovering the artifice of a separate dramatic world.

Not only is the audience—this all-important medium in which the play develops—an object of which stage characters are aware, it becomes integral to the evolution of the play itself: we see the "audience acting with actor, becoming actor" (Doll 1987, 75). Hamm, consummate actor and creator, "plays" to his audience, whether it be Nagg, Clov, or those offstage in the theater. Eventually, however, Hamm exhausts his audience resources on stage, as Nell, Nagg, and finally Clov cease listening to his "auditions." Thus, by the end of the play, Hamm thinks he has no one left to listen to his "last soliloquy" (Beckett 1958, 78) but the audience sitting in the dark of the auditorium. Forced at the end to play the game according to the rules of silence (moments before he claimed he would "Never!" cease playing, asking instead for a coffin in which to be buried), Hamm "speaks no more," denying the audience any simple closure at the end, throwing the dramatic ball back into the audience's court. It is, finally, our game to end or continue: our vision of the play constitutes the reality of it.

This brings us to what is perhaps the centerpiece of *Endgame*, Hamm's recounting the tale of a madman he used to visit in an asylum.

> HAMM:
> Yesterday! What does that mean? Yesterday!
> CLOV *(violently):*
> That means that bloody awful day, long ago, before this bloody awful day. I use words you taught me. If they don't mean anything any more, teach me others. Or let me be silent.
> *(Pause.)*
> HAMM:
> I once knew a madman who thought the end of the world had come. He was a painter—and engraver. I had a great fondness for him. I used to go and see him, in the asylum. I'd take him by the hand and drag him to the window. Look! There! All that rising corn! And there! Look! The sails of the herring fleet! All that loveliness!
> *(Pause.)*
> He'd snatch away his hand and go back into his corner. Appalled. All he had seen was ashes.
> *(Pause.)*
> He alone had been spared.
> *(Pause.)*
> Forgotten.
> *(Pause.)*
> It appears the case is . . . was not so . . . so unusual.[19]
>
> (43–44)

Appearing near the halfway point of the play (page 44 out of 84 in the Grove Press edition), this tale is one of the few moments when Hamm is truly swept up in the tale he is telling.[20] None of the self-conscious verbiage and commentaries (like his favorite line, "Nicely put, that") appears in what obviously is a telling story for a man now trapped in the same world the mad painter had seen. Unable to comprehend the painter's apparently erroneous vision at the time, Hamm now knows all too well the appalling nature of the world.

If we step back one remove and see the present-day Hamm as the surrogate "madman," we, as audience, then take young Hamm's place. Like the younger Hamm, we would now say to him, "Look about you at the flourishing earth and seas" (the two mutually exclusive elements Hamm spoke of to the painter). "How can you see the world around you as a desolate waste, you alone (or nearly so) being spared?" By the end of the play, the game is indeed in our court, as our vision of the play and/versus reality is starkly juxtaposed to the world inhabited by *Endgame*'s characters. We have the choice, it seems, of accepting the (nuclear) holocaust-like vision of the world propounded by those on stage, or, like the younger Hamm, of pointing to the "reality" of a world conceptually ordered and cleanly divided and saying, "Look, everything is fine." If we accept the first of these options, we must basically accept the grinding death of the world and its inhabitants (and say, like Clov "that the world is extinguished, though I never saw it lit" [81]). If we maintain the second point of view, we deny the power of the vision of the play, as well as our complicity in its construction, since we are (re)created by those on stage as much as those on stage are created by us. Apparently, we, like those on stage, can attempt to remain in the "shelter" of order and life, or we can opt for the "death out there" in a disordered, decaying world—or we can choose both and neither. For us, as well, the decision is not as clear-cut as we might at first expect.

The black-and-white, polar options we seem left with are actually mixed together like the light outside Hamm's shelter:

> HAMM:
> Is it night already then?
> CLOV *(looking):*
> No.
> HAMM:
> Then what is it?
> CLOV *(looking):*
> Gray.
> *(Lowering the telescope, turning towards Hamm, louder.)*
> Gray!
> *(Pause. Still louder.)*
> GRRAY! . . . Light Black. From pole to pole.
>
> (31–32)

The poles of our apparent dichotomy curve back toward each other in complex fashion, rendering the "simple" split more complex, and the dynamic pattern richer and more beautiful. The order in the shelter is necessarily mixed with the chaotic, generative suffering of life; the creative disorder of the void outside is intermingled with the closure of a dead or dying world. The world inside the shelter tends toward apparent finality as the "chess" moves become more and more limited. The "without" regenerates itself as a source of both imaginative and physical life. The sides of the dilemma interpenetrate each other, as chaos and order, death and life mingle on either side of the shelter's "hollow" brick walls. Indeed, they are essentially hollow, as there is, in the end, no difference between the "within" and the "without." Only suffering exists for those of us who maintain that there is some real difference between the void without and Hamm's shelter, "a speck in the void, in the dark" (36), within.

At root, the multiple levels of dilemma in the play are, like Zeno's paradox, tied into causality. Hamm states early on his belief in causality—"But we breathe, we change!" (11)—a belief that continues to haunt him (indicated by his repeated question, "What is going on?"). As audience—witness to and participant in this de- and revolving game—we can maintain a belief in a categorical duality between order and chaos—life and death—suffering to forge a causal link between each grain of the impossible heap of our lives. Or we can make the leap Nell seems capable of, relinquishing our need for ego-enforcing, causal thinking and accepting the determinate indeterminacy and dynamic unity of life and death, of beginning and ending. The pressures of life on the edge of the modern existential abyss push us ever closer to the naked dilemma that *Endgame* forces both its characters and us to confront. Watching this play, we, too, exhaust our means of diversion and delusion, slowly "discarding" them like the pieces sacrificed in a lost chess match. In the end, faced with the same Great Doubt as the characters before us, it will be our choice whether to accept the continued suffering of an ambivalent dualism or throw off these conceptual shackles and, seeing the horrors and joys of life as the same, achieve nirvana through the veil of tears. In the end, the play is ambivalent, and thus it

> releases anxieties of disintegration, emptiness, or inundation by the unconscious. Simultaneously, however, it can become a source of delight. We derive pleasure from our positive investment in that original, undifferentiated mode of being which has been forced by the reality principle to survive in the reserves set aside for alternative [fringe] states of consciousness. (Schwab 1984, 201)

We can either view the play in terms of expectations and polarities, or we can apprehend it in the "undifferentiated" state to which Zen and Chaos theory point; the way we "see" the world of the play alters its reality.

Finally, we see that Zeno is the insane painter is Hamm: all three peer out the window of their inescapable conceptual causality. Piling the grains of time before them, they attempt to create from this a fully formed, closed existence with meaning, life, and art. But they succeed only in seeing themselves and their world as a desolate waste. If, on the other hand, we extricate ourselves from this trap, we are free to see Hamm's (the madman's, Zeno's) existence as a much richer, more complex work of art than his flagging attempts at creation can construct. In the end, it is we, throwing off the polarity of stage and audience—of self and other, distinct arrow and target—who can see the meaning and richness of the game Beckett plays.

5

Happy Days, Minutes, Hours: Time's Arrow, Time's Target

April is the cruelest month, breeding
Lilacs out of the dead land, mixing
Memory and desire, stirring
Dull roots with spring rain.

—T. S. Eliot

The way to the goal is not to be measured! Of what importance are weeks, months, years?

—Eugen Herrigel

About four years after *Endgame* was finished, Beckett wrote his first full-length play in English, *Happy Days*. Though in a different language, revolving around a female character (for only the second time in Beckett's drama, and the first time on stage), and written "to comment upon . . . things Irish and English" (Bair 1990, 517), *Happy Days* is to a significant extent a further exploration of the images with which Beckett worked in *Endgame*. As hinted at in chapter 4, Winnie appears to be a fuller development of Nell's smaller role. Just as the major pair in *Endgame*, Hamm and Clov, are developments of the smaller roles of Pozzo and Lucky in *Waiting for Godot*, so Winnie and Willie grow from their precursors, Nell and Nagg. Ash bins are replaced by a mound of earth, and the weight of lines is shifted from male to female character, but the relationship between husband and wife is similar.

One of the clearest indications of the cross-play continuity between *Endgame* and *Happy Days* appears on the first page of Beckett's notebook manuscript of the play. Here, before the first line is written, is a quick sketch (see figure 14).[1]

This figure is obviously a drawing of the mound in which Winnie is ensconced, and the description Beckett writes just below of the "expanse of scorched grass" with a mound rising in the center confirms that this

Fig. 14. Sketch of Winnie's mound (from manuscript notebook)

image is central to, and very likely the inception of, the play. This image of the mound of earth that is slowly swallowing Winnie is essentially a continuation of *Endgame*'s manifestation of Zeno's paradoxical heap of sand, the "grains" of which are burying Winnie as they pile up from one "happy day" to the next. Implying the connection between "impossible heaps," Rosemary Pountney states, "In *Happy Days*, . . . although we see the earth encroaching in linear fashion upon Winnie, the heap can never be completed in a finite universe . . . " (1988, 53). For Winnie, as well as the characters in *Endgame*, the heap of moments she experiences mount steadily up, choking her as she waits for them to do what they logically cannot: come together to connect her life into a meaningful whole. In *Happy Days*, therefore, Zeno's paradox takes on more obvious physical dimensions as Winnie is asymptotically interred under her attempts to connect her life causally.

Happy Days is no mere repetition of *Endgame*, however. Just as *Endgame* shares important elements with *Waiting for Godot*, yet certainly creates its own unique world, so *Happy Days*, while sharing many of the central themes of Beckett's earlier drama, exists on its own terms. This is probably more true of *Happy Days* than of *Endgame*: Beckett's decision to write the later play in English instead of French gives *Happy Days* a very different feel, especially since a great deal of English poetry appears in the context of the play; the play is somewhat less self-consciously metatheatrical than its ancestors (including *Krapp's Last Tape*); and concentration on a female character allows for interesting new dimensions in Winnie and for the play as a whole. Living from day to day, even moment to moment, on whatever invention or ritual she can come up with, Winnie exists in a world that is little more than a pastiche of English literature and common objects. She seems alive only in her daily ritual and web of half-remembered poetry, which she repeats as well as she can.

Aside from *Happy Days*' much more explicit allusiveness, its relation to specific aspects of "proper" society is one of its striking and unusual features. Among the more noticeable Anglicizations of the play (beyond the language itself) is the prim, British nature of the characters. Although

Winnie is "absurdly" buried in a mound of earth and isolated from society, she and Willie maintain a much more social (and specifically British) lifestyle than do Beckett's earlier characters. The piercing bell which dictates "the beginning and end of Winnie's day" (McMullan 1993, 17) acts—like the "without" in *Endgame* and Godot in *Waiting for Godot*—as a destabilizing force for the Winnie/Willie pair. In this case, however, the bell is the manifestation of a vague, potentially malevolent, but much more social force than the two previous "thirds": the bell ensures that Winnie behaves "properly" (that is, being awake for the appropriate length of time each day).[2] In addition, her preening at the beginning of act 1 with toothbrush, lipstick, and hairbrush is a continuation on her part of now obviously obsolete social rituals which only serve to remind her how "near the end" (of toothpaste, lipstick, etc.) she really is. Furthermore, Willie's reading of an old, yellowing newspaper (whose stories must obviously remain the same day after day) caricatures the home life of a world in which a proper social context is maintained. All this must have the effect on Winnie (and Willie, if, as seems likely from his final appearance, he is really aware of what is happening) of further isolating her through constant reminders of the "old style," which no longer exists. Even her half-remembered quotations and her references to "days" and other "old" ways of speaking serve only to reinforce an absent society that may at first seem a comfort to her, but that is in fact (through her memories of it) one of her greatest sources of suffering: "woe woe is me— . . . to see what I see" (Beckett 1961, 10).[3] Though lines like these apparently make Winnie happy for a moment, the manifest meaning in them proclaims the pathetic nature of Winnie's present condition.

Like Hamm, Winnie is torn between the need (or desire) to retain her "things"—whether physical objects or dimly remembered lines of poetry—and the forces of an "entropic universe" (Carey 1987, 147) which push her toward an apparently closed and final state. Though, like the creator/Hamm, Winnie has her story to tell, she is also in partial, "tragicomic" possession of others' creative efforts as well (Carey 1987, 148). She attempts to contextualize herself within her "classics," trying to re-member a complete self in the "old style" of thinking. As we have seen, however, these attachments place Winnie in a very precarious position according to Zen doctrine, as one of the great stumbling blocks (the greatest, in fact) to a perfected life in Taoism and Zen is an overzealous love of the world—possessions, rank, and people (and memories thereof). In terms of the archery metaphor, Winnie, like Hamm, is embroiled in a conflict between the need to maintain a causal distinction and connection between bow, arrow, and target and a growing sense that this mental framework can no longer support itself. More akin to Nell, it is memory specifically that Winnie finds is her most prized possession—and the hardest to release. Although she, like the Zen/archery novitiate, discovers that the conceptual baggage of the past can only cause suffering in the end, Winnie clings to her failing ability to re-create a past because this past, and the re-membering act of memory itself, reifies the ego-consciousness and thus gives her a (false) sense of self-presence in and versus a social context. If Winnie is the archer, her problem is primarily a temporal one: she is mortally afraid of letting go of the "old style" of the past, where one could possess things—both physical and mental—and closure and meaning were still possible. The play, however, is entropic; it can point only in the direction of "lessness." Winnie can never reverse the "film" of life and regain a naive confidence in the way the world was before. She must release the arrow of self and let it fly forward into an open-ended moment of "being-time."

For Zen Buddhism and its precursor, Taoism, the memory and societal propriety Winnie tries to hold onto is something to be rejected outright: the surest way to get a Taoist master to drown himself in a river was to offer him a high position in government. For Zen as well, its roots being in Mahayana Buddhism, it is samsara, or suffering, caused by a "thirst" for the positions, titles, and lusts of society, which constitutes the fundamental predicament of the human condition. In either case, any knowledge of or attempts to objectify one's behavior—even, in fact, knowing that what one does is supposedly bad or good—is a sure sign of trouble in an individual, as well as in a society that encourages this mode of behavior. As Lao Tzu puts it,

> When the Tao is lost, there is goodness.
> When goodness is lost, there is morality.
> When morality is lost, there is ritual.
> Ritual is the husk of true faith,
> the beginning of chaos.[4]
>
> (1988, 38)

In other words, when truly perfect living (which, beyond the concept of good and evil, is inexpressible by words) is lost, then rules of conduct begin to creep in (in three stages, according to the passage), rules that define goodness against something else. And this division precipitates the death of the truly harmonious state.

As we have seen, Zen also teaches that dividing the world into pieces means that these pieces will be objectified, at least half to be seen as "other" and consequently to be manipulated by the subject (the "I") for its momentary pleasures. But these pleasures will only create a thirst for more, a thirst that is unquenchable and will surely bring suffering in the long run, as it continually fragments that which should be left whole. Thus, the "society" to which, in abstentia (or perhaps in toto), Winnie and Willie belong, is effectively one of brittle, useless morality, degenerating perhaps to the state of Lao Tzu's ritual "husk." Yet this world, like the madman's vision in *Endgame*, is not so unlike the present state of the "real" world: Despite their being found in an absurd situation—an absurdity as utterly important to the effect and point of this work as Gregor Samsa's waking up a cockroach is to Kafka's *The Metamorphosis*—Winnie and Willie live under a societal code that buries them beneath its outdated rigidity just as much, if not more, than the mound that slowly swallows Winnie. In fact, the mound is, on one level, a physical manifestation of this quotidian societal baggage.

Some might urge that this play is simply an absurd abstraction, that audience reaction is to the pathos of a "normal" person being placed in a situation outside the bounds of anything that should or could happen—in other words, that Winnie is reacting as we would react to an extraordinary situation. Martin Esslin, for example, states that "the dramatization of the absurd . . . [together with the specifically Kafkaesque vision of the world] are expressions of . . . a loss of contact with the real world" (Esslin 1971, 256), indicating that the predicament of Beckettian characters is that they are trapped within a world alienated from the real, or normal, world in which we exist. Yet, as with *The Metamorphosis*, whereas the surface of the piece is shockingly improbable and alien, what lies underneath is an acute probing into the complex difficulties of living in our everyday world. Gregor is turned into an insect in *The Metamorphosis*, yet it is his family's attitude toward him that truly makes him less than human. Winnie is buried in a mound of earth, yet it is empty habit (the routine of normal life) beneath which she actually sinks.[5]

Hopelessly ill-equipped to deal with the predicament in which she finds herself—life in a malicious or, worse yet, uncontrolled nonclosed universe—Winnie can find comfort only by clinging to an outdated mode of conceptualizing her world, "the old style." What this old style really is is a traditionally Western understanding of the world, where such quasi-absolute concepts as days, nights, God, and so on are valid in an abstract, self-existent sense. But in Winnie's world, of course—a world that amplifies the doubts of a society in the throes of a quantized, post-Nietzschian, post-Sartrian, postnuclear time—it is no longer possible to speak of, and in, absolute abstractions. Winnie is stuck in a serious rut in which "no change" can take place in her attitudes. She tries to comfort herself by stating that it is "no better, no worse" (Beckett 1961, 9); but from the increasing paucity of her belongings and her attenuated ability to move, it is evident that things are indeed getting worse.

This reduction in Winnie's physical "means," far from being the cause of her suffering, is simply the concrete manifestation of a much deeper problem in her (our) understanding of life. Winnie suffers from a vision of the world that necessitates the multitudinous minutiae of propriety, order, faith, and knowledge; and she is buried mentally (and thus physically) beneath the infinite fragments of her life. What is expected of her is too much, and what assurances are given her are too few for Winnie to maintain anything but the last shreds of virtue or even of dignity. The world—an unspecific, hopefully malicious but probably only chaotic, "outside"—encroaches on Winnie's best intentions, forcing her to take more and more drastic measures to uphold an outdated moral code of conduct, a code which evidently only makes her life worse.[6] Even if she is not aware of it, we can see quite clearly that Winnie exemplifies the first stage on the Zen path to enlightenment: she is suffering, and this "pain [which is] heartlessly inflicted on . . . [her] nerves is ineradicable" (Suzuki 1949, 16). If we set aside until later the final tableau of the piece, there is obviously no escape for Winnie from her suffering; she must somehow survive and keep up her spirits, but the job is becoming more and more difficult with each passing "day."

In Winnie's repetitive actions and garbled quotations, we not only see the cycle of suffering in the world (as well as the potential for the Zen novitiate's escape from it), we also become aware of the importance of scaling, iterative repetition and positive "noise" to the play—all of which are elements emblematic of Chaos theory. First of all, the stage directions, which are of such import to this play, reveal both the iterative and scaling functions of Winnie's actions. If we remove the dialogue from an early (and random) selection of Winnie's monologue (the opposite of what most readers do!), we see the following:

> *brings out spectacles in case . . . turns back front . . . takes spectacles from case . . . lays down case . . . opens spectacles . . . puts on spectacles . . . looks for toothbrush . . . takes up toothbrush . . . examines handle of toothbrush . . . lays down brush . . . takes off spectacles . . . lays down spectacles . . . feels in bodice for handkerchief . . . takes out folded handkerchief . . . shakes out handkerchief . . . wipes one eye . . . wipes the other . . . looks for spectacles . . . takes up spectacles . . . starts polishing spectacles, breathing on lenses . . . polishes . . . polishes . . . polishes. . . .*
>
> (Beckett 1961, 10–11)

Aside from the rather fascinating effect this has of showing how the actions form a dramatic movement of their own,[7] this small section (drawn from less than a page of actual text) shows how cyclical—even on the smallest scale—are the actions Winnie performs. Like the more obviously vaudevillian routines performed by Vladimir, Estragon, and Clov, Winnie's actions here cycle around the physical presence of her glasses and on reading more clearly what is printed on the handle of her toothbrush. In this play, however, the "slapstick" routine is reduced from the large scale (problems with boots, hats, ladders, and so forth) to the small scale of hand motions—and even, in the second act, of mere facial movements. While this compression of scale to the more subtle is an important harbinger of things to come in Beckett's later work, it is also important to note in this context that the actions of these different plays are, in terms of self-similar actions, "the same." In other words, while the scale of Winnie's actions has (perforce) been reduced, the same type of action as in earlier plays is being performed.[8] As indicated in chapter 2, this self-similarity over scale differences is the organizing principle from which Chaotic systems derive their complex patterns, and thus Beckett's plays, taken as a whole, manifest behavior which is indicative of the complex boundary layers between order and disorder which constitute Chaos.[9]

Beginning with the large scale of the play itself, we can see how the scaling of self-similar actions operates through the context of the two acts of *Happy Days*. While Winnie's actions are already limited in the first act, she is nonetheless able to move left and right, manipulate her things, and turn to see Willie. By the second act, these movements are reduced to "eyes left" and right, trying to see her bag—"a little blurred perhaps . . . but the bag" (53)—and to imagining that Willie is still around. In both acts, similar actions take place; but the scale is reduced in the second.

Winnie's ritual self-affirmation in each act is also scaled. In act 1, she brushes and then examines her teeth, brushes her hair, and puts on lipstick—societal conventions which affirm her sense of self-worth and propriety (at least in terms of societal norms). In act 2, the only affirmation left Winnie is what she can see of her object-self with her eyes:

> The face. *(Pause.)* The nose. *(She squints down.)* . . . the tip . . . the nostrils . . . breath of life . . . that curve you so admired . . . a hint of lip . . . *(pouts again)* . . . if I put them out . . . *(sticks out tongue)* . . . the tongue of course . . . you so admired. . . .
>
> (52)

In this unlikely blazon, Winnie attempts to affirm herself from an outside, quasi-sexual point of view (appending Willie's approval of her nose and tongue to her description), an act which effectively makes her as much an object to be manipulated as are the contents of her bag in act 1. Thus, while Winnie is no longer able physically to move things around, she moves her own features about before her mind,[10] becoming "the object [both] of the audience's gaze" and of her own (Connor 1988, 183), objectifying herself in an attempt to affirm her existence.

Although Winnie's movements and actions are reduced in the second act, it is effectively this reduction of scale that increases the intensity of her predicament: the movement of Winnie's eyes becomes as important to *Happy Days* as a stage cross or a slap might be to another play. In her scaled-down world, every movement, every twitch, carries with it huge ramifications. It is thus an act of thunderous subtlety when Willie crawls around the mound in the last pages. By far the largest movement of the play, this action seems almost surreal in size and impact when compared with the stillness that precedes it. Willie's slow crawl—because of the reduced scope of action in *Happy Days* as a whole, and especially in the second act—seems of greater significance than would a gunshot in a conventional play. Whatever the outcome of Willie's appearance, it is difficult to overestimate its impact on the audience.

The process of reduction of scale—or "lessness"—which Beckett begins in earnest in *Happy Days,* is intimately connected with another feature of great import to his plays: the quasi-repetitive iteration of actions and themes. Winnie begins her days in acts 1 and 2 with similar rituals, uses similar means to pass the time until the desired "bell for sleep," and works toward the culmination of her day—her song—in both acts. Yet, as in *Waiting for Godot*, the similarity of actions between the two acts by no means produces mere repetition. As already noted, Winnie's morning ritual in the second act is reduced in scale; in this act, deprived of outside means of distractions and no longer assured of Willie's attention, Winnie relies more heavily on her stories of Mr. Shower/Cooker and Mildred, who is "four or five" years old (55); and it is not until act 2 that we finally hear her song. As seen with *Godot* and *Endgame*, this iterative pattern both repeats and differentiates Winnie's and Willie's actions, rendering the specific moments of the play indeterminate (or unpredictable for the first-time viewer), yet allowing us to perceive a larger pattern of behavior in the play as a whole.

A crucial iterative pattern that develops in the course of the play is Winnie's half-remembered poetry quotations. The mental "lifeline" on which Winnie depends is certainly an incarnation of the reduction and repetition we have discussed,[11] but it also exemplifies the "noisy" nature of the Chaotic system that is *Happy Days*. Winnie's quotations are peppered with lapses of memory and injections of her own words. Thus the "information" from these quotations is not merely one of juxtaposition or allusion, but is more like an interference pattern formed between Winnie's mind and the lines she re-creates. Thus, while Winnie's flagging memory has indicated to many critics the pathetic state of both Winnie and the world in which she lives, this is not necessarily the case.

As we have already seen, information theory suggests that noise, or interference, can primarily be seen not as a problem with the meaning being transmitted in a message, but as a valuable source of information in a system. Thus a noisy, open-ended, or more surprising system can, and will, produce more information than a predictable one. Chaos theory itself proclaims that noise enhances the information content—the naturalness or beauty—of a self-similar system. "[N]o matter how much rich and apparently irregular detail appears in fractal curves [or other deterministic mathematical models], they are never exactly like natural phenomena, which is filled with random irregularities" (Stevens 1989, 343). Mandelbrot advocates the use of chance in the quest to emulate the noisy self-similarity of nature: "The goal of achieving a full description [of a natural system] is hopeless, and should not even be entertained" (1983, 210); thus, chance is the only "mathematical tool available to help map the unknown and uncontrollable" (201).

A picture of the so-called Koch curve (see figure 15) clearly reveals the "enhancing" value of noise. The Koch curve is generated by taking a line segment, *L*,[12] removing the middle third (as in the Cantor dust set) and replacing this segment with an equilateral triangle whose legs are each of length L/3:

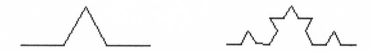

Fig. 15. ***Left:*** **Replacing the middle third of a line segment with (the upper two sides of) an equilateral triangle.** ***Right:*** **Taking the four line segments generated by the first iteration and performing the same process to each of them.**

If we repeat this process over and over, replacing the middle third of each of the straight line segments generated by the iteration before with a triangle one-third its size, we eventually come up with a picture like that shown in figure 16.

While this is a unique—even pretty—figure, it is quite obviously regular, each tiny section mimicking *exactly* (minus problems with computer resolution) what occurs on the larger scale. Thus, this figure is not informationally (or aesthetically) all that exciting. If, however, we insert chance (via pseudorandom alterations of the generative triangles) into the curve, we arrive at pictures that become more and more fascinating and natural-looking (figures 17 and 18).

In the first picture, produced by injecting only a small chance of random noise, there is already a more surprising, information-rich figure, as all lines of the figure are not exactly self-similar. When the chance for minor noise is increased to a large percentage, as in the second figure, the form becomes much more natural-looking. The line it forms could be the outline

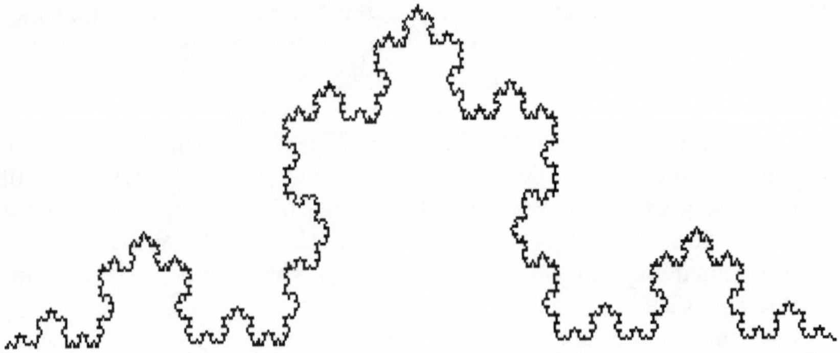

Fig. 16. A "level 5" Koch curve, generated by iterating the "middle third triangle" process through five levels of recursion.

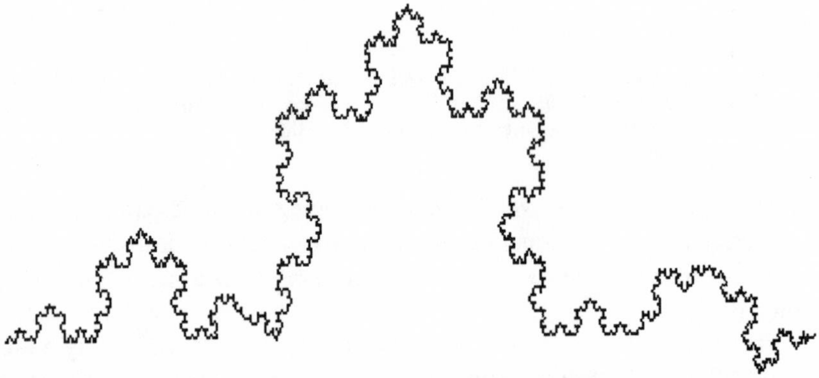

Fig. 17. A "level 5" Koch curve with small chance (7%) of minor Gaussian noise (i.e., small variations in the shapes of the triangles) introduced. A Gaussian distribution of random events is normalized to approach a natural level of noise. In other words, the Gaussian distribution mimicks most natural noise, which remains close to a regular pattern. Only on rare occasions do very-large-scale random events take place. The formula for generating a Gaussian distribution from a random number *n* is as follows: $G = (1/2\pi)e^{(n^2/2)}$.

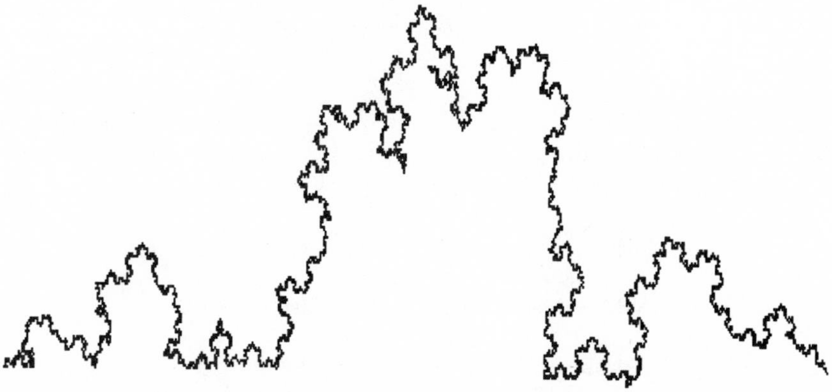

Fig. 18. A "level 6" Koch curve with a large chance (60%) of minor Gaussian fluctuations.

of a "thunderhead" type of cloud, or (as viewed from the sky) the intersection of a rocky coastline with the sea.[13] In any event, the figure here is much richer in information, or surprise; it looks more like something we could see in nature.

The sacrifice for this more natural and richer variation on the Koch curve is that the figure is essentially unrepeatable. Whereas if I run my computer program to generate the "regular" Koch curve, I will invariably get the same figure, if I insert some degree of randomness (even a very small one), I will generate figures which are essentially random themselves. I am able to reproduce curves similar to each other, but the chance that I will be able to reproduce exactly my original figure is infinitesimal.[14] The trade-off for a more complex, rich system is that the system is reproducible only in a general sense; therefore, it is the modified Koch curve that is truly representative of a Chaotic system.

In *Happy Days*, Winnie's quotations fit this "natural" model of interfering and information-creating noise. As opposed to exact quotes (a term which itself is difficult to define, since even the choice of only part of some work is effectively noise, as it does not reproduce the work in its entirety),[15] Winnie's quotations are of half-lines, and even the words—and word order—are garbled. Thus, as opposed merely to reproducing the meaning (or, more precisely, the information) contained in the full quotations, Winnie actually generates new information via her noisy, incomplete memory. An example of this occurs when Winnie quotes a partial line—"beechen green"—from Keats's "Ode to a Nightingale,"[16] the full line of which is:

That thou, light-winged Dryad of the trees,
    In some melodious plot
Of beechen green, and shadows numberless,
    Singest of summer in full-throated ease.[17]

The allusion itself is telling, as the poem is a romantic confrontation of man's sorrow with nature's comfort. Moreover, several other lines from the poem are revealing in relation to the setting of *Happy Days:*

Where but to think is to be full of sorrow
    And leaden-eyed despairs,
Where Beauty cannot keep her lustrous eyes. . . .

Darkling I listen; and, for many a time
    I have been half in love with easeful Death. . . .

Forlorn! the very word is like a bell
    To toll me back from thee to my sole self!

The first two portions of this quote show the overlap of mental states between Winnie (and Willie?) and that of the narrator in Keats's poem. The third quote provides an enticing parallel between the world of the poem and that of the play: the bell (whether physical, as in *Happy Days,* or metaphorical, as in "Ode to a Nightingale") acts as an external force, recalling the sojourner to his/her lonely and sorrowful existence. Therefore, utilizing the "classical" paradigm in which allusions operate unidirectionally on a text or play to deepen significance and meaning, Winnie's allusion to "Ode to a Nightingale" provides valuable information which helps us interpret and broaden the scope of the play's actions.

If, however, we shift paradigms and look at the "noise" surrounding Winnie's quotation of Keats, we see new information/meaning being generated on both planes (that of the play and that of the poem)—information that comes into being in the interstitial space between *Happy Days* and "Ode to a Nightingale." Let us examine the context of Winnie's quotation:

I am the one, I say the one, then the other. *(Pause.)* Now the one, then the other.[18] *(Pause.)* There is so little one can say, one says it all. *(Pause.)* All one can. *(Pause.)* And no truth in it anywhere. *(Pause.)* My arms. *(Pause.)* My breasts. *(Pause.)* What arms? *(Pause.)* What breasts? *(Pause.)* Willie *(Pause.)* What Willie? *(Sudden vehement affirmation.)* My Willie! *(Eyes right, calling.)* Willie! *(Pause. Louder.)* Willie! *(Pause. Eyes front.)* Ah well, not to know, not to know for sure, great mercy, all I ask. *(Pause.)* Ah yes . . . then . . . now . . . beechen green . . . this . . . Charlie . . . kisses . . . this . . . all that . . . deep trouble for the mind. *(Pause.)* But it does not trouble mine. *(Smile.)* Not now. *(Smile broader.)* No no. *(Smile off. Long pause. She closes eyes. Bell rings loudly.)*

(Beckett 1961, 51)

Winnie is obviously skewered on the paradox of causality that is so important for Beckett's plays. She sees herself as one "object" and then as another; but she cannot figure out how the "grains" of her life are connected into the whole to which she feels they must add up. Winnie's prophecy from act 1, when she claimed that if her breasts disappeared, she would never have had them—"And should one day the earth cover my breasts, then I shall never have seen my breasts, no one ever seen my breasts" (38)—has now come true. She can no longer say with certainty that she has arms or breasts. Like the boy in *Waiting for Godot,* who cannot remember having given the same message before, Winnie is no longer sure of her own objecthood. Indeed, it is only through an act of mental violence that she is able to convince herself that her self-affirming audience, Willie, *may* still exist. As the Zen novitiate ensconced in the throws of the Great Doubt—the state in which she, like other Beckettian characters, is trapped—Winnie's object-nature is evaporating beneath the weight of Zeno's paradox: she is, but cannot be, who she was before. This issue of subject/objecthood (whether she is object to her own subject or is object to Willie's audience) is what is "troubling to the mind" for Winnie.

In the context of her suffering state, what is the function of the mini-allusion to her "classics" that Winnie makes? In the immediate context—one of memories of Charlie Hunter and her "first kiss" remembered from the first act (15–16)—the recollection of this line is perhaps a memory of school days when she learned the poems she now tries to quote. Additionally, the words themselves ("beechen green") recall a different, better world of green trees, of "lakes" and "reeds" and boat rides (53). The quote thus helps round out her picture of a remembered better world—with, however, the counterpressure of the sorrowful "now" of the poem providing a strongly ironic, paradoxical element to the recollection. The quote follows on the heels of Winnie's acknowledged need to re-member the world around her (her arms, her breasts, and Willie—"My Willie!"). Thus, to pull up a line of poetry from her memory is an affirmation of memory, continuity and ultimately subject and objecthood.

We may note also that the play enhances the information we see in Keats's poem, as Winnie's confrontation with, and necessary acceptance of, indeterminacy (of her own objecthood and of Willie's existence) points out the fact and value of the indeterminate nature of the poem—the richness of the speaker's inability to determine whether his vision was internal or external ("Was it a vision or a waking dream?"), as well as the question of what will happen next.[19] Therefore, in the interactive space between the surrounding noise of the play and the poem, information is enhanced and generated for both "partners" through an analysis "in which information is created rather than conserved" (Hayles 1990, 176). Like the shift from the Newtonian paradigm (in which information about initial conditions is lost once a system reaches a steady state) to that of Chaos (in which information is created from the surrounding noise as a system evolves), this reading allows us to see that Winnie's garbled quotations are not a loss of information but, rather, act generatively to create more information than was contained in the original. That this increase in information is paid for by a similar increase in noise and indeterminacy is indicative of the Chaotic nature of Winnie and Willie's world.

Winnie's dealings with her noisy quotes also give her a quality of innocence, one which seems a saving grace but at the same time is potentially her downfall. In the opening line of the play, "Another heavenly day," and in the more explicit reference that opens act 2, "Hail, holy light" (from Milton's *Paradise Lost*), Winnie appears to reassert an innocence based on her simple trust in the "old style," as transmitted through the lines she remembers. Content in her world of clichéd quotations, she "remains an incurable optimist" (Knowlson and Pilling 1980, 92). Furthermore, her failing memory only reinforces her childlike innocence in the face of her horrible situation: we get a sense from Winnie's joy at remembering anything at all that she is like a child who tries to remember grownups' words. However, if we note the quotations Winnie forgets in remembering, we find that she is a little more astute than we at first might imagine. "Winnie may live a kind of death in the life she calls 'old style,' but even in quotation she does not utter that dread word [death]" (Cohn 1990, 166). She often shies away from dangerous thoughts and language. At the same time, however, Winnie uses quotations to approach an understanding of herself that is not necessarily aligned with the social propriety of the "old style": "at times—and many more times than one might think—she over-reaches herself to express, sometimes obliquely, more sensitive or more profound concepts or emotions" (Knowlson and Pilling 1980, 94). Winnie is, in effect, increasing the information in the play's "system." Yet these "more profound" ideas which are generated are often ideas of dismay, ideas which she again conveniently avoids through her forgetfulness. Thus, Winnie struggles between an awakening knowledge that her life can no longer be lived according to the rules to which she is accustomed and the fear of that knowledge.

Another example that indicates both the generative and the paradoxical function of Winnie's quotations is her recollection, early in the play, of Milton's rendition of Adam's lament in the Garden of Eden: "O fleeting joys / Of Paradise, dear bought with lasting woes!" (*Paradise Lost* 10.741–

72).[20] Yet what Winnie remembers is, *"(Takes up mirror, starts doing lips.)* What is that wonderful line? *(Lips.)* Oh fleeting joys—*(lips)*—oh something lasting woe. *(Lips.)"* (Beckett 1961, 14). In her half-remembering, Winnie verges on "oh everlasting woe," a rich, even more concise version of Milton's lines. Yet she seems unconscious of the implications this quotation has for her, throwing it out in an offhand manner while applying her lipstick. Like a half-conscious person riding a raft in a rapids, Winnie is only partly aware of the dangerous state she is in; at the same time she is unable to change the direction of her words and actions, regardless of the consequences. Finding solace in these "wonderful lines," as she does in the "small graces" she is granted by whatever forces control her life, Winnie survives for the moment, but survival in this sense costs her the chance to free herself from her predicament: as she cannot fully face her physical and mental interment, she cannot take steps to end it. She is caught in the iterative wheel of samsara, in which—by not allowing herself to see the complex new patterns of the nonclosed world in which she now lives—she trades momentary solace for permanent suffering (as Milton's lines suggest). Thus, Winnie's innocent attitude, while providing temporary shelter from the harshness of her reality, is, in the end, a damning quality that traps her in an endless cycle of suffering.

It is perhaps this inability on Winnie's part to deal with the paradoxically indeterminate world of *Happy Days* and her status in and of it that forms the crux of the play. The discrepancy between Winnie's usually bright, optimistic words—like "That is what I find so wonderful" (49)—and her worsening situation forms the basis of an important dichotomy that begs a solution (for example, why doesn't she do something to alleviate her plight? Or, at least, why can't she talk directly about it?). At times, we even see a Brechtian splitting of Winnie's character, as she momentarily "understands" what her life has come to. For instance, when Willie first speaks to Winnie in act 1 (a one-word response), she cries out: "*(joyful)*. Oh you are going to talk to me today, this is going to be a happy day! *(Pause. Joy off.)* Another happy day. *(Pause.)* Ah well, where was I . . ." (23). More violently, in act 2, Winnie passes from a "broad" smile when recounting the story of Mr. Shower/Cooker to an almost schizophrenic bout of screaming when she recounts how "Suddenly a mouse ran up" Mildred's "little thigh" (58–59).[21] In moments like these, we can see the strain on Winnie to remain upbeat in the endless succession of days during which she becomes more and more conscious of the stark juxtaposition of others with herself—other times, other people, even an "other" self in the form of Mildred. Winnie's scream, then, is a primal one; it is a release of the energy and tension that maintaining a cheery disposition costs.

The crack in her demeanor these scenes indicate—a loss of control which occurs more and more frequently, especially in the second act—is as close as Winnie comes to dealing directly with her position, and it is in these moments when she is most human, her frailties and her courage blending in pathos and potential triumph, that we feel the greatest empathy for her situation. Yet the paradox here lies in Winnie's continual recovery from her vision of what is actually happening to and around her. Perhaps, as T. S. Eliot said so eloquently, "human kind cannot bear very much reality." In order to continue, Winnie (like others, especially Vladimir, before her) must back off from her insights. In the interstitial pauses, however—in the gaps of true silence in Winnie's long-winded monologue—she and we are confronted with the "abyss behind what is taken for reality" (Foster 1989, 27). These moments may be moments of crushing defeat, or they may be moments of victory in Winnie's life (an issue discussed more fully below); but they are definitely times when the paradox between Winnie's attitude (as exemplified by her monologue) and her predicament becomes obvious.

At other times in her monologue, Winnie presents a more cerebral challenge, both for herself and for us. At one point, after remembering "that day" when Willie gave her a bag to go shopping, Winnie says, in a passage reminiscent of *Krapp's Last Tape*,

> I used to pray. *(Pause.)* I say I used to pray. *(Pause.)* Yes, I must confess I did. *(Smile.)* Not now. *(Smile broader.)* No no. *(Smile off. Pause.)* Then . . . now . . . what difficulties here, for the mind. *(Pause.)* To have been always what I am—and so changed from what I was. *(Pause.)* I am the one, I say, the one, then the other. *(Pause.)* There is so little one can say, one says it all.
>
> (Beckett 1961, 50–51)

As Foster says of this passage,

> The dilemma in this dramatic statement is clearly uttered . . . . It is a recognition of change and constancy at the same time. She is the same yet, paradoxically, different. Logically, this is impossible . . . . Logically . . . it should be either 'I am still what I have always been' or 'I am different from what I was.' (Foster 1989, 37)

What Winnie presents in these few sentences is a variation on Zeno's paradox, the classic dilemma often described as "Ulysses' paradox,"[22] the upshot of which is the logical impossibility of sameness-in-difference, both spatially and temporally. The problem for Winnie is that she feels the necessity to reflect on her experiences. She uses memory and a "Kantian" grid over time and space in an attempt to organize her universe into a cohesive set of causally connected moments—an infinitely divisible set to be pieced together by the observing conscious mind.[23] "It is because we [normally] see the world as a collection of discrete things [the grains of sand in Zeno's paradox] that we superimpose causal relationships, to 'glue' these things together. . . . Cause-and-effect is essential to our project of attempting to secure ourselves 'within' the world . . ." (Loy 1992, 247). Unfortunately, the world is not subject to this artificial packaging; thus, attempts to apply the causality paradigm to the world can only create frustration and suffering for the subject. As if to point out the importance of this problem, Winnie cycles back to the same lines at the ends of both acts (as well as at other points in the play):

> *WINNIE gazes before her with happy expression.*
>
> WINNIE Oh this *is* a happy day! This will have been another happy day! *(Pause.)* After all. *(Pause.)* So far.
>
> *Pause. Happy expression off.*
>
> (Beckett 1961, 47–48, repeated on 64)

Winnie is happy (or at least appears to be) because of Willie's actions in each of these cases. She reacts with unthinking pleasure, which is effectively a Zen state: "In Zen, language is evoked by the present occasion itself; it is not merely a mapping of the present in terms of learned structures" (Kasulis 1981, 136).[24] Memory, however, immediately mitigates her emotion, as she reduces the present moment to a past event *(will have been).* Once she attempts to compartmentalize her experience, Winnie has already moved well into the territory of suffering; she becomes acutely aware of conceptualized time as an enemy to her, a source of suffering as she cannot fill the temporal void that stretches before her each day. Thus in the end, all Winnie can safely say (with trepidation) is that it has been a happy day "so far." Her need to encapsulate her experiences necessitates conceptual dichotomy, which leads to the pain and suffering that exemplify her life as she sees it.

Obviously Winnie's trouble is another reiteration of the question of perception as it applies to subjectivity and objectivity: the subject/Winnie, which is effectively unchanging (at least, from the ego's point of view), perceives the causally connected object/Winnie, which must change over time (because each moment must be connected). Therefore, the root of the paradox, on this level at least, is that the *perceiving* subject cannot be and yet must be the same as the *perceived* object. Thus, "it is indeed tempting to raid the Lacanian store-cupboard and declare Winnie to be looker and looked-at within a patriarchal Law which denies her independent access to the un-conscious—as '*object* of scrutiny'" (Bryden 1993, 88). As we have seen, Zen considers the dichotomy between subject and object (as well as between conscious and unconscious) a false one. It is only our inability to efface our rigid egos—our conception of ourselves as autonomous and static—that keeps us from apprehending the interpenetration of "us" and the "outside" world. And it is the need to maintain our autonomy (by possessing things, finding pleasures, and so forth) that is finally responsible for our unhappiness and suffering.

What we see in the stark contrast between most of Winnie's words and her physical situation is a generative, nonstatic portrait of the confrontation of a consciousness and a world, a confrontation that must occur, given Winnie's ego's desire to survive. In *Happy Days*' seemingly endless and changeless environment, change, an iterative cycling back on events, occurs because it must: according to ancient Chinese tradition, "everything in the world was animate and changing, and these changes were not linear, but cyclic" (Kaltenmark 1969, 26). Chaos theory, of course, is intimately concerned with the intermixture of noise and self-similar iterations. Winnie's round of asymptotically worsening days and nights is nothing short of a crystallization of the Zen/Chaos theory vision of the world as a "without-causal," self-similar web.

Winnie's conflict, then, is that she is unable to accept and work within this changing universe, needing instead to maintain an outdated, impossibly rigid conceptual framework in order to survive (as she would consider her pathetic state). It is, in fact, the act of thought itself—deemed by Suzuki as Ignorance (the capital letter indicating a state not so much mental as spiritual)—that forces Winnie to maintain a bipolar view of life, one that brings only suffering:

> In Ignorance knowing is separated from acting, and the knower from that which is to be known; in Ignorance the world is asserted as distinct from the self; that is, there are always two elements standing in opposition. This is, however, the fundamental condition of cognition, which means that as soon as cognition takes place there is Ignorance clinging to its very act. When we think that we know something, there is something we do not know. (Suzuki 1949, 128)

There is, in fact, no division between self and object (if one "understands" that both are "without-existence")—it is only Ignorance that creates a chimera of difference. Moreover, in an argument that sounds like it could have come from Socrates, Zen attacks the very notion of knowing (or thinking) as being the root of not-knowing: as one cannot consciously know everything in the universe—all lines of poetry, for example—at once, every *act* or assertion of knowledge deconstructs itself in a multitude of acts of ignorance. (A similar type of reasoning leading to Socrates' statement that all he knew was that he knew nothing.)

Thus, there is an intimate connection between the dichotomy of "time present and time past" (to quote Eliot's *Four Quartets* again) that is contained in the above examples, as well as other of Winnie's musings and the dilemma of self versus object:

> The idea of Time, according to Buddhist experience, is a subjective conception, which develops, as the child becomes adult, with the formation of the ego and the notion of self. Its attributes of past, present and future are wholly bound up with the idea of ourselves as 'object.' Indeed, our conception of such a three-faceted phenomenon is merely our memory, our idea of the present in terms of the past and future, and our anticipations. All three, Buddhism urges, are self-oriented. (Foster 1989, 38)

The differentiation of time into past, or the "old style" (days and nights), and present (and, by implication, the intractable future), which is obviously a topic of great concern and distress on Winnie's part, is a difference only to the conceptualizing mind, which has constructed this "grid" in order to break down the constant flux of the world and our lives into finite, easily digestible pieces. For Zen, this erroneous division of self and object through time is a mistake with important consequences: using a flowing stream as a metaphor for life, Suzuki states: "If you are at all tempted to look into it [the stream], do so while letting it flow. The fact of flowing must under no circumstances be arrested or meddled with . . ." (1949, 19). Yet the mental action of dividing time, and subject from object, does arrest this process. Compartmentalization and simplification (or abstraction) form an important basis of the Newtonian paradigm—indeed, of mainstream Western thought and teaching as a whole. The consequence of causal division, however, is to divide things over and over again. As the world is, under these circumstances, infinitely divisible, there is no end to this futile quest. If, on the other hand, we accept the "new" paradigms of Zen and Chaos theory, we see that letting go of the causal (or stochastically abstracted) framework "leaves behind it not chance [or complete chaos] (its binary opposite) but a sense of mystery [or Chaos], of being part of something that we can never grasp [in an abstracted, deterministic fashion], since we are a manifestation of it" (Loy 1992, 247). Chaos theory and Zen, though operating on different planes, both indicate that releasing our common perception of reality is a necessary step toward a freedom to apprehend the entirety of each moment in a prereflective state.[25] For Winnie, this means that, in order to free herself, she must let go of her object nature—her habitual frame of mental reference.

Near the end of the play, we see the consequences of Winnie's failure to free herself from empty ritual and habit grow to alarming proportions: whereas before, Winnie had concerned herself with changes occurring in her object-self and in the world over macroscopic periods of time (the "old style," and her former, younger self versus the present), she now becomes more and more concerned with small increments of time (to be sure, partly because she is running out of things to say and do to keep busy—evinced by her more and more frequent litany, "one says it all"). The moment when this is clearest is when Winnie says,

> I used to think there was no difference between one fraction of a second and the next. *(Pause.)* I used to say . . . *(pause)* . . . I say I used to say, Winnie, you are changeless, there is never any difference between one fraction of a second and the next.
>
> (Beckett 1961, 59–60)

A moment later, she brushes this concern off—"Why bring that up again?"—yet we can see from this statement the reductio ad absurdum toward which Winnie is headed: her ability to believe in "happy days" is being destabilized and deconstructed. The "sides" of the paradoxes of temporal closure and of perceptible object-existence are growing closer and closer to each other, the gaps between the sides becoming more and more evident and violent in their closing intensity, and eventually the disparate elements will prove too much for Winnie, her ability to rationalize (or shrug off) the differences will collapse, and she will be left squarely facing the schism that is her life.

Winnie's story about Mildred (a sort of combination of Willie and Winnie, as well as Beckett's name for Winnie in an earlier draft of the play)[26] who is at once innocent and sexual like herself, her attempts to convince herself that all is well, that this will be "another happy day," that she is not talking to herself—"Ergo" Willie is listening to her (50)—are all evidence of how Winnie's almost continuous monologue presents an ever clearer picture of her frustrated situation, a situation arising from her conflicting desires and needs. From fairly numerous examples, such as her evocation of the final lines of *The Unnamable*—"I can do no more. *(Pause.)* Say no more. *(Pause.)* But I must say more" (60)—it is evident that Winnie is forced into the state of the Great Doubt, in which she must be aware of the paradoxical futility of her need to maintain a hollow mode of existence when she can "do no more."

She (and, indirectly, Willie) is at the mercy of the destabilizing "social" pressure of the bell, a vague but powerful force that tells her when to wake and when to sleep (if she ever really does get the signal to sleep—we never see this part of her day). During her waking moments, she seems driven to fulfill a "pensum," as Malone would put it, by speaking and otherwise filling the time she has been allotted to remain conscious. Winnie often refers to Willie's "marvelous gift" of being able to sleep the day away, and she looks forward longingly to night, when she can put all her things away and go to bed herself. At the same time, however, Winnie cannot resist the bell's call—whether, like the screams she hears, it is inside her head or it is actually audible—however much she might want to (in the second act, she tries unsuccessfully to sleep through the sound). This bell, which at the same time represents part of the "old style" in the form of an alarm clock (the original prop Beckett used) and the auditory embodiment of the "without," begins (and ostensibly ends) Winnie's daily ritual, a ritual embodying the worst "husk" of true living that Lao Tzu indicates in the above-quoted lines of the *Tao Te Ching*. Winnie's mumbled prayers and admonition to herself, "Begin, Winnie. *(Pause.)* Begin your day . . . " (8), for example, clearly indicate how ritualized her day has become, how unchanging and prearranged her daily routine.[27]

As the play continues, we find that, like the characters in *Endgame*, Winnie attempts to plan in advance every event, every moment, and even her stories, in order to make easier her attempts to maintain the categorical "old style." Even her song, which we finally hear near the end of the second act, has its proper place as the last event of each day. The objects Winnie removes from her bag each have their time and place as well. For whatever reason, this daily ritual must be played out in proper sequence and at the proper times, because, though Winnie had first assumed that all her objects could be taken out of her bag "indefinitely—back into the bag—back out of the bag—until the bell—went" (45), it turns out that she has only one chance to perform each ritual act per day. That there is no apparent reason for Winnie to perform any of the actions she does or say anything she says (except, of course, to survive the day), and that there are seemingly arbitrary rules governing what and when she can do things, clearly indicates the hollow social order of her existence.

Against the pressures of a Chaotic, always changing world, Winnie, in her state of Great Doubt, clings to the "old" paradigm: that the world is conceptual and ordered. This clinging need/belief reduces Winnie's preferred mode of existence to trivial insignificance. What Winnie is pleased to learn each day is so paltry and fleeting it does not seem worth "the pains" it takes for her to learn it. Thus, all of her talk of learning something new each day—"hardly a day [goes by], without some addition to one's knowledge" (18)—only serves to reinforce how little her life means as long as she refuses to open herself to the richer patterns which exist around (and within) her mound of earth. What Winnie somehow continually manages to keep at bay are the horrors and potential salvation of seeing the world as "Just chance . . . happy chance" (60).

What becomes most evident in Winnie's necessarily static battle with herself and her universe is that, as with *Godot* and *Endgame*, her speech and actions are the externalization of the final stages of meditation (the Great Doubt) a Zen novitiate must go through to achieve the state of satori, or enlightenment. As Zen Buddhism, which is eminently concrete, is "ultimately a state of mind" (or, better, "without-mind"), an end toward which each person must move through his or her confrontation with the dilemmas of life, the pains of meditation are ultimately the agony of casting off the old way of seeing the world through a new understanding of "realized experience" (Foster 1989, 30). As is evident from Winnie's struggles, the experience of meditation, far from being a peaceful period of calm and rest, is one of the most difficult, trying experiences a Zen student can practice; it is in the Great doubt of the final sessions of meditation that the student finally learns to let go of the ego and all its trappings and becomes capable of breaking through into a new way of seeing the universe.

During the Great Doubt—a period that can last seconds or days, or more—the student appears quiet, even half-dead, staring blankly with half-closed eyes and barely breathing. Inside, however, her mind plays tricks, cries out, and in general fights for survival of the "old style," where ego and suffering are secure. This period is a "still-point of terrible tension in which one gives oneself up to the feeling of nowhere to go" (Kasulis 1981, 114). This time, probably *the* ultimate trial for the Zen student, is actually an active period of "fight or flight" in a struggle for the ego-consciousness's life or death within an apparently static, unmoving world. In a metaphorical description of the Great Doubt which evokes the world of *Happy Days*, Hakuin states:

> Supposing a man should find himself in some desolate area where no man has ever walked before. Below him are the perpendicular walls of a bottomless chasm. His feet rest precariously on a patch of slippery moss, and there is no spot of earth on which he can steady himself. He can neither advance nor retreat; he only faces death. (Yampolsky 1971, 135)

Though all elements are not identical by any means, it is evident from this description of the Great Doubt (leading to the Great Death when the person finally lets go the ego and falls from the precipice) that Winnie is buried in this "slippery" slope, unable to turn away from herself no matter how hard she tries. While she struggles to divert her attention from her predicament, she is, in the end, left facing the void that lies between her supposed subject and object selves.

As we have seen, however, Winnie puts up a pretty good fight against the destabilizing forces of her necessary meditation. Although she grows aware that the "old style"—the old way of seeing the world—is no longer tenable (perhaps she has seen or suffered too much to imagine it could ever again be reinstated), Winnie nonetheless continues the old habits of speaking and doing that keep her from really confronting her situation. One of the best examples of Winnie's reluctance to face her situation—as well as the way in which the play cycles inward, forcing her deeper into the horrifying predicament of the Great Doubt—is her use of the things inside of her "bag." In the first act, Winnie is highly involved in the objects she possesses in her bag, often using them to help her maintain a semblance of the way life used to be for her, thus providing distraction from a full-fledged "meditation." These objects thus maintain Winnie's bipolar, causal, and therefore suffering vision of life.

Near the beginning of the play, when Winnie brushes her teeth, she sees that the toothpaste is nearly gone: "*(examines tube, smile off)*—running out . . ." (Beckett 1961, 9). Her consternation at the sight of her tube of toothpaste is shrugged off, but this event begins an undercurrent in her speech which indicates Winnie's unhappy knowledge that things cannot long remain even in the sorry state they are now. Another of Winnie's prized possessions, her parasol, is either used violently (when she strikes Willie with it) or is of no real use to her, as it catches fire when she tries to use it to protect herself from the rays of what is clearly a postholocaust sun. These and other possessions may give Winnie temporary relief through the habit and memories associated with them, but they actually extend her suffering because they seduce her back into the divisive world of ordered distinctions, where the self is conceptually separated from, able to understand, and possess other things. Even the looming threat of "Browny," her gun, does not ensure relief, since according to Buddhist tradition death cannot alleviate her suffering consciousness.

In the second act, Winnie is forced by circumstance to go deeper into her meditative state: now, although she can still make out her belongings, she can no longer use them as distraction from the mound of moments piling up around and burying her like Zeno's sands, moments which she still valiantly tries to forge into a causally connected life. Unable to maintain her distracted state under the relentless destabilizing influence of the insistent bell, her suffering grows worse and worse, as it must to provide the energy and impetus for her to break with the old, ego-centered ways. Yet, Winnie will not relent in her struggle for "survival"; deprived of her possessions, she turns to herself, both present and in memorialized past, for affirmation of the "old style." The stakes raised, Winnie treats herself as object, defining what she sees and even using others' impressions of her as evidence of her object-existence.

Once again, we are down to the crux of the play: Winnie's troubles can be reduced to the essential matter of whether she can be perceiving subject of her own objecthood. However, the paradoxical position of trying subjectively to see herself as object places Winnie in the unenviable position of playing the traditional male to her own womanhood. By trying to perceive her own objectivity, Winnie becomes both subject and object of the traditionally male gaze. As deLauretis says (of cinema, but the analysis applies to the theatrical gaze as well),

> The woman is . . . icon, or object of the gaze: an image made to be looked at by the spectator, whose look is relayed by the look of the male character(s). The latter not only controls the events and narrative action but is "the bearer" of the look of the spectator. The male protagonist is thus "a figure in a landscape," she [Laura Mulvey] adds, "free to command the stage . . . of spatial illusion in which he articulates the look and creates the action" (p. 13). . . . In that landscape, stage, or portion of plot-space, the female character may be all along . . . representing and literally marking out the place (to) which the hero will cross. (1987, 139; quotation from Mulvey 1975, 13)

How does Winnie fit into this scheme? To begin at the end, she is quite literally marking out a single spot in a "landscape," and thus is essentially playing out a stereotypical female/object role. In addition, Winnie—over and over again, as when she states, "Someone is looking at me still. . . . That is what I find so wonderful" (Beckett 1961, 49)—attempts to construct herself as object of a "male" gaze (often linked explicitly to Willie). For Winnie, "Knowledge of one's own presence is . . . a matter to be confirmed by the acknowledgment of others. When self seems to fade, reaffirmation may come from another's gaze. . . . [Thus] Winnie . . . feels herself ebbing and recharging under an anonymous eye" (Bryden 1993, 102). In light of this, Winnie envisions herself as marking out the role of the female protagonist in the realm of standard oedipal narrative. *Oedipus Rex*, the "master narrative" of this type, leads us along the path of (male) narrative desire—the desire to uncover, or "denude" the truth: "*Oedipus Rex* is an instance of the question of an identity dependent upon the unraveling of history and a gradual enlightenment open to the gaze of the [positionally male] audience" (Roof 1987, 154).

Notably, the two main tools we have been using to study Beckett's drama, though shifting away from the traditional paradigm, fall fully within a similar realm of male-dominated ideology, an ideology that defines itself against and through a feminine "other." As Hayles says, science is normally projected to be "an exclusively male domain; but it is the peculiar project of this domain [of Chaos theory] to have intercourse with a feminine principle" (1990, 174). Thus, it is chaos itself that is engendered as feminine—a world that, in opposition to the masculine rigidity of the classical paradigm, is mysterious and beckoning. As for Zen Buddhism—which, until a few years ago, excluded women to such an extent that even to touch one was taboo[28]—there has always been a tendency, through its Taoist influence, to maintain a vision of the void—the indefinable realm of undifferentiation, the ineffable "Tao"—as essentially feminine. Thus, both Zen and Chaos theory construct their "narratives" in terms of solitary (or unencumbered) males in a quasi-sexual affair with an all-encompassing female principle. At the same time, these men must abstain from interaction with real women (whose physical presence can be distracting) and attempt to immerse themselves within the *Ur*-female they seek to understand.

In patriarchal schemes like these, who or what is Winnie? Is she merely the female object of a standard oedipal narrative? Undoubtedly, no. Although she apparently would like to construct *herself* within this "old style" of vision, Winnie's situation is much more complex. First, the man in the world of the play, Willie, is not a "proper" male protagonist; like the castrated swine of which he speaks, he is essentially impotent and nearly nonexistent. This leaves Winnie to create the male gaze herself through a sort-of virtual Willie that she postulates is audience to her monologue and is gazing at her, affirming her disappearing physicality. When Willie finally does appear ("dressed to kill," as Beckett paradoxically puts it), Winnie's fantasy spectator crumbles before the reality of her male counterpart: at the same time she attacks his lack of manliness —"Reminds me of the day you came whining for my hand" (Beckett 1961, 61)—and fears the real gaze of a male—"Don't look at me like that! *(Pause. Vehement.)* Don't look at me like that!" (63). Winnie, though attempting throughout the play to reinsert herself into a traditional role as female object, has by this point become so conscious of her problematic subject/object nature that she cannot return to her traditional state of simple objecthood.

As we have seen, the quasi-narrative patterning that describes *Happy Days* is far from traditional. This play revolves in iterative cycles that are more presentational than expositionally denuding, finally giving us a tableau of information in which *meaning* is only incidental. "This technique has the advantage of avoiding for the most part the over-explicit. Its ambiguity and its openness seem well suited to express the vision of a world which eludes definition and reduction to closed systems of any kind and is characterized above all by mystery and bewilderment" (Knowlson and Pilling 1980, 99). The "mystery and bewilderment" Knowlson and Pilling describe is, again, a description of the female principle (that "other" which beckons but always remains just beyond understanding). That this narrative process is emblematic of both the feedback loops of a Chaotic system and the ever devolving spiral of Zen meditation indicates how essential the feminine principle is to the function of these processes—as well as the common feeling of "bewilderment" of the audience that arrives expecting a traditionally oedipal narrative pattern.

We see, then, another schism over which Winnie has been stretched: she wants (or so she says) to be the simple, unconscious object to the traditional male gaze,[29] trying even to construct the gaze herself; yet she *is* that feminine other which beckons her "male" self toward a realm which cannot be described in terms of the "old style," which gives her the words to conceptualize her world. Winnie is thus heading straight for the silence of "nothing left to say," a silence in which the impossibility of continuing to re-member the old paradigm of rigid conceptualization and differentiation butts up against the impossibility of letting go into a new, nonclosed, prereflective world in which words and concepts have no permanent meaning—only relative information. "What *Happy Days* becomes, aesthetically, it would seem is a ritualistic prelude, designed to prepare the audience for a moment of silent meditation when Winnie and Willie look at each other in the '*Long Pause*' that concludes the play" (Carey 1987, 149).

Therefore, when Willie rounds the front of the mound of earth and tries to climb it (in obvious response to Winnie's complete desperation), the moment of truth is at hand. Although Winnie tries to brush off the significance of the situation by attacking Willie's pathetic need for her (a cruelty made poignant by the situation), they each realize the import of the moment. When, as the curtain drops, "*They look at each other*," Willie, as "outside" perceiver, can either reinforce Winnie's sense of self-as-object through a traditionally male gaze, or, as seems more likely, he can act as Zen master—perhaps through this same gaze—and give her the shock she needs to get out of her state of extreme suffering. In the latter case, the gun lying beside Winnie is an important element in this scene: in order to give Winnie the shock she needs to break out of her state of paralyzed fear, he may need to use the gun on her. Yet the significance of Willie's possible use of the gun is more symbolic than real. The threat of annihilation from "Browny" may be directed toward the perceiving subject (either Winnie *or* Willie) or toward the object of perception. However, it is only if both are killed at the same time—if subject and object are no longer perceived as separate—that Winnie can truly achieve the state of mental freedom, or nirvana, she needs so much more than physical liberation. Like a snapshot of the metaphorical arrow flying across the distance between self and other, Winnie, Willie, and we are left suspended in a moment of time which could be the instant preceding death or freedom (or both). However, unlike Zen anecdotes in which the student is granted the gift of vision, Beckett once again ends the play in the pregnant moment before we know which way the scales will tip. However, as opposed to *Godot* and *Endgame*—and foretelling later plays—in *Happy Days*, the potential space is reduced, compressed to a more violent, and therefore concrete point, a grain of time in which all possibilities resonate. Thus, Willie and Winnie are essentially our metaphorical arrow and target: they "gaze" at each other across an ever-closing distance in which a violent, potentially liberating "connection" will be made. Either the "system" of the play will collapse completely under its own weight, or the world will be created new from Winnie's and Willie's gaze across this explosive point.

6

Iterative *Footfalls*, "However Faint They Fall": Lessness in Arrow, Target

A good traveler has no fixed plans and is not intent upon arriving.

—*Tao Te Ching*

"How can the shot be loosed if 'I' do not do it?"
"'It' shoots."

—Eugen Herrigel

When, nearly a decade and a half after completing *Happy Days*, Beckett wrote the short, ghostly, Noh-like play, *Footfalls*, his tendency toward reduction in the earlier play had already evolved through a group of shorter plays (notably all in English). In the short pieces, *Play*, *Come and Go*, *Breath*, *Not I*, and *That Time* (whose writing time overlapped that of *Footfalls*), the apparent drive toward "lessness," which began in *Endgame* and especially in *Happy Days*, had already resulted in smaller-scale, highly textured plays ranging in length from more than a half hour (as in *Play*) to about a minute (in the case of the actorless *Breath*). *Footfalls* thus fits somewhere in the middle of this range, though, with the exception of the unusually conceived play, *Breath*, it is one of Beckett's shortest up to that period. After the intervening decade of reduction, then, it would seem likely that by the time he wrote *Footfalls*, Beckett would be far from the longer, more normative form and content of *Happy Days*. Notably, however, the focus on a central female character, as well as the imagistic inception of the play, give us a first indication of how *Footfalls* continues revolving similar concerns to those of its older relative, albeit in a more confined space.

As Beckett publicly noted (see, for example, Knowlson and Pilling 1980, 220; Gontarski 1985, 164), the inception and "central image" of *Footfalls* is the picture of May (or "M") pacing the slim, shrinking strip of gray light, tracing out what Enoch Brater has noted is the sideways eight of infinity—∞.[1] The words and script were "'built up around this picture.'"[2] Like Winnie in her mound of scorched earth, this image both contains and reflects the actions of the play as a whole. While May performs her intermittent ritual pacing, her mother (we are told, though she is only indicated as "V") speaks from a dark distance, wakened from her "deep sleep" by her "daughter," May. Here, then, is another—yet unique—permutation of paired Beckettian characters: the relationship we surmise we witness this time is one between mother and daughter—a new relational pairing for Beckett's drama[3]—and this time half of the pair is invisible.

In terms of the archery metaphor used throughout this work, the Zen/archery student is now entering the final stages of training. She slowly awakens from her dream of causality but is consequently no longer sure of the reality, or presence, of bow, arrow, and target. Her world contracts into a tight spiral which revolves around the question: What are these elements of perception when the premade categories of conceptual language fails? The relational context of arrow and target remains destabilized by the "active" force of the bow, but when the student is able to reject some a priori absolute reality for these pieces of her moment of being-time, the causal action of an arrow flying toward a target because of the force of a bow is radically reduced to one of flickering absence.

As the student's mind loses its hold on causality, the elements of her world, like a poorly run silent film, cycle rapidly between instants of blank confusion and clearly defined, prereflective apprehension of "what's there." At this point, the student loses any conscious conviction of who or what is loosing the arrow, approaching a feeling that "'It' shot and 'It' made the hit" (Herrigel 1953, 59). This moment, during which the student grows "more uncertain than ever" (Herrigel 1953, 28), is both infinitely quick and eternally frozen like an "expanse of ice" as presence and absence spin, locked into a decaying orbit around each other. It is this revolving interplay of the competing paradigms that defines the central image of *Footfalls:* the pacing figure of May. As opposed to the numerous readings of the play which have investigated the psychological impetus for the play—whence comes May's pacing, the struggle which is going on between daughter and mother, and even "where" V is—this examination of the play takes a more existential approach. Rather than try to figure out what historical event(s) have caused May and V to arrive at the situation in which we see them, we will consider the stark, minimal landscape of the play as manifestation of being in the latter stages of the Great Doubt.[4]

To reflect this reduced, starker world, the setting has also changed considerably since Beckett's longer plays (generating the humorous impetus to term Beckett's earlier work "conventional" in relation to his later plays). In *Play*, no longer is any attempt made to stage anything resembling a trompe l'oeil background (as in *Happy Days*) or even a quasi-realistic setting; instead, the players (or "victims") are interred inside urns that are only three feet in height—apparently too short to allow the players to sit or stand within them, and thus necessitating trapdoors for the actors (Beckett 1984e, 159). In *Not I*, only a hooded figure and a pair of lips (impossibly high above the stage) are visible; the rest is in darkness. And in *Footfalls*, the stage is almost completely dark, with only May's strip of light visible (and then, dimly so) throughout the play. There is not even a suggestion from the staging as to where or on what May paces. We have moved, as Garner puts it, from "the anthropomorphic signatures of 'inhabited space' . . . [to] the aesthetic surface of visual abstraction" (1987, 351).

Simultaneous with the move away from obeisance to representational staging appears a movement toward a formalization or "musicality" of the aural element in the plays, as well as a tendency to constitute the "listener" as an important factor or even as a controlling one. In *Happy Days,* and in Beckett's earlier plays, listening is, of course, an important part of the pairing of characters—it is especially important to Winnie's mental health to "know" Willie is listening to her—yet, in the later plays, the listener begins to have a direct effect on what is said and done by speaking characters, as well as on how the audience interprets the actions and words spoken on stage. Beginning with *Play*—with the spotlight "expressive of a unique inquisitor" (Beckett 1984e, 158), and developed into a physical presence in *Not I* and *That Time,* where only the listener is visible—the growing focus on the silent, reactive element of the pair is tantamount to a shift within these plays toward the aural, with words and especially sound becoming equal to, if not more important than, the visual elements of staging.[5] Thus, as the plays become less representational (or more formalized) visually, there is a shift in staging toward an equality between sound and vision, a trend that continues into Beckett's last works.

In *Footfalls*, the element of sound is obviously of great importance, as is evident from both the aural "image" of May's steps and from what the characters say. V, for example, tells us that her daughter needs to "hear the feet, however faint they fall" (Beckett 1984b, 241); and both characters select words—"stark," "feat," "rack"—whose sound is striking and archaic. Because of the importance of sound to the verbal, emotional, and physical layers of the play, some even claim that "the entire emphasis [of the play] is on the sound and pattern of the footfalls" (Anna McMullan 1993, 102). Yet at the same time, the play seems to revert to a form closer to that of Beckett's earlier drama, in which the speaker has greater control over what occurs on stage.

Closer examination of the play itself, however, reveals an underlying stress on the listener as generative element. In section 1, May and her mother carry on a fairly normal, straightforward dialogue that reveals that mother/ V is sickly and needs her daughter's aid ("but it is too soon"), as well as the relative ages of the two players. In this section, most of the questions and responses are concrete, providing haiku-like images of the here and now of the two. With almost no adjectival ornamentation, the two converse in images at once present and repeated:

> M: Would you like me to inject you again?
> V: Yes, but it is too soon.
> [*Pause.*]
> M: Would you like me to change your position again?
> V: Yes, but it is too soon.
>
> (Beckett 1984b, 240)

Even at this early stage, however, the iterative nature of their discussion, as well as other elements in the play, indicates its later evolution. Most obviously, V is not a visible presence but a voice from the dark "without." In addition, V, after waking from her "deep sleep," briefly objectifies May as she counts her paces; and, of course, the section ends with V asking if May will ever have done "revolving it all" in her "poor mind," raising the daughter's pacing to the level of metaphorical icon. However, by virtue of physical presence—as well as the fact that V is "brought to consciousness" (or being) by May, generating only two questions in section 1—it seems that May has the active, speaking role in this section, whereas V takes on the more passive role of listening and responding. Thus, an apparently straightforward dichotomy is set up between the pair, with the speaking role being the generative one.

As we have come to expect from Beckett, this supposedly simple relationship is radically destabilized as soon as the next section starts. With the lines

> I walk here now. *[Pause.]* Rather I come and stand. *[Pause.]* At nightfall. *[Pause.]* She fancies she is alone.
>
> (241)

V returns to her nascent objective, objectifying role, watching an "absent" May as her "absent" voice begins a narrative account of May's youth. At the same time, V's opening statement that *she* is walking "here now" throws into question who exactly is whom in the play, an undermining of the "stable self" characteristic of Beckett's work of this period, and allows a more fluid, fragmented persona to develop (Bryden 1993, 114–15), a multiple persona in which any sharp distinction between listener and speaker is lost as individuality dissolves. As with Beckett's other plays, "The [simple] binary divisions between daughter/mother, self/other, author/fictional creation [which are set up at the beginning] . . . become increasingly blurred" as the play progresses (Anna McMullan 1993, 100). The nonpresence that is V becomes objective narrator, the all-important, omnipresent filter of experience that parcels out understanding as May paces the strip of light:

> V: I walk her now. *[Pause.]* Rather I come and stand. *[Pause.]* At nightfall. *[Pause.]* She fancies she is alone. *[Pause.]* See how still she stands, how stark, with her face to the wall. *[Pause.]* How outwardly unmoved. *[Pause.]* She has not been out since girlhood.
>
> (Beckett 1984b, 241)

May becomes the objectified "poor" listener (in many senses), pacing the strip, believing she is alone. Yet, as Beckett's drafts reveal (Pountney 1988, 280–81; Brater 1987, 53), V is more or less contained within May's mind; thus, potentially, the "present absence" of May onstage dictates the "absent presence" of V offstage. The "poorly" listening May still may (as her name implies) be the generative element of this section.

In section 3, May speaks her own narrative (a "sequel" to her mother's), continuing the story of a girl who had to pace the floor (yet, in a church this time), then moving on to the time when that girl will fade away "like moon passing through rack" (Beckett 1984b, 242), and finally recounting the story of Amy, her mother, Mrs. Winter, and an incident at church vespers. In this section, May presumably moves through an account of the past to an account of the future—as seems confirmed by the empty stage in section 4—to a narrative of a mythologized present. This cyclical, temporal progression resonates with the fluidity of time in Eliot's "Burnt Norton," indicating that it is her "footfalls [which] echo in the memory" (Eliot 1963, 117) and that she, the speaker, is the generative element in the play. Again, however, the issue is complicated: May, like Mouth in *Not I*, refuses to refer to her (presumable) self in the first-person, instead resorting to use of the third person—"A little later, when as though she had never been, it never been, she began to walk" (Beckett 1984e, 242)—and even of an anagrammatic representation of herself—Amy—in this section. Although V is conspicuously absent now, May has effectively become audience to her own words, acting as listener and speaker at the same time; now, like the novitiate archer, May embodies both presence and absence.

In section 4, then, when the light fades up again "a little less," revealing this time an empty stage, it is the audience alone which now listens intently (with both ears and eyes) to the dying sound of the chime, the failing light—the fading echoes of *Footfalls*—listening by this time being the only presence on stage. In this resonating potential space, May and V, as well as their complementing and contrasting words, intermix freely;

questions of duality or unity, of who is speaking truth and who is lying, are no longer valid or useful. The "resonance chamber" of section 4 is that "other" frame of reference in Beckett's plays—the "without" of Zen, the deterministic Chaos of dynamic systems theory—with which we have by now become familiar. In *Footfalls*, though, this frame of reference no longer exists as a potentiality at the fringes of the play. May's pacing figure, the stark, archaic vocabulary, and V's ambiguous existence establish this frame more firmly here than in any of Beckett's earlier plays.

How, more specifically, has *Footfalls* shifted this far "off center"?[6] Through the more focused, formalized, ritualized nature of the play itself. *Footfalls* is, in effect, the Zen "without-causal" frame of reference. The fluidity of focus, staging, and character already revealed by our brief look at the play has the striking (and potentially unsettling) effect of exposing how formal and ritualized is the space and time in which *Footfalls* takes place—which is *Footfalls*. We previously noted the ritual repetition and doubling that lies just below the surface of Beckett's earlier work; but, by the time we reach *Footfalls*, all representational distractions have been removed, allowing us a direct confrontation with the iterative temporal and spatial patterns of the work. As Mary Doll has noted about Beckett's plays in general, but which is especially true of his later plays, this type of time and space is the "sacred" or ritualized space-time that Mircea Eliade describes in *The Sacred and the Profane*.[7] In this work, which over the years has proved influential in many areas, Eliade lays out the differences between secular (or common) space and time, which is essentially homogeneous—in other words, there is no essential difference between one moment and the next, or between one place and another—and sacred space and time, where discontinuities exist.

In *Footfalls*, there is definitely something special about the place May paces: though we are never sure where this place is—whether it is within her house, the "little church," or simply in Peter Brook's "holy" stage space—there is something about it that attracts May to it, to hear her own steps, "however faint they fall" (Beckett 1984e, 241). This space, then, appears to be "qualitatively different from others," a factor which arises not from rational choice or "theoretical speculation," but from "a primary religious experience that precedes all reflection on the world" (Eliade 1957, 20, 21). It is this experience of discontinuity between the "sacred" and the "profane" that orients space about a central, "fixed point," which (as it positions the universe around it) effectively defines and creates the world (21–22).

Time itself is cyclic and repeatable during and in the sacred, ritualized, space of the play, creating "a sort of eternal mythical present that is periodically reintegrated by means of rites" (70). In the Christian context of

Eliot's "Burnt Norton"—in whose opening lines some (James Acheson and Enoch Brater, for example) find an important source for *Footfalls*[8]—"If all time is eternally present / All time is unredeemable" (Eliot 1963, 117) in a concrete sense, since potential and possibility never can be realized in the "present" moment. Beckett's play rejects the specifically Christian context of Eliot's poem (Acheson 1987, 129), but play and poem share an "echoing" atmosphere of lost possibilities and potential flux, to be apprehended by the mind's eye:

> Footfalls echo in the memory
> Down the passage which we did not take
> Towards the door we never opened
> Into the rose-garden. My words echo
> Thus, in your mind.
>
> (Eliot 1963, 117)

Certainly the overlapping imagery of footfalls, doors, and "perpetual possibility" reveals the similar circularity of time and space in both works, thus strengthening our perception of the play as ritual iteration in a potential space. Additionally, Eliot's lines indicate that the cost for May and V of an eternal, mythical present is that iterated past and future can be recovered only *as present* moment, since conceptual time's ability to exist outside this discontinuous space is nullified. Thus, the present must always remain, in some sense, "unredeemable," because redemption can never arrive.[9] Therefore, May "Tells how it was. *[Pause.]* Tries to tell how it was. *[Pause.]* It all. *[Pause.]* It all" (Beckett 1984e, 241) in a never-ending present in which "It all" revolves incessantly.

As these observations indicate, there is, at the same time, good reason to see *Footfalls* in light of Eliade's sacred time and space and an apparent discrepancy between Eliade's vision of the sacred and the worldviews of Chaos theory, and especially of Zen Buddhism, which I have been utilizing to re-present Beckett's work. First of all, both stage space and time are ritualized and circular in *Footfalls*: May's pacing is at once present and extruded over years of nightly repetition; her pattern on the floor is a repeated, closed form. Eliade's observations about the sacred vision's "reintegration" of a "mythical time made present," which arises through ritual repetition (1957, 68–69), therefore describe the space and time we witness within the play. In addition, some of the conclusions Eliade draws coincide with the Zen position that the world must be absorbed in a pre-reflective state, the world-as-it-is being fundamentally different from our usual experience of it. In the normal ("profane") mode of existence, experience is "a *reconstruction* in that it imposes categories that were not present in that experience when it originally occurred. . . . For Zen [however] . . . reality is protean, always changing its shape as soon as we come into contact with it" (Kasulis 1981, 60).

Zen goes on to claim that, if we can learn to live in this a-causal state, "there is no longer the tendency to make reality into something static or reified" (Kasulis 1981, 60–61). Therefore time, space, and person are infinitely fluid and malleable. Here, then, lies an apparent problem: for Eliade, sacred space and time *are* reified and quasi-static, centering the world about a fixed time and place of the origin, for "no world can come to birth in the chaos of the homogeneity and relativity of profane space [and time]" (Eliade 1957, 22). Thus, there is apparently a large schism between the Zen doctrine that portions of reality cannot be "reified" and Eliade's claim that temporal and spatial reification are necessary for a religious experience of the world.

At the same time, Zen depends on ritual meditation and routine to allow students (and masters) to find and maintain the state of enlightenment: "Practice, repetition, and repetition of the repeated with ever increasing intensity are its [the path to enlightenment via archery's] distinctive features for long stretches of the way" (Herrigel 1953, 40). How do we reconcile the need for ritual time and space in Zen with its radical relativity? The answer to this apparent problem, which has important repercussions for *Footfalls*, lies in Eliade's definition of the sacred as "eternally present," or pre-reflective:[10] for Zen, *all* time and space is "sacred," as life itself is—or should be—experienced (at all times) in a pre-reflective state. As the entire world is effectively reified, no time or place is relatively more important than any other; time becomes infinitely cyclic and space becomes motilely fixed. Time is both discontinuous and continuous since there is no necessary (causal) connection between moments, yet iteration continually recovers the past and future into the "now." Space is both continuity and discontinuity since (as we saw in chapter 3) absolute stillness (discontinuity) and absolute motion (continuity) are one and the same. Thus, every moment and space is sacralized, each instant of "being-time" a unique one of death and birth—which explains the Zen aphorism, "Live each moment as if it were your last."[11]

For May, pacing the strip of gray light, these observations reveal the universality of the sacred in her world. She and her mother exist in a world completely without-time and without-space (as per Kasulis's convention) in which the focus achieved through the iterative compression of scale effectively augments the scope of their world. The reduced scale of *Footfalls*, as well as the iterative reduction of scale that takes place within the play itself, "creates a strong impression of cyclic progression. The pacing figure becomes steadily more memorable as she is seen to be fading, so that the echo of her presence exists strongly for the audience in her final absence from the stage" (Pountney 1988, 284). Thus, the tiny, shrinking world in which May and Mother live becomes, by virtue of its restrictive, formalized and nonspecific place and time, invariant and universalized—like the scaling constant that Feigenbaum discovered in Chaotic systems.

What Feigenbaum (using renormalization group theory) realized about systems exhibiting Chaotic behavior is that they all approach disorder by bifurcating in a series of strict geometric steps in a ratio of 4.669 (see Gleick 1987, 171–75). What this implies is that in a system tending toward Chaotic behavior, a new quantity is being conserved: instead of mass or length remaining constant,[12] this fixed ratio of bifurcations indicates that the "roughness" or "scaling factor" of a Chaotic system remains invariant across scales (Hayles 1990, 155). The picture of the Mandelbrot set (see figure 19) reveals how the Feigenbaum scaling factor works in this particular instance. In this set, the area of each of the smaller "bulbs" attached to the main body are in a relation of some multiple of 4.669. The second bulb along the real line segment, for example, is 1/4.669 times the area of the main body.

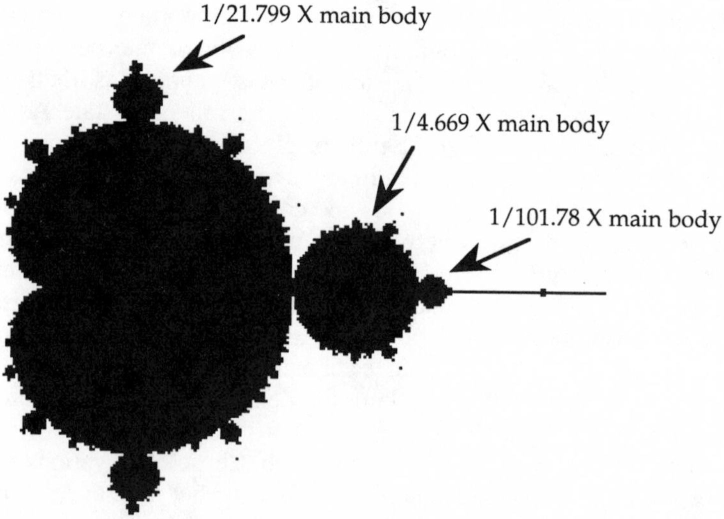

Fig. 19. The Feigenbaum scaling constant revealed in the Mandelbrot set.

Systems that are scale invariant contain fixed points in which "perturbations on the smallest scale are quickly transmitted throughout the system, affecting even the largest macroscopic level" (Hayles 1990, 156). Essentially, this means that fluctuations in motion or spatial construction which exist in the tiniest of scales are universalized, thus explaining how Chaotic behavior can arise from perturbations too small to be measured.

Referring to the Cantor dust once again,[13] we can see how at each level of generation, the dust mirrors the level above it—in fact, multiplying the lower line segment by three returns one to the level above (see figure 20).

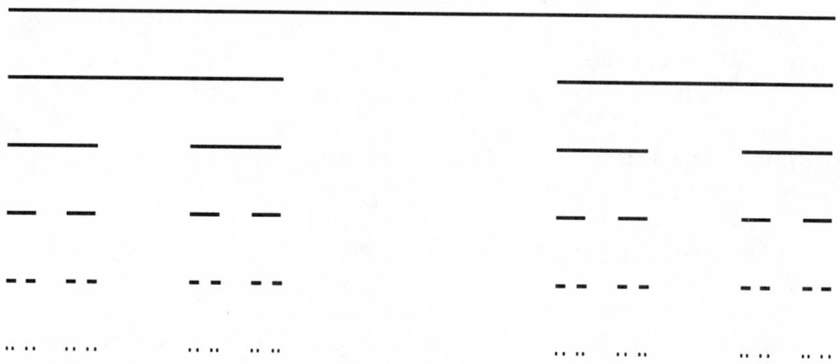

Fig. 20. The first five generations of what will eventually become the Cantor dust. Each level is produced by removing the middle third of the line segment(s) that lies above it.

At each of the infinitely many infinitesimally small "fixed" points resulting from a sufficient number of iterations of this process, the entire "universe" of the original line segment exists in its entirety through scale invariance and fixed-point symmetry. Therefore in a Chaotic system, the "conserved" tendency toward "lessness" is, at the same time, a universalizing, Chaotic trend. Thus, for *Footfalls*, the reduced temporal and spatial arena of the stage is scale-invariant, the sacred stage space—like the Christian church May characterizes it as—actually encompassing and *being* (in actuality, not metaphorically) the world itself. Each moment and each place is therefore linked, or mingled, with every other moment and place, creating a world that is a stage.[14]

In similar fashion, within the world-stage of *Footfalls* the conservative forces of lessness and self-similarity are operating. In the structure of the play, a pattern of diminishing threes is set up. There are three main, or verbal, sections to the play, the third of which is divided into three itself (a smaller version of the whole) and finally, on the empty stage, the lessening pattern of three occurs once again. Sections 1 and 2 each have, more or less, a single basic thrust: in section 1 it is the dialogue, and in section 2 it is the observational monologue of V. Section 3, however, is divided into three distinct phases: May's "Sequel" to her mother's story, a blazon of "The semblance" that is May, and the tale of Amy and Mrs. Winter (see Cohn 1990, 168). The triplet of this third section, like the Cantor dust, reflects the whole of the play in lesser fashion: the sequel to V's story—"she began to walk. *[Pause.]* At nightfall. *[Pause.]* Slip out at nightfall and into the little church by the north door . . . " (Beckett 1984b, 242)—the dialogue between Amy and Mrs. Winter—"Amy. *[Pause.]* Yes, Mother. *[Pause.]* Will you never have done? *[Pause.]* Will you never have done . . . revolving it all?" (243)—and May's self-description all reflect and permute elements of the play that appeared in the previous two sections. In addition, May's description of "The semblance" which is herself directs us toward the next iteration of the ritualized pattern of the play:

> The semblance. Faint, though by no means invisible, in a certain light. *[Pause.]* Given the right light. *[Pause.]* Grey rather than white, a pale shade of grey. *[Pause.]* Tattered. *[Pause.]* A tangle of tatters. *[Pause.]* Watch it pass—*[Pause.]*—watch her pass before the candelabrum, how its flames, their light . . . like moon through rack. *[Pause.]* Soon then after she was gone, as though never there, began to walk, up and down, up and down, that poor arm.
>
> (242)

In the commingling of images that make up this description—images strongly reminiscent of Prospero's famous speech in *The Tempest*—we see the dissolution of persona, the final near invisibility of May's existential self, the girl "never properly born"[15] who now dissolves like scattering clouds before the moonlight.

Section 4, which, as we have discussed, acts as a resonance chamber for the first three parts, is also constructed of three—the chime, fade-up, and fade-down of light that constitutes the superstructure of the other sections as well.[16] This section is much less an equal fourth to the three that preceded it than it is the next level of iteration in a series: the tripartite commingling of images we witness here is the next step toward the zero point of lessness, encompassing via scale-invariance the steps of the play preceding it. The play is thus a triple iteration of threes: the first iteration—three verbal sections; the second iteration—the third section made up of three subsections; and the third iteration—chime, fade-up, and fade-down on an empty stage. Like the chime and the lights, there is a diminishing spiral tectonic structure of three to the play itself, an iteration of a middle-third "Cantor dust" toward the infinite, infinitesimal stage of zero. As Alan Schneider and Billie Whitelaw observe in the filmed rehearsal process for *Rockaby*,

Schneider: Every line of Beckett's contains the whole of Beckett . . . . He's always choosing different means . . .
Whitelaw: To say the same thing?
Schneider: Yeah.

(Beckett 1985)

It is via this fixed-point linkage between the infinitesimal and the largest scales that Beckett's work, like a holograph—each portion of which contains the information for the whole—derives universality through lessness.

Beyond mere reduction, we can see how the set of threes effectively creates overdetermined referents in *Footfalls* by noting Hoon-sung Hwang's semiotic study of the play. Likening the play to a hall of mirrors[17] that reflect one another without referring to any "objective" referent, Hwang explains how "The audience of *Footfalls* is bombarded with triple echoes of a specific image, 'a woman walking up and down' at three levels of signification: 1/ the visual, 2/ the aural, and 3/ the imaginary (the fictional)" (1993, 373). The first two of these we have discussed specifically; the imaginary/fictional we have to some extent spoken of as the potential space within which the play echoes.[18] In a traditional play, the audience member

> derives from the conventionalized onstage happenings a range of dramatic information which enables him to translate what he sees and hears into something quite different: a fictional dramatic world characterized by a set of physical properties, a set of agents and a course of time-bound events. (Elam 1980, 98)

In this type of play, each image refers back to a single referent, so that we can piece together like a jigsaw puzzle the meaning of the metaplay. However, in *Footfalls* (as—to some extent—in all of Beckett's plays), signs are not related back to any stable referent, the images refuse to refer to anything but each other. When, for example, V begins section 2 with "I walk here now. *[Pause.]* Rather I come and stand" (Beckett 1984b, 241), we are thrust into a world in which stable distinctions are no longer valid. In the stage "presence" of *Footfalls* as a whole there is a fluid triple entendre, so to speak, that destabilizes the primacy or presence of any one element.

Also, at the "outer" level, the play reveals three types of semiotic reflexivity: between author and text, between character and audience, and between subtexts within the play. The first type arises from self-knowledge on the author's part, a competition between author and text for truth-value. For example, as Bair points out, this play has strong biographical sources; Beckett's mother (May Beckett) would, on sleepless nights, pace the floor of their house (1990, 23), and (fictional) May's pacing has strongly Parkinsonian arrhythmia, which Beckett might have picked up watching the progression of his mother's disease. Within the play, May/V create their own versions of how and when the pacing began, whether it was when "other girls of her age were out at . . . lacrosse" or "when she was quite forgotten" (Beckett 1984b, 241–42); thus an irresolvable competition is set up between fictional and biographical referents. The second type, between character and audience, is complicated by the character's consciousness of herself *as* character, "often manifested by an audience on stage" (Hwang 1993, 370), be it May or V. Thus, as "The two women are an internalized audience of each other" (Levy 1990, 97), their act(s) of listening to each other on stage destabilizes any static distinction between character, actor, and audience. The third type, that between subtexts, is related to the differing signals we receive from visual and aural sources (what we see and what we are told we should see). We are told of a very physical (physically ill) mother, but hear only a voice from offstage. We are told May paces either in a church or in her home, but see her walking on a blank stage in a thin strip of light.

By complicating the relationship between each set of signifiers and referents, each sign being refracted into three by the prism of the visual, aural, and imaginary planes, the audience's "conventional reception of theatrical performance, locating meaning in the referent, is frustrated, since the referent is shared by . . . three images." Thus the audience "is induced to realize that the meaning resides less in the image re-enacted [on these different planes] . . . than in the shaping of these messages or in the mode of the relationship among the theatrical signs that create them" (Hwang 1993, 374). Rather than reside in any concrete, specific referent, the meaning—or better, *information* (as conceptual meaning is at best elusive in Beckett's plays)—of the play resides in the relational context of triple resonances between signs.

Through these reflecting signs and the iterative lessness of the play, the fluid mother-daughter, May/V, pair is locked into a universe created from infinitesimal points refracting one another, one wherein even the smallest events are reflected in and by the triple-image on stage and are thus profoundly important. By "revolving it all," the women are, at the same time, living in and creating Eliade's "sacred" realm, in which permutative iterations in space and time forever regenerate and amplify time and space itself. May's walks lead nowhere, yet they are everywhere; time, like May's steps, leads backward and forward in constant cycling iteration. The two women exist in a world—heaven or hell, nirvana or samsara (there is no difference but point of view)—in which their relationship can be played out in miniature or infinitely (there is no difference but point of view).

Like the familiar yet strange specter of May fading to view each time, we see once more that Beckett's essential paired relationship—bisected by a destabilizing third element—iterated and permuted, yet scale-invariant (or "conserved"), forms the crux of this play as well. Here again, arrow and target are set in motion by the bow that has "cut right through you" (Herrigel 1953, 61). This time, however, it is the essential female relationship we see: in *Footfalls*, mother and daughter play out their relationship on the (r)evolving stage. How does this pairing reflect and uniquely rework Beckett's penchant for doubles? Let us look more closely at the fundamentals of the relationship between (this) mother and daughter by considering the historically "undramatic" nature of the mother-daughter relationship.[19] From Penelope on, the wife and mother in European literature has been associated with stillness and home, a counterpart to her husband who travels and interacts with the outside world. The "good" daughter will, of course, follow her mother and perpetuate this counterpoint with her future husband. Thus, in most Western literature the normative female character is relating either with her husband or with suitors to be her future husband; and she does this either in or near her home—or, as Christendom spread its influence, in her one other appropriate setting: the church. The proper woman, therefore, has significant relationships only with men and does so only at home or in its appropriate extension, the church. Thus, as Jenny S. Spencer puts it, "[A] woman's scope of action was sorely circumscribed" (Spencer 1989, 147).

At the same time, however, the household became the domain of women, men traditionally giving over control of domestic space (and often expressing an inability to understand the minutia of its quotidian routine). Thus, the house becomes both a sanctuary from the pressures of the external (male) world and a private, closed arena in which mother and daughter are forced to be permanent compatriots and combatants. Mother and daughter are trapped in a relational context which—in opposition to the male context of one versus another—makes separation and identity difficult. This concept is not new:

> Nancy Chodorow, a leading spokesperson for early socialization experience of females, proposes that the mother-daughter relationship is characterized by an essential continuity not present in mother-son relationships. While mothers treat sons as separate beings, encouraging their autonomy, mothers identify with their daughters, treating them as extensions of themselves. (Browder 1989, 111)

Drawn and/or forced back to the household setting and to each other, women find it difficult to succeed according to the rules of "difference" set up by the male world outside. Mother and daughter daily (re)iterate a world—a relational context—of sameness from which difference must be wrenched and which carries with it potentials and problems that differ from those of the male world outside the home.[20]

As noted in chapter 2, this idea that individuals (women) fit within an a priori context is an important aspect of Zen Buddhism (and of Japanese culture as a whole):

> The notion that the world is a stage and we are the actors is not Japanese. For the Japanese the world, the human context, is not a static backdrop against which people play out their individual roles. Rather the context is an organic reality, transforming itself to the rhythm of its own necessity, establishing the interrelations that define individual persons. In Japan, personal significance always occurs *in medias res*; it arises out of the demands of the social, linguistic, or philosophical framework. The individual becomes meaningful insofar as he or she is an outgrowth of the relationships established by the operative context, not vice versa. (Kasulis 1981, 9)

Aside from the fascinating reversal of the great Shakespearean metaphor,[21] we can see from what Kasulis states that in this *Weltanschauung*, a set of people or characters is defined by the relational, external/internal context that surrounds them. For May and her mother (and Beckett's pairs, in general), this means that it is the *relationship*—the interstitial space and time around and through which the two interact—that defines them both. It is not the characters who create a pair, but this unique paired relationship between *characters* that creates May and her mother.[22]

Furthermore, May and V are inscribed within the specifically Zen context of "without-context," the *Mu*, or nothingness toward which Zen points. Their world, which resists signification as anything but what it *is* (any singular external references), calls to mind the Zen aphorism, "one must *be Mu*, not think about it" (Kasulis 1981, 11). Although *Footfalls* as a whole re-presents this context, it is May's all-important, emotionally charged negative prefix "un–" ("What is it, Mother, said the daughter, a most strange girl, though scarcely a girl any more . . . *[Brokenly.]* . . . dreadfully un– . . . *[Pause.]*" [Beckett 1984b, 242]) that most pregnantly reflects the inability of concepts to capture the experience that is occurring. The hanging negative, the emotional center of the play, expresses almost perfectly the inability of words to encompass the experience of the play. This is a context, a play, a pair of characters, which must be experienced first-hand, without conceptual distinctions.[23] It is within this context of a-conceptual sameness, of immediately shared space and routine, that May and mother (and audience) are defined—and against which they struggle in a futile and (according to Zen) misguided attempt to establish any concrete, fundamental difference between them*selves*.

How can we better characterize this "without-context"? The words of the play itself give us the means: the litany of repetition that ends each of the first three sections centers on "it all," a vague, encompassing term that May must revolve in her "poor mind." This unspecified pair of words is, at one and the same time, May's eternal problem and the context within which the women play out their ritual repetition. The "it" is, on one level, the third element that destabilizes the mother-daughter pair. Like Godot in the earlier play, "it" motivates, is the goal of, and provides the context for the play. Without this potential character, we might simply contextualize mother and daughter as static, discernible individuals, but, as with the third element in the other plays we have examined thus far, "it" reveals the ultimate relativity of any fundamental distinction.

"It" is also Hwang's "fictional/imaginative" level of signs which destabilizes the aural and visual elements of the play. "It" is May's problem of presence, as she can never fully exist so long as she must "revolve it all" physically and mentally. "It" is that self-abnegating force which should loose the arrow in archery. "It" is Derrida's "trace," which is uncharacterizable because it is the without-context on which writing (signs to referents) is based—thus "it" reveals the chaos upon which supposed order is predicated.

> Residing at a deeper level than words can reach, the Derridean trace remains inaccessible to direct verbalization. It is "always already" present, the elusive and ineffable difference from which all subsequent inscription derives. . . . By making the trace inaccessible and indeed unknowable, Derrida opens writing to radical indeterminacy. . . . First a received duality (speech/writing) [signifier/signified] is destabilized by inversion; then the existence of a third term (the trace) is revealed whose nature is undecidable because by definition it falls outside the realm of discourse. . . . The vertigo characteristic of deconstruction appears when we realize that texts are always already open to infinite dissemination. Far from being ordered sets of words bounded by book covers, they are reservoirs of chaos. Derrida initiates us into this moment in *Of Grammatology* through his concept of iteration. (Hayles 1990, 179–80)

The iterative permutation of signs with overdetermined referents—the "trace"—reveals the fundamental "lack" that lies at the heart of all discourse and that destabilizes the apparently distinct polarity which occurs within its context. For May/V (and Beckett), the only term able to point out the magnitude and multivalency of this third element is "it all." "It" is, in effect, Beckett's Unnamable, the decentering third whose new without-context reveals the invalidity of our traditional, conceptual paradigm. Like the Derridean trace, May's "it" "epistemologically" divorces any supposedly concrete referent from the sign, "bracketing . . . the question of meaning" (deLauretis 1987, 110–11), therefore projecting us once again into the world of information theory as it relates to dynamic systems.

As we have discussed in previous chapters, information theory is closely aligned with Chaos theory in professing that the most information-packed message (as opposed to the one with the most meaning-value, though the two can coincide) is one in which a large dose of "noise" or chaos resides in its content. May's "it," like Derrida's trace, is able to uncover the radical relativity of any meaning by revealing the multiplicity of the potential referents and the fundamental "without" on which meaning and presence are constructed. Thus, in the groupings of three (which "Implies Chaos") and the trace-like nature of the third element, "it all," the information content of the play becomes "noisy" (at least conceptually), and the play becomes much richer than it would if meaning were conserved.

Using the idea of Chaotic patterning as a starting point, it is possible to construct a rudimentary "phase-space" diagram of the play in order to see its information content pattern in a graphically more revealing way.[24] Starting with *Footfalls*' carefully defined, almost musical precision, we can begin decomposing the play (a term taken from music theory) back toward its fundamental "chords."[25] First we abstract the play into component units such as pauses, May's steps, and "vocal units" (a "beat" of language, often bracketed by pauses). Though parts, like the vocal units, are of necessity somewhat vague, the play is so tightly constructed on so few elements that a reasonably accurate diagram of the play can be fashioned in this manner (see the appendix). Once this is done, we immediately see how "regular" portions of the play are, event following event with great predictability.

Into this regularity, however, unexpected or noisy events occur in such a manner that the information content of the play is always high, while at the same time, meaning accretes through repetition of the regular patterns. For example, in section 2 (the most "regular" section of the play) a predictably repeating pattern occurs from V's first words until just after V asks (for us) the question, "But this, when did this begin?" Here a break in the pattern occurs in the form of a longer, or divided "vocal unit": "When the other girls were out at . . . lacrosse she was already here." Then the familiar pattern returns for a couple of beats—"At this. *[Pause.]* The floor here, now bare, once was—"—at which point she is interrupted as May begins pacing again (Beckett 1984b, 241). Following are a few irregular "measures" (a bridge section, if you will) followed by a new regular pattern of faster-cadenced speech. Although, obviously, this system of reduction loses the finer detail and art of *Footfalls* (much as the decomposition of music loses the beauty of the melodic line), and thus the observations below can be only crude approximations of the reality of what happens on stage, the trade-off is ease of dealing with and visualizing the underlying pattern and structure of the play.

This type of patterning, which occurs throughout the play, can be mapped out and counted, showing a structure of long regular patterns followed by mixtures of irregular/regular sections akin (though not an exact functional match) to the Cantor dust set. If we take the "dust" of points that remain after several iterations of removing the middle third of a line-segment and count those as our "irregular" moments, we find that these moments come in separated by the following intervals (calling the shortest distance one "unit"): 1, then 3, then 1, 9, 1, 3, 1, 27 . . . .[26] This patterning, incidentally, is an extremely important aspect of natural systems: Mandelbrot, working to filter out errors from noise in phone transmissions, discovered that errors occur in a scale-invariant fashion—exactly as the Cantor dust set. From the smallest to the largest scale, noise and predictability will always appear in precisely the same geometric relationship—a patterning that fits the cyclic scale invariance of Beckett's works.[27] In the alternations of regular, predictable segments of pacing and rhythmic speech, with unexpected events in *Footfalls*, we "see" this dust-type patterning—for example, a 1, 3, 2, 7 pattern (a good approximation to the 1, 3, 1, 9 sequence in the Cantor dust) near the beginning of section 3 (see the appendix). And in the characters' iterative, quasi-redundant patterns on stage, we see them at the same time resisting and creating the harmony of noisy meaning that is the play.

We can further relate the play to naturally occurring Chaotic patterns if we examine more closely May's pacing on the strip of light. If we refer to biographical material for a moment (a move which, yielding the information it does, seems justified here), we find that Beckett's mother, May, used to pace the household at night after her children went to bed; and that she became ill with and died of Parkinson's disease which causes, among other things, "the tendency toward relentless pacing alternating with difficulty in initiating movement" (Culik 1993, 367). All in all, then, May's movement patterns seem to emulate Beckett's mother's propensities.[28] With this similarity in mind, we may regard (the fictional) May's pacing as partially determined by the rhythm of Parkinson's disease, which, as Dr. Oliver Sacks has noted, is demonstrably Chaotic in nature.[29] Notably, the irregular pacing of Parkinson's disease has been characterized in terms of fractal, self-similar geometry (see, for example, Gantert, Honerkamp, and Timmer 1992).[30] Thus May's movement may reflect the naturally Chaotic patterning of the disease. This remarkable fact reinforces the argument that what occurs in the miniature world of the stage *is* in a very real sense what occurs offstage. Whatever the exact case of this relationship, the play itself reveals, in the specific a-rhythmic sequence of May's pacing, the same

"Cantor" patterning of short-long-short between periods of stillness and movement, a patterning that remains self-similar in its structure even while May's movement lessens as *Footfalls* progresses (see the appendix).

If we now take one step further back and try to picture the underlying patterns of the play as a whole, we can construct our "phase-space" diagram of the play in order to see if what happens on stage is, at some level, patterned on something like the strange attractor so important to Chaos theory. Mapping the type of event on one axis, the "change in event over time" on another, and May's position in time (on the strip) on the third, we produce the three-dimensional phase-space diagram shown in figure 21.

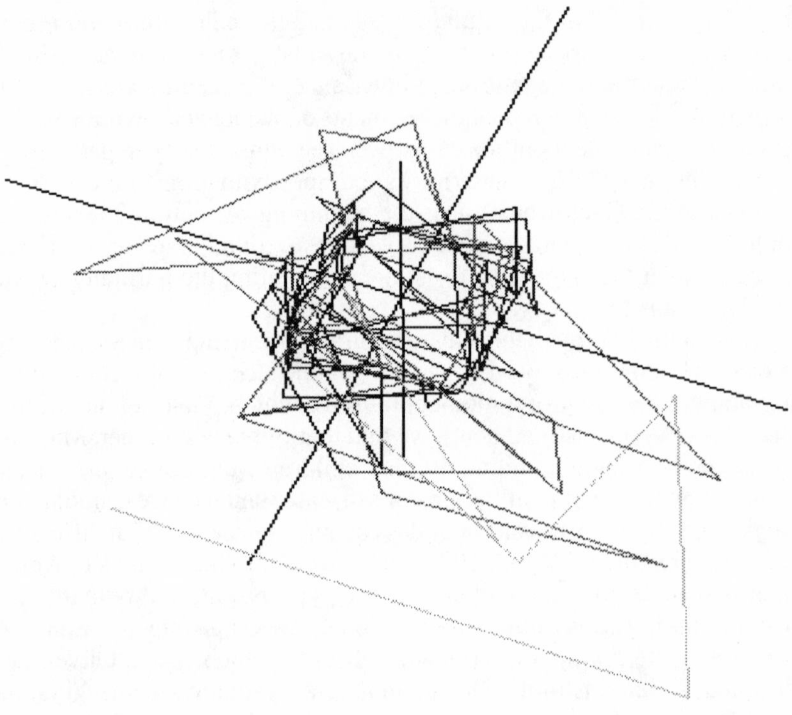

Fig. 21. A three-dimensional phase-space mapping of the entire play, *Footfalls*. See the appendix for a detailed discussion of how this figure is generated.

Although necessarily crude (as no rudimentary mapping of the play can capture the nuances of each moment), the "strange" pattern looks similar to one arm of the Lorenz attractor (see figure 6): never repeating, but circling around a closed space, the diagram reveals that the structure of the play, like May on the strip of light, never has done "revolving it all."

At a first pass, then, *Footfalls* appears structured about a strange attractor whose loops cycle orderly progression and Chaotic movement arbitrarily close to one another. This crude picture reveals more clearly than almost any words the vital interplay between Beckett's plays and the fundamentals of Chaos theory. Here we can see the whole of May's halting movements, the interplay of the pair's voices with silence, the fading lights and chimes in one spatial, pictorial image that is effectively a translation of the play from a medium that is a combination of temporal and spatial to one that is essentially spatial; and this image is Chaotic. Thus our observations that the play displays so much self-similarity from smallest to largest scale, as well as richly patterned information, is borne out in the underlying structure of the play as a whole, a structure that reveals at once the complexity and the unity of pattern underlying *Footfalls*. And thus if we attempted to pattern Beckett's plays in their entirety, we should expect to see a similar underlying structure for the entire oeuvre.

Where does this leave May and V? They are afloat, it seems, within the deterministic indeterminacy of this potential (and real) world, ever revolving "it all" and searching for a meaning which in fact can only be the "without-meaning" of the play itself—"it all." May (and presumably V) suffers in this "dreadfully un-" state because of her inability to let go of her quest for definition of and control over her identity. Flickering in the twilight between presence and absence, she must, in order to free herself from her own hell, let go of rigid dichotomies and completely abandon herself to the Chaotic without-context that surrounds her. May/V is, like Winnie and others before her, in the Zen state of the Great Doubt, but now we as audience participate in the world of her mind and physically see the revolutions of the psyche as it encounters its own imminent demise.

In this state, her greatest battle is for a presence that she feels she needs but has not attained, and one of her greatest weapons (as with other Beckettian characters before) is her/their narrative. Through May's slow, yet implacable movement and the iterative accretion of information (in V's monologue and May's "Sequel")—which becomes the sad story of a daughter who "was never there" (Beckett 1984b, 243)—May/V fight to create a (mythological) history of May's existence. Beginning with V's confession, "I had you late. *[Pause.]* In life," the two cooperate with and combat each other in (re)constructing the narrative of May's youth, and the beginnings of her pacing. This history, however, is not a simple one; there are obvious discrepancies between V and May's monologues, as well as within May's monologue itself. As we have already noted, V places May in her house, while May places herself within a "little church"; and, after recounting the origins of her pacing, May jumps in startling fashion to the story of Amy and "Old Mrs. Winter, whom the reader will remember" (242), throwing into question even the proper medium for what occurs. Around this story (or stories), built in pieces like Zeno's grains of sand trying "to mount up to" a heap, May attempts to build her sense of presence. When V tells her version of the story—in "objective" third-person narrative form—we are given what seems to be a straightforward tale of the growth of the unusual habit in her daughter, who must hear her feet, "however faint they fall" (remember that, in our analysis, this is the most regular, or predictable of the sections—and that the opening lines of even this ostensibly simple section generate confusion or blurring of character). We are thus inclined to believe what we hear to be the "facts" of May's life: V knows and controls the flow of information—and, therefore, her daughter's life.

When May begins her "Sequel," however, V's apparently objective frame-history is immediately thrown into question. Although May claims to follow her mother's narrative, she tells us (notably, like Mouth in *Not I*, in the third person) that her walking began, not at home, but in the other "appropriate" sphere for women: the church. "[S]he began to walk. [*Pause.*] At nightfall. [*Pause.*] Slip out at nightfall and into the little church by the north door, always locked at that hour, and walk, up and down, up and down, his poor arm" (242). Thus, as May begins her version of what took place, the straightforward account of V is immediately thrown into question.

If, on the other hand, we are tempted to imbue May's version of the story with greater veracity, discrepancies immediately crop up, indicating not only that May's version is no more true, but that she is, in some sense, writing her own history: "A little later, when she was quite forgotten, she began to— *[Pause.]* A little later, when as though she had never been, it never been, she began to walk" (242). In Chaotic, iterative fashion, a Hamm-like *racontrice* creating her story, May circles back on her narrative, adjusting it as she goes. Additionally, by absorbing her mother's speech patterns and tone during the tale of Mrs. Winter, May and V are commingled, their variant versions of May's predicament becoming, like the pair of characters themselves, unified in the without-context of radical relativity. Thus, as expected, no frame of reference is privileged with any more conceptual truth-value than any other, the whole of the play determined by this indeterminate patterning.

What, then, happens in *Footfalls*? We could certainly be tempted to answer, with Estragon, "Nothing happens"; but the narratives that eventually revolve around to the "future," the fading chimes and light, and May's slowing revolutions indicate some forward thrust to the play. If we consider once more Beckett's professed impetus to create this play—the young girl "never properly born" (in Maddy Rooney's words) of Jung's lecture—we perhaps have an answer: May, having never achieved existence through "proper" birth, is attempting to create, or "birth" herself. One aspect of the play that resonates almost mythologically with birth and creation is the number of steps May paces out each time: nine.[31] As she and her mother relate May's problematic life, she continually steps out the months of pregnancy, attempting through ritual, or "sacred" time and space to give birth to herself.

Beyond the "creative" act of listening to May's resonating footsteps, she and V attempt to gestate a being or self via their/her narrative of her life. As Gontarski points out, "In her story, the incompletely born May is creating a fictive self. Fiction is May's attempt to give birth to herself, or a self . . ." (1985, 165). Creating and listening to her words, *and* the sound of her footsteps, "however faint they fall," May/V attempts to create herself through (self-)perception, an act in which the audience, as "best" perceivers, is invited to participate.

> The text emphasizes the activities of seeing and hearing: V seems to exist mainly to hear May in the first section and to see her in the second. The audience are thus made aware of their own perceptual experience of the play. The momentum of the play would therefore seem to be the production of the self: the rhythm of birth, at which the audience assists . . . like a mid-wife. (Anna McMullan 1993, 102)

May/V attempts to birth their/herself in an act of perception and presence.[32]

This attempt to gain being, however, seems to falter and fail: "[I]nstead of rising towards completion or creation, the rhythm [of birth through perception] increasingly loses momentum and simply fades out. By the third section, all perception has become fainter and more problematical" (102). Thus it would appear that May/V's attempt is not working very successfully; not only is May/V unable to arrive at any unified, concrete fictive/factual history, she "narrates" her future self as "rack" passing before the moon. May's birth into perception and presence is at risk, as she is unable to string herself together into a causal being. Her pacing counts out the moments of a life that cannot be created fully. When she tries to add up "all the microscopic pieces" of her existence, she finds that she "cannot extend them to the long term" of a "real" life (Gleick 1987, 175), and therefore she can never achieve any actual presence. May's feet echo like grains of sand falling atop one another, trying to add up to Zeno's paradoxical heap.

Through the deterministically acausal eyes of Zen and Chaos theory, however, May's plight is not, in reality, a problem: she simply must let go of her desire for relative causality via conceptual perception and narrative "connections," and see herself and her world instead in a prereflective state.

If she passes through her Great Doubt to the Great Death (of the ego-consciousness), May/V will be released from her need to be perceived (either by us or by herself) as something *other*—Amy, Mrs. Winter, "she"; she will no longer need words, narrative connections, or even the faint sounds of her steps on the boards of the stage. In each moment of being-time—each grain of sand which falls on Zeno's heap—May/V can exist as she is, needing no future or past to frame her present presence. She can stop needing and "revolving it all": because she is "it all": she *is* the without-context of the potential space that surrounds her. May's "dreadfully un-" is no longer a "broken" expression of an object-desire thwarted around which she must wheel constantly; it is now identified with her. Like the successful Zen student, May, V, and the negative prefix—her "un-," Joshu's *Mu*, their contextless context—become one. These supposedly disparate elements are no longer at odds; instead, they identify with and through each other. Therefore, May/V does not have to be frozen any longer in her eternally revolving world; she can be freed to silence and stillness. If she can shift the paradigm of her vision, May/V can escape the slowly pacing prison of her infinity.

When, therefore, the final iteration of the play reveals the empty strip of light on the potential space of the stage, it is possible that May has finally achieved stillness, escaping through the nexus of her (r)evolving world. The twilight world between causal presence and without-causal absence through which May and V—like arrow and target—cross fades into the stillness of self-fulfilled moments of resonating categorical absence as simply as "snow slips" from a "bamboo leaf" (Herrigel 1953, 48). If *Footfalls* reveals May/V, objectifying her via her (our) own dissociated and listening self, the pressures of this dissociation also re-create her "dreadfully un-" existence: she becomes fully one with the negative prefix as she is successfully born into non-presence. In the end, all that remains is the echoes of her scattering pieces which fall, like the grains of Zeno's heap, echoing fainter and fainter across the infinity she inhabited.

7

What Is the Sound of *Ohio Impromptu*? No Arrow, No Target

Seeing into Nothingness—this is the true seeing, the eternal seeing.

—Shen-hui

"Bow, arrow, goal and ego, all melt into one another, so that I can no longer separate them. And even the need to separate has gone. . . ." "Now at last," the Master broke in, "the bowstring has cut right through you."

—Eugen Herrigel

When, after the approximately ten minutes of static, nearly motionless monologue that comprises *Ohio Impromptu*, we hear R pronounce "nothing is left to tell," it is quite apparent that Beckett's work has taken yet another step toward the zero point of lessness. In *Footfalls*, we saw a "winding down" of motion and interaction as May and V began with dialogue and fairly consistent movement, only to (d)evolve into monologue, then silence and stillness (in the final level of iteration that ends the piece). Right from the start of *Ohio Impromptu*, nearly all motion and interaction between characters has been removed. Two characters, owning only the titles L and R, simply sit, R reading a story from a "worn volume" of two other, implicitly related characters who eventually sit and read from a "worn volume" themselves. The only motion and interaction we see for the bulk of the play are L's knocks on the table at which they sit, which cause R to repeat the last sentence from the book he reads.[1]

We seem far here from the relatively easier comprehensibility of Beckett's earlier, more representational plays like *Waiting for Godot;* yet, *Ohio Impromptu*'s internal narrative and physical representation are each remarkably straightforward (akin to the immediate context of *Catastrophe*). We hear a story of a man who tries, but fails, to escape the memory of his lost love by moving to what seems fairly obviously to be the right bank of the Seine River in Paris (see Astier 1982, 336–38). After a time, the man is successfully comforted by one sent from his Beloved, who comes to him at night and reads him a narrative from a "worn volume." We see two men sitting at a white "deal table" with a "Latin Quarter" hat resting at its center, R reading from a book, L apparently listening. Why, then, the frustrating strangeness of the play? Quite simply, because of slippage: slippage between what we see on stage and what we hear in R's narrative; slippage between the categories of "play" and "fiction." One finds, in these later plays especially (as has already been noted in the case of *Footfalls*), that there is no straightforward way to assign all our sensory information into any single set of complementary referents. *Ohio Impromptu* is multivocal (or, in Bakhtin's words, polyvalent), its elements in continuous flux, combining harmoniously and dissonantly as they rub against one another.

Metaphorically, *Ohio Impromptu* reaches the final stages of Zen training in archery. No longer do the concepts bow, arrow, and target exist. There is simply a moment of plenary absence in whose "always already" dynamic flux "it all" exists as one. No longer do arrow and target exist separately, to be forced together via the manipulation of a drawn bow; now arrow and target (and bow) are actively one, no subjective vision separating their polyvalent interaction. Essentially, then, there is no arrow or target—or better yet, to make use again of Kasulis's terminology, "without-arrow" and "without-target"—as no polarizing consciousness claims objective self-existence for them. Without a conceptual consciousness *waiting* for "something" to happen, the present moment is freed to flow unhindered, carrying all down the river of nirvana.

How does *Ohio Impromptu* reach this "enlightened" state? The nature and structure of the play are crucial to the "awakening" process that takes place: *Ohio Impromptu* is certainly a play on the edges of drama, size, and comprehension. As Beckett plays with dramatic conventions in this piece, we are able to see, crystallized, the focus and work of his entire oeuvre, permuted yet one more time. We see the familiar Beckettian "less is more" at work. Though apparently nearly static, the minimalized actions that occur on stage (by virtue of their "lessness," as in *Footfalls*), carry a weight that is much greater than their physical dimensions. Because of this, the final image of the pair looking up at each other is profoundly important and moving.

We also see iteration and destabilization: in *Ohio Impromptu*,

> the visual image constitutes a[n apparently] stable point of reference throughout the performance, but its essentially static nature is undermined, firstly by the gestures, which introduce a dynamic element into the stage image, and which may radically affect, even challenge our interpretation of it, and also by the continual modification or [iterative] re-view of the scenic image in light of the text. (Audrey McMullan 1987, 24)

Thus, image is effectively destabilized by action, and both are destabilized by the repeated words and images generated by the narrative read. Like the protagonist of the narrative who walks out to the Isle of Swans over and over seeking "some measure of relief" (Beckett 1984d, 285), the text replays words and events, constantly affecting and altering the "reality" we see before us.

Furthermore, we see the richness of information produced by the interplay of regular and irregular patterns: as with *Footfalls*, the text of *Ohio Impromptu* sets up a dynamic of expectation and surprise. The bulk of the emotionally charged story told by R is related in simple, third-person, neutral speech; but words like "conflowed" appear from time to time, increasing the information we receive. The reading "occurs as a circular function on the micro level" of the play (Klaver 1991, 368); through this circularity, the pair creates "a rhythm through their repetition, so that any variation becomes significant" (Audrey McMullan 1987, 27). L's knocks are, at the same time, surprising in their timing and "expected," because, as the audience quickly learns, R will repeat the last sentence he read at L's request. Once, having reading the odd, "quintessentially" Beckettian sentence, "After so long a lapse that as if never been," R pauses, and then exclaims, "Yes." As has been noted, this word is almost the only qualitative match to the title word, "Impromptu," as it seems the only spontaneous event in R's speech. It is the "sudden appearance of the unanticipated" (Abbott 1991, 15) that thrusts the "strange attractor" of the play off to a distant point.[2]

We thus see another permutation, or "avatar," of many of the features with which we have been dealing, aspects of the play which once again reveal and are revealed by the "mindlessness" (Beckett 1984d, 288) of Zen Buddhism and the interplay of Chaos and order. In light of these systems, *Ohio Impromptu* potentiates—and this time realizes (as closely as is possible on a stage)—a paradigm shift. The play is, on many levels, a Zen koan read, meditated on, and finally identified with and through. This device, used especially by the Rinzai school to force the Great Doubt and Great Death, which have been so important to our study, can, if meditated on with all of one's being, produce an intense "state of thought without thinking, of consciousness beyond thought" (Deshimaru 1985, 10)—in other words, "Profounds of mind. Of mindlessness" (Beckett 1984d, 288)—which leads to the state of satori, or nirvana. Like a koan, the brief, paradoxical, sometimes humorous narrative and staged framework of meditative ritual reading which constitutes *Ohio Impromptu* presents us with many seemingly contradictory concepts and juxtapositions that cannot be resolved systematically, necessitating the shift in vision to the "without-causal" state arising from the Great Death.[3]

If Beckett's earlier plays are the slow accretive practice of Dogen's

"Cultivation-authentication,"[4] *Ohio Impromptu* is at the culminating point, a period wherein the months or years of practice and gradual buildup of enlightenment are intensified and foreshortened as the former ego-centered paradigm is cast off in favor of the "without-context" of satori. This quiet, still, yet intensely suffering period is what we see before us on stage. As with Zen practice (and the iterative process of Chaos theory as well), this critical moment is brought on by intensity of repetition, on both large and small scales. For Zen, repetition is the key to perfecting any act, be it zazen (sitting in the lotus position and concentrating on *mujo*—no mind, or no-thing), martial arts, or simply breathing. Perfection comes through repetition (Deshimaru 1982, 49), and only then can enlightenment come. Attempting to achieve *mujo* (or "without mind") purposefully[5] requires endless repetitive practice, as any form of striving for, or desiring the enlightened state will invariably call the ego (or active conscious mind) into play, which will create a state of waiting for "something" to happen, thus destroying the subject's chance of finding a "consciousness beyond consciousness."

Finally, after "revolving it all" in an endless series of ritual iterations, the student ceases to wait for something to happen while sitting in zazen.

> No longer sitting to be enlightened, one merely sits to sit. Feeling almost dead in any case, no longer protecting any part of the self, the disciple sits with abandonment, totally unconcerned with the consequences. At this point, the Great Doubt may arise: a still-point of terrible tension in which one gives oneself up to the feeling of nowhere to go. (Kasulis 1981, 113–14)

At this point, a "fixed point" in whose lessness lies universality, scales of time and space cease to exist in a logically connected, continuous sense. Once this state comes to pass, the Great Death (of the ego-consciousness) can occur, allowing enlightenment to fill the void. It is only through repetition of "right action," and especially of zazen, that one can purposely attain the state of satori, or nirvana. There is no great mystery, then, why Zen monks spend their entire lives repeating zazen meditation and question-answer periods many hours a day: to achieve the new vision of the world that enlightenment affords, any cost is deemed acceptable.

As far as *Ohio Impromptu* is concerned, the Zen practice of ritual repetition can help explain the ostensibly repeated reading of the "sad tale," as well as R's repetition of certain pieces of the narrative on L's command: the two (or four, if we include the narrative pair) are involved in the process of zazen; they sit in meditative poses and ask questions of each other (via the knocks). This iterative patterning of reading, knocks, and repeated text will "grind text, wear down the book in the center of the deal table . . . , softening meaning—until . . . [the] mind reawakens to true mindlessness"

(Doll 1988, 52)—a re-visioning of the patterning of reality that takes "the mind out of a rationalistic habit of thought into true mindlessness" (Doll 1987, 73).[6] The characters are working toward enlightenment—escape from the suffering of the singular "I"—and use the repeated zazen ritual of reading and mulling over "their" koan to achieve this state (or *as* this state).

At this point, we might be inclined to try to figure out "who is who" in *Ohio Impromptu.* As with the other plays we have studied, a pair is present—and in this case one exists in the narrative as well. Is one a Zen master, the other(s) student(s)? Again, as with the other plays, this is not a simple issue, as this pair of pairs is in constant flux, the relationship(s) changing as identity shifts and recombines from moment to moment. To simplify matters, then, we will momentarily dissect the play into pieces, each populated by a pair of characters or a doubled event. Although this effectively destroys the organic unity of the play, we are still trapped within the normative logical framework, and thus a distillation of arbitrary parts is momentarily necessary.[7]

If we first consider the play's internal narrative (the "sad tale") as a koan in itself, it follows that either of the stage characters reading this koan—L or R—can be master or student. The next logical question is, of course, Which is which? Apparently, L is the student, as he listens to R's reading; yet, other possibilities are also viable. Perhaps R is the student, as L forces him to read and reread a text which he, as Doll puts it, "seems at a loss to comprehend" (Doll 1988, 50). Perhaps both are students, reading the printed words of some unidentified master—possibly (and recursively) themselves—in an attempt to understand it. Within the narrative, the apparently distinct reader and listener/protagonist are also mingled in a dynamic pairing as they grow "to be as one" during their repeated ritual of reading (another koan?). They, we are told, find a state of "mindlessness" together. Reflecting this internal event, L and R apparently also come to an understanding of the narrative's koan by the end of the piece, as they "replay" what has happened within the story when they themselves turn "to stone." Although the characters L and R, reader and listener, are in flux, there is good evidence that their relational pairing approaches the new vision of "without context" that is nirvana. As opposed to the other works we have examined, the final tableau we witness is a "visual realization of intimacy and communion longed for, but never achieved in *Berceuse [Rockaby]* or other plays," a "closure" that can "only be achieved in the formless state of being/non-being beyond temporal existence" (Audrey McMullan, 1987, 31).

The dynamic interplay of the pairs L and R, narrator and listener, narrative and stage, as well as the destabilizing of our conventional paradigm to make way for a new, discontinuous visioning of the world, can be explicated to a remarkable extent by the play's powerful image of the (Seine) river dividing about the Isle of Swans.

> From its single window he could see the downstream extremity of the Isle of Swans. . . . Day after day he could be seen slowly pacing the islet. Hour after hour. In his long black coat no matter what the weather and old world Latin Quarter hat. At the tip he would always pause to dwell on the receding stream. How in joyous eddies its two arms conflowed and flowed united on.
>
> (Beckett 1984d, 285–86)

Apart from the nice complication of the issue of perception (who sees whom?), here we have, metaphorically, our by now anticipated third element which destabilizes the two arms of the river, forcing them into an apparent pair. Yet here also is the image of reunification as the river reclaims its wholeness via the re-visioning of itself on the "downstream" tip of the isle. This same type of image is utilized by Loy to describe Buddhism's rejection of conceptual absolutism:

> Buddhism denies that there is any rock [or island dividing the current], asserting that there is only a flux. The rock is a thought-construction[, a destabilizing force,] and the sense-of-self might better be compared to a bubble which flows like the water because it is part of the water [of change]. . . . (Loy 1988, 218)

Once we lock onto the implications and importance of this analogy/identity, the dynamic flux of characters and actions takes on a richer, more positive aspect. L and R, and the pair in the internal narrative by association, are "as alike as possible," not only in appearance, but also in the way they sit and their sharing of the single "Latin quarter hat" between them. Whether these pairs are taken to represent the halves of the divided river, left and right, two aspects of a brain (as in *Endgame*), listener and reader (or speaker, as in *Not I*), "real" and "projected," psychotherapist and patient, mother and child (*Molloy*, *Footfalls*, and others), just two pairs of unrelated characters,[8] or all of the above and more, L and R (and the narrative pair) are twinned—at the same time definitely two "ones," and a single "whole." The destabilizing "trace" of the Isle of Swans—and the destabilizing force of memories of the protagonist's ubiquitously absent, potentiated Beloved—necessitates a re-visioning of the pair in terms of their relational "without-context": they are beyond the categorical distinctions of two or one, "identity and difference" (Audrey McMullan 1987, 28), even L or R, as they "conflow" around distinctions and "flow united on." While the play appears to be comprised of simple, static halves or doubles with no gray areas, these distinctions are effectively destabilized like the river around the Isle, signs and referents turbulently dividing and mingling like the interpenetrating halves of the white-on-black, black-on-white field of the Yin-Yang symbol.[9]

L and R are thus one and not-one; they are beyond the pigeonholed distinction of one or the other. Similarly, the relationship between L and R and the characters in the internal narrative cannot be categorized: L is and is not the listener in the story; R is and is not the reader; L is and is not the reader; R is and is not the listener. Yet what, presented in this light, seems to make *Ohio Impromptu* frustratingly complex, appears much simpler if one can achieve the "enlightened" state spoken of by Zen philosophers: there is no need for any one of the possible distinctions and connections between L and R and listener and reader to be any truer than the others. They are all true, while at the same time none of them is true. By making this assertion, we are taking the Buddhist "middle way," which "means not setting up any opposition between subject [me] and object [you]" (Deshimaru 1985, 4)—not making a distinction because that would belittle, or even destroy, the vastness and simplicity of the koan that is *Ohio Impromptu*.

One of the reasons L and R originally perceive themselves (or are perceived) as different is that they have not yet found their "original faces," their (original) enlightened selves. From the internal narrative (and assuming a contingent relationship between what's going on onstage and in the narrative), we are told that since the listener's separation from his Beloved (the owner of "the dear name"), he has been subject to "his old terror of the night" (Beckett 1984d, 286)—he, like Vladimir, Estragon, and many other Beckettian characters, is a conscious, wanting, and waiting "I" suffering from desire: desire to perceive and be perceived; desire for "another living soul" (Beckett 1984g, 278) with whom to interact and from whom hopefully to find relief. This other (more exactly, the messenger of this other) is perceived as someone separate, a distinct (and therefore unknowable) being. According to Zen philosophy, however, it is only because the listener maintains a causal, historically influenced frame of reference that he perceives the reader as separate, or even feels the anguish of separation and waiting/longing for his Beloved. The listener is both correct and incorrect when he claims that "Nothing he had ever done alone could ever be undone. By him alone" (Beckett 1984d, 286). So long as he maintains a distinction between self and other, he is correct: nothing can be undone by him alone. If, however, he changes his vision to that of the marginalized frame of reference—the without-context of Zen, the fixed-point scale invariance of Chaos theory—he will perceive all around him without the need for self-reifying categories like "alone," and he will therefore be released from everything he ever did "alone" (in the old frame of reference).

From the new frame of reference, what plagues the listener (and thus L—and/or R) is not the loss of his Beloved one but the loss of his true nature—his prereflective consciousness beyond consciousness—or equally, his inability to return to the state of without-subjectivity. This changes during the play, however. Although the listener (and L, R, and us, along with him) initially regards the messenger as a completely separate entity, as the play progresses we are told that "with never a word exchanged they grew to be as one" (287). Through the repeated ritual of reading the story/koan, the two lose their distinctness, slowly merging into a single "one." What occurs at the end of the narrative, then, is a final "mindless" union of the two into a whole—not a whole where there are no longer protagonist and reader (for that would be to make an absolute distinction) but a dynamic one in which the two are "without-separation." In other words, the two are still individual, but their categorical individuality has been destabilized by the koan that is the play. Via this radically decentering force, they subsume their egos, their "I-ness," or their subjectivity. They are able to pass beyond individual consciousness to a state that precedes reflective consciousness and in which the conceptual distinction between self and other cannot be made. They are, therefore, two-in-one and one-in-two.

If we next expand the study beyond the confines of the internal narrative, the relationship of L and R to the listener and the reader can be described in similar manner. At first, what happens on stage and what is taking place in the narrative appear to have nothing in common, but as the play progresses, these two "individual entities" as well conflow, growing to be "as one." The narrative passes through the present moment on stage to its future, and stage and story achieve a dynamic, intersecting relational cohesion (though they are never simply identical). Similarly, the L and R pair also becomes one-in-two as they merge with the characters of the internal narrative and with each other. What is left is both utterly complex and "absurdly simple."[10] All the possible pairings of characters, relationships, and actions become a moving montage that, if we drew connecting lines between possibly linked characters, would have the complexity of a spiderweb. Yet, if we step back from the perplexing picture, we can look at the "spiderweb" of the play as a simple and beautiful whole. To carry the spiderweb analogy one step further, the whole is composed of indispensable and individual parts, yet each part is nothing without the whole to give it shape and function. Through their repeated ritual readings, the characters have learned a new way of "being" themselves and their world: "when the senses reawaken, words fill and flow, becoming so much more than the things signified" (Doll 1988, 50). Once this "reawakening" takes place, the world becomes "green again with wonder" (Smith 1986, vii). Without the need to connect causally any two points of time or space, each moment falls like the grains of Zeno's heap, but now each grain is self-sufficient, creating a heap of "being-time" (Loy 1988, 222) all its own.

The "divided arms" of distinction are radically destabilized in the staging of the play as well. For example, the stage directions require darkness on the bulk of the stage surrounding the white of the deal table—a clear case of light and/separated-from dark—yet the Latin Quarter hat lying at the center of the table puts a black blot at the center of the light table. Similarly, the table reflects white light inside the circle of darkness of the stage. Light flows around the dark hat, darkness flows around the pool of light "midstage," like isles within rivers within isles. Dark interpenetrates light, which interpenetrates dark in scale-invariant fashion. As with his use of white and black in *Ill Seen Ill Said*, in *Ohio Impromptu* Beckett seems to use apparently simple divisions only to point out the impossibility of determining where one "half" stops and the other starts. In *Ill Seen Ill Said*, Beckett writes, "Nothing left but black sky. White earth. Or inversely" (1981, 31). First, we are given an ostensibly simple division between black and white; then Beckett pulls the rug out from under us by unequivocally stating that the division could just as easily be the other way around.

Additionally, the apparently static physicality of the staging is destabilized. From first to last, there are only table, hat, book, chairs, and two men, "as alike as possible." Nothing moves much, the staging not at all. As opposed to Beckett's other late plays, the table is even positioned "midstage," allowing an apparent centrality missing in other of his later works. But this apparently stable image is, in fact, no such thing: the table may be midstage, the "Black, wide-brimmed hat at center of table" (Beckett 1984d, 285), but L and R are both "audience right." The image, then, is "weighted" to the right, and an implicit rotational motion is potentiated (figure 22).

Viewed from above, the hat resting at the table's center acts as a pivot point around which the table seems destined to rotate because of the mass (both physical and dramatic) situated at the right end of the table. Thus, within the stasis of the staging is a physical and emotional decentering, an implicit motion that destabilizes any centrality in the staging of the play. The radical relativity of Zen tells us that the table, like the "still" Isle in the river, must of necessity be destabilized, as it is only "a thought-construction": there can be "no rock at rest relative to the water" (Loy 1988, 218), since there is no causal connection to provide stability from one moment of being-time to another. Stasis and stability (and movement, for that matter) are results merely of our vision of what occurs, not what necessarily is.

Apparently, then, even in the static, stable staging of *Ohio Impromptu*, none of the distinctions which on first viewing seem so clean and easy are, on closer look, valid. Light and dark intermingle, forming a simple whole that contains both; motion and stillness interpenetrate. Order, distinction,

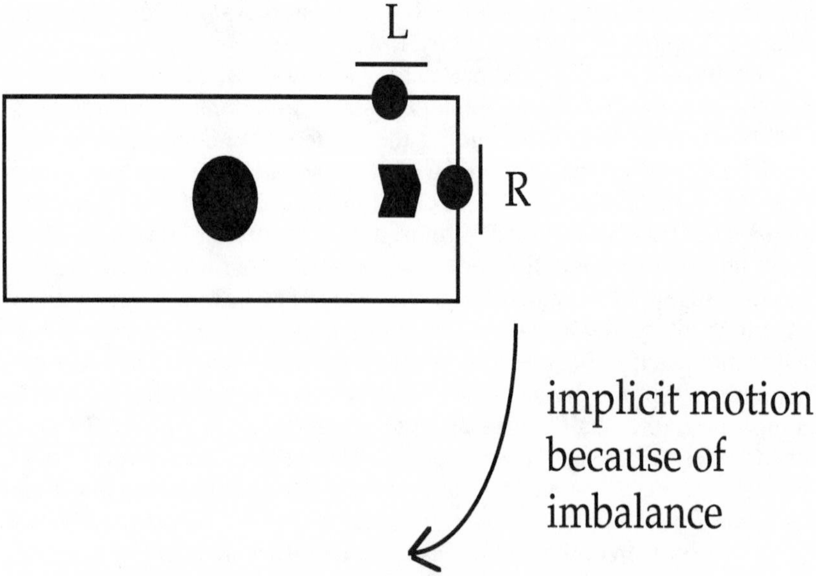

Fig. 22. Instability in the staging of *Ohio Impromptu*

and stability give way to the richer pattern of Chaos. From our causal point of view these interfering images present a complex, daunting problem.[11] If, on the other hand, we are willing to shift our vision to the radical relativity of Zen and the holistic graphical presentation of Chaos theory, we can apprehend in a prereflective manner that which is before us: a moment of experience that simply *is*. "The one is a predicament, the other not" (Beckett 1949, 102).

If we now refer to the previous work on *Footfalls*, we can once again find the interplay of two versus three—of an apparently stable two forced apart and destabilized by a marginal, radicalizing third—in the superstructure of *Ohio Impromptu* as well. If we look at the form of the narrative/play which is *Ohio Impromptu*, we see that, while the play is unitary, there are definite "beats" in its internal workings. Audrey McMullan identifies two halves in the play, defined by the repetition of "'Il reste peu à dire [Little is left to tell]'" (Audrey McMullan 1987, 26). Interestingly, this division is marked not only by R's repeated words but also by his only physical action (until the final moment): turning a page in the "worn volume." Here, at nearly the absolute center of the play, R turns the page, effectively slicing the work into two pieces: "No sleep no braving sleep till—*[Turns page.]*—dawn of day" (Beckett 1984d, 286). The play, like the river and the characters, breaks into halves about the turned page, each of the halves apparently self-sufficient and distinct (one-half of the protagonist alone, the other, of the two men together).

If we look at the play in a slightly different light, we see an alternate way of dividing it: like *Footfalls*, there are three like sections which constitute the bulk of the play, and a different kind of section at the end. First, there is the description of the protagonist's physical actions: his move from bank to bank and his walks that physically mediate between the two banks (as the isle is in the middle of the river). Second is the description of his emotional response, his dreams and "his old terror of night" (286). Third is the description of the two men together reading from the "worn volume." The final section, in which "Nothing is left to tell" (288), is akin to the empty stage revealed by the final fade-up in *Footfalls*. Being necessarily reductive, we might characterize the first three sections as action (moving from one bank to the other, then walking the middle), anguish (the resultant emotional fears), and relief or resolution (via a new ritual of reading which replaces the old one of walking). Thus we see twos and threes are at play here as well, as *Ohio Impromptu* neatly falls into three "beats," the median section of the "old terrors" emotionally dividing the first and last, allowing them to reflect and refract each other.

If, taking a cue from *Footfalls* once again, we examine the third of these sections, we find that in this play as well there are iterative levels within levels. Part A of the third section involves the arrival of the Beloved's messenger "to comfort" the protagonist. Part B tells how they, "With never a word exchanged . . . grew to be as one" (287). Part C relates what happens when the tale is "a last time told" (287): the "Profounds of mind. Of mindlessness" (288) that ensues. Once again, there is roughly an action (the reader arrives), a response (they grow to be "as one"), and relief/resolution ("they sat on as though turned to stone"). Thus, the structure of the play is iterated on a reduced scale within the third section.

The final iteration occurs when "Nothing is left to tell." First, R announces that the narrative has finished; second, the two sit in silence for "Five seconds"; and third, they lower their hands and raise their heads simultaneously. Again, there is action, (emotional) pause, and resolution, this time played out in a matter of seconds. Yet this is a new "level" of iteration, not merely the same thing repeated; "There is more than a difference of degree" (Beckett 1949, 102) between what comes before and this. One subtle but extremely important factor is in the rhythm, or pattern of knocks that L performs. In the previous "beats," after L knocked once to have R repeat the last sentence read, R would pause for another knock before proceeding. Here, however, the sequence is altered:

> Nothing is left to tell.
> *[Pause. R makes to close book.*
> *Knock. Book half closed.]*
> Nothing is left to tell.

[Pause. R closes book.
Knock.
Silence . . .].

(Beckett 1984d, 288)

R finishes his action, closing the book, *before* L knocks this time, an event which signals at once the now intimate relational context of the pair—as R seems to understand L well enough now to "pre-perform" closing the book—and the new, comforting, without-context into which they have both (all) entered. The infinitesimal fixed point of this subtle, dramatic moment literally erupts with a wealth of information that has universal consequences, not only for the play, but for Beckett's oeuvre as a whole. In the potential space of this brief action, and the look that follows it, is the crystallization of a lifetime of looking for contact with "another living soul / one other living soul" (Beckett 1984g, 278).

The culminating universality of lessness, the triples that occur in iterative fashion, and the fixed-point symmetry displayed in this final stage moment might cause us to ponder in what further ways the "lens" of Chaos theory can be focused on the play, a question that leads us to examine the multitude of convergent levels operating within *Ohio Impromptu*. As we have seen, many levels of character and staging operate around and through each other in the play, constituting a rationally "insoluble structure, a Möbius strip that forecloses on rational logic and defeats reconciliation" (Klaver 1991, 367). We have already seen how listener and reader intersect with each other and with L and R on stage, pairs mirroring pairs; how light interpenetrates dark, and vice versa; how stillness and movement merge in the potential space of the play; how the image of the divided river informs (and is informed by) everything from narrative characters to the appearance of the hat on the deal table; how the internal narrative, the iterative reading, even the play itself operate as a koan.

There are many more layers at work within the play, further eroding any stable, centered meaning. As I have already hinted, the duality of past and future are destabilized, as what occurs in the narrative being read—which is ostensibly the narrative of the two before us—crosses over from relating past events to relating the "impossible": what will take place next in stage reality. Our common notions about how past and future are divided and interrelate is fragmented by the immediacy of the stage present. Intimately related to this is the relationship between genres: in *Ohio Impromptu*, drama is fiction and fiction drama, the two combining in a form that defies pigeonholing, yet is compelling in its uniqueness.

Furthermore, in addition to the iterative nature of L and R's (re)reading, there are other ways in which the apparent linearity of the play is destabilized, most notably, the "tidal" ebb and flow of language, movement, lighting—and, of course, reading as well. To take one example (there are many others), let us examine the use of language to instantiate the waterlike nature of the play. Aside from the obvious use of the river metaphor, other linguistic pointers to water imagery abound in the play. In the sentences following R's description of the "downstream extremity of the Isle of Swans" (which alerts us to this water imagery), he describes the protagonist's move as follows:

> Relief he had hoped would *flow* from unfamiliarity. . . . *Out* to where nothing ever shared. *Back* to where nothing ever shared. From this he had once half hoped some measure of relief might *flow*.
>
> (Beckett 1984d, 285; my emphasis)

Here a flowing motion is set up in both imagery (flowing relief), motion (of the character), language (flowing), and even rhythm (the "Out . . . Back" movement of the language). In the description of the protagonist's walks on the Isle of Swans, we are treated to a doubling up of the tidal nature of the play: the protagonist's walks are an out and back motion—"Then turn and his slow steps retrace"—and L's knock on the table creates a repetition of this last sentence, effectively turning the motion around again. Thus we begin to sense that the play is more circular than linear; yet even here, circularity, ebb and flow, is destabilized: "Could he not now turn back? . . . No" (286). Like a river flowing, or a wave in the ocean, a constant ebb and flow occurs, but all the while, each wave is different and "the river is never the same." Each moment is like, but never the same as, the moment before; a strange attractor at their cores, the loop of repetition is never closed in nature or in *Ohio Impromptu*.

As a spoken, visceral element of drama, language itself is destabilized, approaching a level of "effacement" and reduction which might carry it out to the still, silent point of "Nothing is left to tell." "One of the important ways in which this is attempted is by a return to the repetitive and autocitational devices of the fiction" (Connor 1988, 126). In other words, in deconstructive fashion, the immediacy of the spoken word is eroded by the iterative self-referentiality of the words being spoken. The pair on stage "quote themselves" (126), their present linguistic moment intermeshing with past (and future) language and reality.

If we move from the temporal and spatial axes to another "axis of motion"—perhaps Hwang's imaginative level (as referred to in the previous chapter)—we can also see that narrative, stage characters, stage set, and lighting function as recursive levels which interfere and inform one another in a flux of imaginative re-visions. If, for example, we look at the interplay between text and stage context, we find the two are open to an infinite Derridean rereading of themselves in a cyclic, creative manner.

> The stage image can be seen as a metaphor for self-creation: the creator creates himself through the narrative, or is created by it (the self being as much a fiction as the fictional self) in a process of scissiparity (schizogenesis) presented on stage: a dramatic concretisation of the play between creator and created. . . . (Audrey McMullan, 1987, 29)

On this imaginative "vertical axis"—at right angles to the dimensions of space and time—creation is the iterative interpenetration of levels of text and con-text with one another.

If we are not yet exhausted by the multitude of layers functioning simultaneously in *Ohio Impromptu*, and will allow a momentary look outside the immediate context of the play itself, we unearth yet more layers of information that intersect the play tangentially. First, as H. Porter Abbott has pointed out, the play is partially a humorous send-up of the conference that commissioned the work.

> It is hard not to entertain the idea that a dramatic piece consisting entirely of two ancient white-haired men, "As alike in appearance as possible," poring over a text, was intended to cast back an image, however refracted, of the audience for which it was composed—scholars whose professional life is spent poring over texts and reading them to each other. (1991, 8)

Those who read and reread texts for a living watch two who read and reread texts for life. The cycle of refractions exhibited by this level of information destabilizes the distinction between audience and stage (a relationship with which we will have further dealings later) in a backhanded ironic manner.

To explore the extratextual further, we can examine Beckett's aborted poem on the back of the first page of his first holograph.[12] This rather humorous, impromptu poem ends with the lines,

> Be yourself, they said, [you're (   )] stay yourself.
> Myself? I said. What are you insinuating?
> [Yourself before, they said.]
> *Pause.*
> [And after.*]*
> *[Pause.*]
> [Not during? I said.][13]

Though never used thereafter, these lines (those deleted making matters more obvious) give the first indication of the temporal and personal discontinuity that colors the final play. It appears Beckett envisioned that Self is a relative impossibility in any real sense. Discontinuity between time, space, and self is the normative environment of both poem and play. In other words, in *Ohio Impromptu*'s system, Zeno's grains of sand cannot and should not ever "mount up to a life" (Beckett 1958, 70). The implications extend beyond the borders of the play. This poem is highly biographical (indicating in its lines the request that conference coordinators in Ohio made to Beckett for an original work). Thus, it is Beckett's "self," as well, that is implicitly discontinuous and insubstantial. Like the title, which contains within it the "new world" location where the play was commissioned (thereby helping make it fit the description of an "old world" impromptu), Beckett's life and art here reflect one another, creator and created illuminating and decentering each other, making both life and art insubstantial.

In a further destabilization of the distinction between fact/biography and fiction, the Isle of Swans that figures so prominently in the play is, as noted above, a real island in the Seine.[14] Thus, the narrative as told *could* actually take place in our reality. We could (as I have done) walk out to the downstream tip of the Isle of Swans and, beneath a replica of the Statue of Liberty (a further fixed-point conflation—this time of old and new worlds), contemplate the Seine, "How in joyous eddies its two arms conflowed and flowed united on" (Beckett 1984d, 286). Biography and reality could effectively trade places with the stage, as the narrative subsumes reality within its fictional confines. Fact and fiction lose meaning but gain vast informational "surprise" in their commingling.

Finally, should we care to speculate on the reality/universality of the infinitesimal point of the "worn volume" which rests between L and R, we might find that it is somehow emblematic of Beckett's work as a whole. "[T]he book would thus constitute a writer's lifework, a whole *oeuvre* representing in this case, I think, that of Beckett himself in the form of a make-believe compilation of all his writings so far" (Astier 1982, 338). Scale-invariant, this tiny book iterates and encapsulates the entirety of Beckett's work. An entire biographical life exists in the quantum flux of a fictional book. If this is so, R's closing the book at the end of the play is an image that calls to mind Prospero's (and, so it is felt, Shakespeare's) relinquishing of the powers of "magic"—speech and knowledge—at the end of *The Tempest*. On a biographical level, Beckett, at the time seventy-five years old and already the most studied living playwright, could compare to the Shakespeare who wrote *The Tempest,* both in relative age and notoriety. And of course the Shakespearean shadow cast on the play adds even richer overtones to *Ohio Impromptu*. For example, the fact that *The Tempest* is also a water-and-island play, with language and imagery that "flows and ebbs" (V.i.270), adds another level of allusion to that which we have already examined.

Lengthy and mind-boggling merely to lay out in brief, the vast number of mutually intersecting and interfering layers that constitute *Ohio Im-*

promptu seem simply to fall outside any attempt to describe or visualize them fully. If we consider how the representational aspect of Chaos theory has related to the rest of our work, however, we can discover a better, vastly simpler way of visualizing what occurs in *Ohio Impromptu*: while the layers of the play, like individual bubbles in a turbulent river, can never be followed or projected to any significant distance, the dynamics of the play—or river—as a whole can be understood if we look at the system in terms of self-similarity and deterministic Chaos. As we have already seen in several contexts, scale-invariance is a hallmark of Chaotic systems, as every scale "looks like" every other; but none are exactly identical in natural, nonlinear systems—a facet definitely true of *Ohio Impromptu.*[15] Like the iterative space of nature, which is not continuous (or integrally dimensional) but broken up and "pocked," cycling back on itself in constant re-visioning of its own image, *Ohio Impromptu* is fractionally dimensional. Each moment and layer is different; neither time nor space nor signified is conserved, yet the roughness, or impact, of the play *is* conserved over all scales, as the play attains its own unity, albeit a nonrational one.[16] To use an analogy from modern astronomy, the "system" of the play is like the discontinuous, but scale-invariant placement of matter in the universe: many of the levels in the play are effectively "dark matter," hidden from all but the most persevering eyes; yet it is the weight of these elements, along with the more readily visible ones, that guarantees cohesion of the elements we see, and, in addition, potentiates the regenerative force of the play. In its very discontinuity and "lessness," the play generates a kind of rebirth into another state—a state, as we will see, beyond the presence and absence of our common mode of thought.[17]

Utilizing the tools of Chaos theory, we can make another important observation about the interrelationships of the various image levels of *Ohio Impromptu*: the play is itself analogous to a Mandelbrot set. As we discovered in *Footfalls*, the scale-invariant moments of the play reduce at each iteration like the bulbs growing off the main set, a patterning that reveals the progressive movement toward the zero point of lessness. Here we can make a further observation, one that is invaluable in understanding the interaction of the elements laid out above, as well as an observation that is related to the inner workings of the Mandelbrot set. In the pictures of the Mandelbrot set generated above, we took what is effectively a limited vision of the set (for reasons of two-dimensional representation for one thing). Looked at a different way, the Mandelbrot set reveals layers within its already infinitely layered self: the set acts as "a catalogue of Julia sets, a guide to each and every one" (Gleick 1987, 222). These Julia sets pop out of each and every point of the Mandelbrot set, revealing patterns that are at once similar and distinct from their "mother" set.[18] (See the inset, photos 9–11.)

As we can see, "if a particular portion of the Mandelbrot set is expanded to a large enough scale, the resulting pattern is very much like the Julia set for the value of *c* at the center of the expansion" (Stevens 1989, 275–76). Thus an entirely new level of information—an infinite number of new sets—appears from the depths of the Mandelbrot set, if only we know how to look for it. Each set is its own unique and beautiful entity, but at the same time the set of sets interact with each other tangentially, each informing, augmenting, and revealing aspects of the other in their relationship. Broken down, each set may appear to be independently viable, but its infinitely recursive generation, as well as its relationship with all the rest of the Julia sets and the Mandelbrot set, reveals a complex interdependence that destabilizes any static level of meaning, while at the same time containing a vastly complex amount of interrelation within an utterly simple form: $z \rightarrow z^2 + c$. Broken down, each level of *Ohio Impromptu* may seem self-sufficient and independent, but when we see all the interrelating levels—which are like a Chinese box, or Ezekiel's "wheels within wheels"—in light of the cross-relating self-similarity of Chaos theory, we perceive the immediacy of the "utterly simple" pattern of the play as a whole: a tiny form that contains and generates all of the complex information and rich patterns we have seen precisely because it is primarily relational. We must see the play not as a series of distinct signs and images but as a dynamic system of relationships which, while altering all its double and triple parts in a dense, impenetrable flux, is stable as a system, a system beyond logic and causality, the system of *Mu*,[19] or No-thing-ness into which L and R (etc.) apparently enter during the play's final moment. Presence and absence, stage and narrative, and so on, are abandoned as viable constructs, and, "if being or lack of being cannot be figured, at least some shape or pattern, however faint, can be traced against the void" (Anna McMullan 1993, 102–3).

If *Ohio Impromptu* is primarily systemic and relational, then the images with which we have been dealing reveal that these relationships are the "without-context" of self-reflecting and refracting images with no stable "thing" to reflect. In other words, the play can be described in terms of a specific koan: "What do two facing mirrors reflect?"[20] Without a subject (or object) between them, the mirrors can only reflect each other—but what image would that produce? If we choose an element of the play that most readily reveals this vision, the final image of L and R facing each other in "Profounds of Mind. Of mindlessness" must certainly jump out. These two men, "As alike in appearance as possible . . . , raise their heads and look at each other. Unblinking. Expressionless" (Beckett 1984d, 285, 288). In their "stone" stare, these two lose subjectivity, "thus blindly mirroring each other" (Astier 1982, 338) across a relational context of "without-self." This final tableau is at once (again, pairs being destabilized) the "mirror koan" and its resolution, as the two *become* the koan, losing any sense of subjectivity in their "stone" stares.

Because of their subjective absence, the myriad signifiers cycling around the empty "hole" at the center of the play (Klaver 1991, 373) tear themselves apart under their own conceptual weight. With subjectivity and causality dispersed, all distinctions, all dualities—all conceptual frameworks—die, fading away into the "without-relationship" that exists between all the elements within and without *Ohio Impromptu,* and that can only be prereflective reality. By the end of the play, there are no longer objects like bows and arrows, or even actions like archery; so pairs like the "without-arrow" and "without-target" are free to be one in the plenary absence. Thus, the characters, the set, the "sad tale"—all the elements we have broken apart—no longer exist, as the play in its entirety, and consequently Beckett's oeuvre as a whole, is "properly" born into the "without-perception" and "without-presence" of No-thing.[21]

8
Conclusion

> Access to the spiritual life always entails death to the profane condition, followed by a new birth.
>
> —Mircea Eliade

> "Indeed, he is the artless art itself and thus Master and No-Master in one. At this point, archery, considered as the unmoved movement, the undanced dance, passes over into Zen."
>
> —Eugen Herrigel

Into the complex/simple pattern that, we have discovered, constitutes Beckett's plays, we must now reincorporate another, all-important level of iteration: the audience. Although I have consistently referred to the "marginal" element of audience throughout this work, I should, finally, reconsider this element as central to the project. The ultimate forum for Beckett's plays must be those who view its performance; and, in this instance as well, we find that the plays function as a Zen koan. Via the fluid multiplicity of images at work in the plays examined, Beckett skillfully pulls us into the world and language of the characters until we ourselves begin to feel like L and R in *Ohio Impromptu*: confused and agonized, listening intently to try to find relief from the vast levels of signification that assault our senses in the few words and fewer actions we observe. As we have discovered, Beckett consistently assaults our conventional sense of logic on many levels and in many ways, from the two windows in *Endgame,* which face the same direction but look out on ocean and desert, to the temporal destabilization of past, present, and future by the intersection of the narrative with stage time in *Ohio Impromptu*. Over and over, we are frustrated in our attempts to pile the "grains of sand" of these plays into a heap of meaning. Yet, here again, it is only our need to connect these self-sufficient, dynamically interacting moments of "being-time" that creates a problem. If we allow each moment to fall where it may, a pattern of discontinuity appears, more strongly in each play, which finally releases us from the logical death of the late play, *Ohio Impromptu*—and implicitly, at least, from Beckett's earlier drama.

As is true of its internal elements, the structure of each play grows more and more similar to that of a traditional koan: a short, sometimes humorous riddle "with no rational entrance or exit." The upshot of these brief Zen stories is usually a mental (and/or physical) blow which we are told finally jars students out of their old, causal frame of mind and "enlightens" them (and us as well, if we devote ourselves unreservedly to the problem the master presents). Thus, for us the answer to the "mirror koan" of *Ohio Impromptu* is the same as Joshu's answer to the question put to him, and L and R's answer to theirs: *Mu*, or no-thing. In order to understand the answer (or answers) to a koan, one must cease thinking in the old yes-or-no way—or, as Winnie in *Happy Days* puts it, using the "old style."

To succeed with the audience, Beckett's plays must turn inward in us—becoming, in effect, the drama of the Great Death within each of the audience members as the egoistic, logical, controlling Self struggles against the impossibility of what it perceives on stage and in the narrative, finally "shorting out" as recursive words, sentences, actions, and staging float beyond their denotative space into that of a connotative flux. In the interplay between Zen, Chaos theory and Beckett's plays, we have discovered how each of these "systems," using pairs that are destabilized by a third element, decenters the entrenched order of bipolar vision, replacing it with a vision of reality not based on meaning and concepts, but rather of experiencing each moment of reality in holistic fashion.

Each of the plays we have studied exemplifies the ways in which characters and audience alike are led to this new, holistic vision. In *Waiting for Godot*, the twinned relationship between Vladimir and Estragon, as well as the antithetical one between Pozzo and Lucky, is both defined and disrupted via the characters' reaction to the ephemeral "Mr. Godot." Hamm and Clov, Nagg and Nell, exist in relation to (or, better, in spite of) the hostile "without." This environment, threatening in its devastation, robs Hamm and Clov (and Nagg and Nell) of their former, causal relationship and forces them to re-create themselves moment by moment. For Winnie and Willie in *Happy Days*, the malevolent force that traps Winnie and bakes them both beneath a blazing sun is also the source of potential release, as it slowly removes all possible distractions to the reality of the moment qua moment. In *Footfalls*, the densely connotative "it all" refracts May and V until any semblance of separation between the characters breaks down into multiple shadings of without-presence that must resonate with the audience in the brief final moment of emptiness on stage. Finally, in *Ohio Impromptu*, the pair of pairs—L and R and listener and reader—"conflow" about the quasi presence of "the dear name," with character, time, and even stage presence intermingling in a moment that thrusts both characters and audience beyond the linear logic of conceptual differentiation.

In Zen, Chaos theory, and Beckett's drama alike, a progressive movement from the "old style" of traditional Western thought to this new paradigm occurs via a series of iterations of supposedly fringe elements of reality: nonlinear equations, the "without-context" of *Mu*, discontinuous yet repetitive characters, language, and action. These iterations, occurring at once within and throughout Beckett's plays, first lay bare the paradoxical nature of the causal paradigm, then recenter the semiotic, moral, and dramatic codes of the works, allowing both characters and audience, finally, to experience a cathartic moment—the Great Death—in whose potential space this new vision of the world takes form. In the milieus of Beckett's plays, what seems manifestly nihilistic is, instead, a space imbued with the possibility of positive change. The void that infuses his works is not the terminus to which all spirals down but the source from which patterns of beauty, if not of traditional meaning, spring.

To return to the archery metaphor, in *Waiting for Godot*, the common notion that objects like arrows and targets have a distinct, extralingual existence that can be manipulated and causally connected into continuous, narrative events ("shooting an arrow at a target") is rejected by the form and content of the play. By the end, the pairs in the play—like arrow and target—are poised to enter a dynamic union through the tension of the drawn "bow" of this moment of Great Doubt. Audience and characters, however, are cast adrift in this moment of stillness when the Vladimir and Estragon "do not move." The potential for Godot's nonarrival comes as the two cease moving and speaking at the end of each act. In this repeated moment is the space to cease waiting and wanting for a presence whose ability to fulfill our and their wants and needs is, at most, illusory. Like the characters, however, we are, in the end, left in the state of the Great Doubt, knowing now that the old way of seeing stage and reality cannot be valid, but still needing to find closure—to find out who Godot really is.

In *Endgame*, we see further into the suffering created by the characters' battle to extricate themselves from their need to causally connect the "grains" of Zeno's paradox into some meaningful whole. In a highly entropic but self-regenerating universe, Hamm and the others fight for an order and control that is no longer theirs to command. They are forced to discard concepts like bow and arrow, but—with the possible exception of Nell—feel a (modernist) loss when forced to this extreme; the characters therefore cannot completely let go of their old ways and end up trapped between the two paradigms. The multiple levels of paradox that *Endgame* generates are at root linked to the characters' (especially Hamm's) need to maintain causal and logical continuity in a world in which the non sequitur is the rule rather than the exception. Primarily, then, it is the belief in a categorical duality between order and chaos—or life and death—that creates the impending sense of entropic decay and dissolution, impelling the characters and audience to a desperate search for meaning—or, at least, for distraction. Only Nell seems somehow able to escape this dilemma, accepting the determinate indeterminacy and dynamic unity of life and death, of beginning and ending. Following her lead, we, as audience, may be able to do what the other characters cannot: we may see "down to the bottom" (Beckett 1958, 23) of existence, discarding concepts of meaning, causality, and connection, and see instead the beautiful, generative Chaotic patterning which underlies their—and our—world.

By *Happy Days*, Beckett's trend toward "lessness" reduces Winnie to first a body, then only a head, forcing her deeper into the meditative state of the Great Doubt than other characters before her. Winnie, the first major female character in Beckett's drama, struggles through time—the "old style"—and memory to maintain an order that is being effaced by the natural and, according to Chaos theory, positive noise of her world. In an ironic twist, she even pursues an objectifying patriarchal vision of herself as a means to maintain what is familiar to her. However, even the comfort of this familiar, debasing means of conceptualizing herself is eradicated as Winnie's object-body sinks into the mound of scorched earth. Her distractions—the contents of her bag and her objectified body—removed, Winnie is forced to the edge of a new world in which the words and concepts of the old order are no longer valid. The Chaotic noise that drowns out Winnie's memories and words is the embodiment of a new, immediate, nonclosed world in which sound and patterns, rather than meaning, dominate. It is likely the violence of this impending collision between these two paradigms that in the end draws Willie out of his hovel. Whether he comes to hinder or further Winnie's journey—to act as male subject or to break apart the distinction between subject and object—is unclear, and perhaps unimportant. What matters most is that both have now reached a point of maximum constriction. They must either grow into a new vision of the world or die—and in a sense they must do both. As *Happy Days* ends, however, Winnie and Willie are left trapped in a state of Great Doubt. While similar to the earlier plays, though, the noise of this play pushes them, and us, ever closer to the Great Death wherein the temporal connection of events like drawing a bow and shooting an arrow ceases to exist, the rich noise of the moment drowning static memory. In the meditative "Long pause" shared by Winnie and Willie, we sense that all that went before is mere prelude to what must occur next.

Footfalls moves both characters and audience further into the potential space between the two paradigmatic views of the world. Here, the inseparably meshed pair which is May/V exists in a universe that simply has no stable referents, even ones like stage presence and determinate physicality that Beckett's earlier plays contain. Here "all perception has become fainter and more problematical" (Anna McMullan, 1993, 102). The audience is thus pulled ever more strongly into a world in which two (or one) are once again struggling, but this time more to be "born" into nonpresence than to somehow maintain a conceptual sense of self. The final section, or iteration, of the play indicates that May/V may have successfully crossed the moment of the Great Doubt to the state of the Great Death, letting go of the need for words, narrative connection, and even the ghostly sound of her footsteps. Whereas throughout the iterations of her life and the play May/V is unable to find a way to bring herself fully into presence, the final moments of the play provide a way to collapse the disparities and paradoxes of her existence. In the end, May/V becomes identified with her unattached negative prefix, "un-," shifting its dismaying denotation to a new connotation in which past and future dissolve within a self-fulfilled present. In the end, she is released from having to revolve "it all" as she seems successfully to be born into a rich "without-presence," a state to which the audience is also invited as the lights fade up, "even a little less," the fourth and final time. The fluid/static structure of the play and May's steps break down causality until only the moment before us exists. In the dynamic absent-presence of *Footfalls*, the closing arrow and target flicker and fade into the universally resonating void of the emptied stage.

Finally, in the miniature world of *Ohio Impromptu*, the compression of levels of imagery, the koanlike nature of the internal narrative and the play itself, and the "conflowing" nature of the characters themselves allows a complete break with the old paradigm, "relief" flowing from the erasure of subjectivity into the relational context of *Mu*, or no-thing. In the final moments of the play, nothing exists—not arrows, targets, or individuals—but everything *is* in the plenary void of self-sufficient existence. In the earlier plays, the audience is asked to transcend the characters (if we would pass beyond the samsaric world), but in *Ohio Impromptu*, Beckett presents a koan that allows us to join the characters in achieving a state of prereflective "without-consciousness." In both form and content, *Ohio Impromptu* destabilizes any logical, meaningful (as opposed to informational) cohesion. "Generated out of a friction among texts, genres, and writing processes, the work has no center at all and no rational entrance or exit" (Klaver 1991, 372).

As audience members, then, we must join the characters in the state of Great Doubt, iterating the play over and over again in a silent "expanse of ice" (Kasulis 1981, 114) as our need for, and ability to hold onto, a categorical consciousness drops away. To solve the dilemma of understanding caused by the play, we must participate in the shock of the Great Death, changing the paradigm from which we view *Ohio Impromptu* and all Beckett's plays: we must see the play(s) relationally instead of "meaningfully." We must *become* the koan that is Beckett's drama, apprehending the mingling layers in a state which comes before logic and distinction. Thus *Ohio Impromptu* is its own riddle and its own answer:[1] to understand it fully, we must cease looking into the play, trying to "break" its code; instead we must look within ourselves, trying to see the play—and therefore the world—differently.

Why, then, we might ask, are Beckett's plays even necessary? If we are to look within ourselves to find a play's meaning, why do we need a play like *Ohio Impromptu* at all? The answer is that the play, like a koan, is " 'a piece of brick to knock at a gate' " (Reps 1975, 88). Once L and R attain their "true nature," they no longer need the text from which they are reading; once the audience achieves this state of satori, once "the gate is opened[,] the brick is useless and is thrown away" (Reps 1975, 88).[2] Beckett's plays, like the elements within them, are an indicator, a signpost showing us the path (the "Tao," or "way") to escape his vision of the terrifying world of ourSelves. Thus,

> If we do not take perceptions as signs of named things, the most fundamental and problematic dualism of all—that between my fragile sense of being and the nothingness that threatens it—is conflated; if we do not need to fixate ourselves, if we can "let go" of ourselves, we *un*find ourselves "in" the dreamlike world . . . , and plunge into the horizontality of moving and light surfaces where there are no objects, only an incessant shifting of masks; where there is no security and also no need for security, because everything that can be lost has been, including oneself. Especially oneself. (Loy 1992, 250)

Therefore the (non)actions of L and R, listener and reader, light and dark, mother and daughter, present and past, master and slave, birth and death—in fact, all the destabilized dualities of Beckett's plays—are eventually redirected toward us, the audience. Across the void between ourselves and the stage, it is we who must learn to see correctly, ceasing to value those elements conserved in the paradigm of the "old style"—linearity, logic, division—apprehending, instead, the scale-invariance and radically relational without-context within which "we" actually function.

Once we gain the vision of this new paradigm, we are free to absorb the information of these plays in a prereflective state in which fragments are universal, and vice versa. We learn to make "without-sense" of the plays by seeing, "not something different, but in a different way" (Smith 1986, vii). Or, as Arthur Schopenhauer, who was heavily influenced by contact with Buddhism, describes the profound, mind-numbing experience of witnessing a great work of art, "aesthetic pleasure in the beautiful consists . . . in the fact that, when we enter the state of pure contemplation [when logic and linearity are destabilized and association begins], we are raised for the moment above all willing, above all desires and cares; we are, so to speak rid of ourselves" (Schopenhauer 1969, 390). We can then stop *waiting* for relief from some other quarter—waiting for the arrow of comprehension to connect with the target of Beckett's plays—as we find the relief is already there in the stillness and fading light that fills the plenary, relational void in the final moment of each (every) play. Only then, once we are "rid of ourselves," can R's final words, "Nothing is left to tell," begin to make sense in a different way. It is only after Beckett, his characters, and we ourselves have struggled through the plays *together* and discovered *Mu shin*—the state of no mind, or "consciousness beyond thought"—that we can understand No-thing the "positive nothingness of non-being" (Esslin 1969, 58), as the path to the plays' (and our) enlightenment.

Appendix

Evolution of the Decomposition and Phase-Space Diagram of *Footfalls*

> I squashed a bug here
> look here at the stain!
> Am I more substance than this?
>
> — Anonymous

> And who knows whether these images, born of centuries of practice, may not go deeper than all our carefully calculated knowledge?
>
> —Eugen Herrigel

The impetus to quantify *Footfalls* comes from the strict, almost musical nature of the piece. The resultant regularity made strikingly evident the apparently random variations that arise from time to time. Additionally, May's pacing—the stopping and starting motion—seemed to follow a pseudorandom pattern. The interplay between the apparently well-defined behavior of parts of the play and the seemingly Chaotic nature of other elements made me suspect that a scale-invariant patterning might "define" *Footfalls*. Below is an indication of some of the steps I took to "map" the play onto a quasi phase-space.

Step 1 was to parse each of the "events," categorized by type, of the play. The differing events fell into the following categories:

- C: Chime (and echoes); about 7 seconds in Beckett's direction
- F: Fade-up (and down); about 7 seconds in Beckett's direction
- L: May pacing toward left
- R: May pacing toward right
- P: Pause
- V: Vocal "unit": a "beat" of speech (often bracketed between pauses)
- LP: Long pause

At times the physical events (L and R) overlap with the spoken elements (P and V). At these points, I chose to consider the events to be additive, or interfering. Using these codes, a crude mapping of the lines and movement of the play can be done, as in table 4 (see below).[1]

From here, I noted the groupings these elements usually took:

- *WU: A walking unit (pacing the floor L-R and back, or vice versa, once)
- #SU: A speech unit (pause followed by vocal beat)
- -FU: A fader unit (chime followed by lights up—or lights down)
- |: Stand-alone vocal unit
-]: Stand-alone pause

Carrying this out for the play produces table 5 (see below). Note in this table that the units sometimes overlap; thus, WU, for example, is bracketed by *s to indicate its beginning and ending points.

At this point, I condensed the signs to single markers to denote when regular events occur:

- *: Walking unit
- #: Speech unit
- -: Fader unit
- &: Long voice unit (for three uninterrupted voice beats)
- %: Rogue event (the Chaotic, irregular event not covered by the above)

Utilizing this method, I generated table 6 (see below).

Having done all this preliminary work, we can now do some "counting" to examine how scale-invariance is at work within the play. First, we can add up blocks of the different types of events by section (a block being uninterrupted groups of each event type). (See table 1.)

Table 1. Blocks of Events by Section in *Footfalls*

Event type	Section I	Section II	Section III	Section IV
#	5	3	6	0
*	0	1	1	0
&	8	4	5	0
-	2	2	2	2
%	8	6	15	1

A quick look at the last line of this table (and at table 3) reveals very clearly that section 2 is the most regular of the sections (leaving out the very different section 4, which is difficult to measure).

We can also count how many regular events occur between each irregular (%) one. (See table 2.)

The same type of table can be generated for May's movement (number of "bars" between movement units). (See table 3.)

Aside from showing how much movement slows down (note the number of bars versus the number of movements per section),[2] this table and table 2 show a Cantor "dustlike" spacing of movement and irregular events. Like the middle-third Cantor dust, whose spacing follows a short-long-short-longer pattern,[3] these two patterns in *Footfalls* reveal a quasi-scale-invariant structure. In section 2, for example, we get a 1-3-2-7 pattern which is very close to that of a Cantor dust. While not a perfect match with this particular dust, the pattern of dispersion is very much in line with that of a self-similar, scale-invariant, fractal structure.

In order to produce figure 21, on page 154, I first had to consider what could be "measured" in the play. The following is a list of measurable items I considered using to map the play onto "phase-space":

- The kind of event which occurs
- The length (or measure) of the event
- May's physical position
- The differing sections of the play
- Changes in lighting
- Changes in sound

I finally made my decision based on what I feel are the most useful, informative and accurate (closest to a real phase-space mapping) measurables: event-type, position, and "change in event-type."[4] This provides the axes for a three-dimensional phase-space on which to map elements of the play. As this is not a real system, the numerical values of the event-type, position and ∂event-type are arbitrary (the shape is what counts, not the size), but I tried to give more unusual events (and changes) a greater number to indicate the greater amount of information or surprise they provide. The event-types I mapped are:

- Movement right
- Movement left
- Lights up
- Lights down
- Pause

- Voice
- Chime
- Long pause
- Hold (for *x* seconds)

Some of the ∂event-types I mapped are:

- Pause—vocal (value of +*x*)
- Vocal—pause (value of -*x*)
- Walk left—Walk right (value of +*y*)
- Walk right—Walk left (value of -*y*)
- Walk left—Pause (value of +*z*)
- Pause—Walk left (value of -*z*)

By assigning opposite changes negative values, I establish a correspondence between changes that happen in reverse order of each other. Also note that both events and ∂events are additive or interfering; thus if two different ∂events take place simultaneously, their numbers add (or subtract), giving a result which is the combination of both. The last three columns of table 4 show the evolution of these three terms throughout the play. Taking the numbers produced in this table, I generated figure 21.

Table 2. Spacing of Regular and Irregular Events in *Footfalls*

Section I	Section II	Section III	Section IV
7	16	2	1
%	%	%	
%	2	2	1
4	%	%	
%	1	3	
1	%	%	
%	%	1	
1	10	%	
%	%	3	
1	%	%	
%	5 (+2)	2	
12		%	
%		7	
8		%	
%		3	
8 (+16)[5]		%	
		5	
		%	
		%	
		11	

Table 2 *(continued)*

		%	
		1	
		%	
		1	
		%	
		1	
		%	
		10	
		%	
		1 (+1)	

Table 3. Spacing of Motion and Stillness in *Footfalls*

Section I	Section II	Section III	Section IV
*	20	3	3
*	*	*	
8	2	12	
*	*	*	
1	8	14	
*	*	*	
23	3	20	
*	*	*	
3	3 (+3)	1	
*		*	
*		13 (+3)	
4			
*			
1 (+20)			

Table 4. Parsing of *Footfalls* (First Pass)

Lines (≈ beated out)	Mvmnt	Event	Pos	Evnt#	∂Evnt
I: Faint single chime.		C	2	-9	8
Pause as echoes die.		P	1	1	7
Fade up to dim on strip. Rest in darkness.		FU L	0	-6	-6
M discovered pacing towards L.	Length 1	L	-1	4	-8
		L	-2	4	0
		L	-3	4	0
		L	-4	4	0
Turns at L.	Length 2	R	-4	-4	2
		R	-3	-4	0
		R	-2	-4	0
		R	-1	-4	0
		R	0	-4	0
		R	1	-4	0
		R	2	-4	0
		R	3	-4	0
		R	4	-4	0
		R	5	-4	0
	Length 3	L	5	4	-2
		L	4	4	0
		L	3	4	0
		L	2	4	0
		L	1	4	0
		L	0	4	0
		L	-1	4	0
		L	-2	4	0
		L	-3	4	0
		L	-4	4	0
	Length 4	R	-4	-4	2
		R	-3	-4	0
		R	-2	-4	0
		R	-1	-4	0
		R	0	-4	0
		R	1	-4	0
		R	2	-4	0
		R	3	-4	0
		R	4	-4	0
		R	5	-4	0
halts, facing front at R.		H	5	6	-11
Pause.		P	5	1	13
M: Mother.		V	5	-1	1
[*Pause.* No louder.]		P	5	1	-1
Mother.		V	5	-1	1
[*Pause.*]		P	5	1	-1
V: Yes, May.		V	5	-1	1
M: We're you asleep?		V	5	-1	0
V: Deep asleep.		V	5	-1	0

Table 4 *(continued)*

[*Pause.*]		P	5	1	-1
I heard you in my deep sleep.		V	5	-1	1
[*Pause.*]		P	5	1	-1
There is no sleep so deep I would not hear you there.		V	5	-1	1
[*Pause.*		P	5	1	-1
M resumes pacing.	Length 1	L	4	4	3
		L	3	4	0
		L	2	4	0
		L	1	4	0
		L	0	4	0
		L	-1	4	0
		L	-2	4	0
		L	-3	4	0
One two three four five six seven *eight nine* wheel	Length 2	V R	-4	-5	7
		V R	-4	-5	-6
		V R	-3	-5	0
		V R	-2	-5	0
		V R	-1	-5	0
		V R	0	-5	0
		V R	1	-5	0
		V R	2	-5	0
		V R	3	-5	0
		V R	4	-5	0
		V R	5	-5	0
one two three four five six seven *eight nine* wheel.	Length 3	V L	5	3	1
		V L	4	3	0
		V L	3	3	0
		V L	2	3	0
		V L	1	3	0
		V L	0	3	0
		V L	-1	3	0
		V L	-2	3	0
		V L	-3	3	0
		V L	-4	3	0
Will you not try to snatch a little sleep?	Length 4	V R	-4	-5	-1
		V R	-3	-5	0
		V R	-2	-5	0
		V R	-1	-5	0
		V R	0	-5	0
		R	1	-4	-6
		R	2	-4	0
		R	3	-4	0
		R	4	-4	0
[M halts face front at R.		H	5	6	-11
Pause.]		P	5	1	13

Table 4 *(continued)*

M: Would you like me to inject you again?		V	5	-1	1
V: Yes, but it is too soon.		V	5	-1	0
[*Pause.*]		P	5	1	-1
M: Would you like me to change your position again?		V	5	-1	1
V: Yes, but it is too soon.		V	5	-1	0
[*Pause.*]		P	5	1	-1
M: Straighten your pillows?		V	5	-1	1
[*Pause.*]		P	5	1	-1
Change your drawsheets?		V	5	-1	1
[*Pause.*]		P	5	1	-1
Pass you the bedpan?		V	5	-1	1
[*Pause.*]		P	5	1	-1
The warming-pan?		V	5	-1	1
[*Pause.*]		P	5	1	-1
Dress your sores?		V	5	-1	1
[*Pause.*]		P	5	1	-1
Sponge you down?		V	5	-1	1
[*Pause.*]		P	5	1	-1
Moisten your poor lips?		V	5	-1	1
[*Pause.*]		P	5	1	-1
Pray with you?		V	5	-1	1
[*Pause.*]		P	5	1	-1
For you?		V	5	-1	1
[*Pause.*]		P	5	1	-1
Again.		V	5	-1	1
[*Pause.*]		P	5	1	-1
V: Yes, but it is too soon.		V	5	-1	1
[*Pause.*]		P	5	1	-1
M: What age am I now?		V	5	-1	1
V: And I?		V	5	-1	0
[*Pause.* No louder.]		P	5	1	-1
And I?		V	5	-1	1
M: Ninety.		V	5	-1	0
V: So much?		V	5	-1	0
M: Eighty-nine, ninety.		V	5	-1	0
V: I had you late.		V	5	-1	0
[*Pause.*]		P	5	1	-1
In life.		V	5	-1	1
[*Pause.*]		P	5	1	-1
Forgive me again.		V	5	-1	1
[*Pause.* No louder.]		P	5	1	-1
Forgive me again.		V	5	-1	1
[M resumes pacing.	Length 1	L	4	4	-5
		L	3	4	0
		L	2	4	0
		L	1	4	0
		L	0	4	0

Table 4 *(continued)*

		L	-1	4	0
		L	-2	4	0
		L	-3	4	0
halts facing front at L.		H	-4	6	11
Pause.]		P	-4	1	13
M: What age am I now?		V	-4	-1	1
V: In your forties.		V	-4	-1	0
M: So little?		V	-4	-1	0
V: I'm afraid so.		V	-4	-1	0
[*Pause*.		P	-4	1	-1
May.	Length 2	V R	-3	-5	5
[*Pause*. No louder.]		P R	-2	-3	-11
		P R	-1	-3	0
		P R	0	-3	0
May.		V R	1	-5	11
		V R	2	-5	0
M: [Pacing.] Yes, Mother.		V R	3	-5	0
		V R	4	-5	0
		V R	5	-5	0
V: Will you	Length 3	V L	5	3	-1
never		V L	4	3	0
have done?		V L	3	3	0
[*Pause*.]		P L	2	5	-9
		P L	1	5	0
		P L	0	5	0
Will you never		V L	-1	3	9
have done…		V L	-2	3	0
		V L	-3	3	0
revolving it all?		V L	-4	3	0
M: [Halting.]		H	-4	6	1
It?		V	-4	-1	-12
V: It all.		V	-4	-1	0
[*Pause*.]		P	-4	1	-1
In your poor mind.		V	-4	-1	1
[*Pause*.]		P	-4	1	-1
It all.		V	-4	-1	1
[*Pause*.]		P	-4	1	-1
It all.		V	-4	-1	1
Five seconds.	Length 4	R	-3	-4	-6
Fade out on strip.		FD R	-2	6	-13
		FD R	-1	6	0
		FD R	0	6	0
		FD R	1	6	0
		FD R	2	6	0
		FD R	3	6	0
		FD R	4	6	0
Pause.		P	5	1	-14

Table 4 *(continued)*

II: Chime a little fainter.		C	5	-9	-7
Pause for echoes.		P	5	1	7
Fade up to a little less on strip. Rest in darkness.		FU	5	-10	-9
M discovered facing front at R.		FU	5	-10	0
Pause.]		P	5	1	9
V: I walk here now.		V	5	-1	1
[*Pause.*]		P	5	1	-1
Rather I come and stand.		V	5	-1	1
[*Pause.*]		P	5	1	-1
At nightfall.		V	5	-1	1
[*Pause.*]		P	5	1	-1
She fancies she is alone.		V	5	-1	1
[*Pause.*]		P	5	1	-1
See how still she stands, how stark, with her face to the wall.		V	5	-1	1
[*Pause.*]		P	5	1	-1
How outwardly unmoved.		V	5	-1	1
[*Pause.*]		P	5	1	-1
She has not been out since girlhood.		V	5	-1	1
[*Pause.*]		P	5	1	-1
Not out since girlhood.		V	5	-1	1
[*Pause.*]		P	5	1	-1
Where is she, it may be asked.		V	5	-1	1
[*Pause.*]		P	5	1	-1
Why, in the old home, the same where she—		V	5	-1	1
[*Pause.*]		P	5	1	-1
The same where she began.		V	5	-1	1
[*Pause.*]		P	5	1	-1
Where it began.		V	5	-1	1
[*Pause.*]		P	5	1	-1
It all began.		V	5	-1	1
[*Pause.*]		P	5	1	-1
But this, this, when did this begin?		V	5	-1	1
[*Pause.*]		P	5	1	-1
When other girls of her age were out at… lacrosse she was already here.		V	5	-1	1
[*Pause.*]		P	5	1	-1
At this.		V	5	-1	1
[*Pause.*]		P	5	1	-1
The floor here, now bare, once was—		V	5	-1	1
[M begins pacing. Steps a little slower.] But let us watch her move in silence.	Length 1	L V	4	3	-5
		L V	3	3	0
		L V	2	3	0
		L V	1	3	0
		L V	0	3	0
		L V	-1	3	0

Table 4 *(continued)*

		L	-2	4	-5
		L	-3	4	0
		L	-4	4	0
[M paces. Towards end of second length.] Watch how feat she wheels.	Length 2	R	-4	-4	2
		R	-3	-4	0
		R	-2	-4	0
		R	-1	-4	0
		R	0	-4	0
		R	1	-4	0
		R	2	-4	0
		V R	3	-5	6
		V R	4	-5	0
		V R	5	-5	0
[M turns, paces. Synchronous with steps third length.] Seven, eight, nine, wheel.	Length 3	L	5	4	-7
		L	4	4	0
		L	3	4	0
		L	2	4	0
		L	1	4	0
		L	0	4	0
		L V	-1	3	5
		L V	-2	3	0
		L V	-3	3	0
		L V	-4	3	0
[M turns at L, paces one more length,] I say the floor here, now bare, this strip of floor, once was carpeted, a deep pile.	Length 4	R V	-4	-5	1
		R V	-3	-5	0
		R V	-2	-5	0
		R V	-1	-5	0
		R V	0	-5	0
		R V	1	-5	0
		R V	2	-5	0
		R V	3	-5	0
		R V	4	-5	0
halts facing front at R.]		H V	5	5	7
Till one night, while still little more than a child, she called her mother and said, Mother, this is not enough.		V	5	-1	-12
The mother: Not enough?		V	5	-1	0
May—the child's given name—May: Not enough.		V	5	-1	0
The mother: What do you mean, May, not enough,		V	5	-1	0
what can you possibly mean, May, not enough?		V	5	-1	0
May: I mean, Mother, that I must hear the feet, however faint they fall.		V	5	-1	0

Table 4 *(continued)*

The mother: The motion alone is not enough?		V	5	-1	0
May: No, Mother, the motion alone is not enough, I must hear the feet, however faint they fall.		V	5	-1	0
[*Pause.*		P	5	1	-1
With pacing.] Does she still sleep, it may be asked?	Length 1	V L	4	3	4
		V L	3	3	0
		V L	2	3	0
		V L	1	3	0
Yes, some nights she does, in snatches, bows her poor head against the wall and snatches a little sleep.		V L	0	3	0
		V L	-1	3	0
		V L	-2	3	0
		V L	-3	3	0
[*Pause.*]		P L	-4	5	-4
	Length 2	P R	-4	-3	6
Still speak?		V R	-3	-5	11
		V R	-2	-5	0
		V R	-1	-5	0
Yes, some nights she does, when she fancies none can hear.		V R	0	-5	0
		V R	1	-5	0
		V R	2	-5	0
		V R	3	-5	0
[*Pause.*]		P R	4	-3	-5
		P R	5	-3	0
Tells how it was.	Length 3	V L	5	3	8
[*Pause.*]		P L	4	5	-4
		P L	3	5	0
Tries to tell how it was.		V L	2	3	6
[*Pause.*]		P L	1	5	-4
		P L	0	5	0
It all.		V L	-1	3	6
[*Pause.*]		P L	-2	5	-4
		P L	-3	5	0
It all.		V L	-4	3	6
	Length 4	R	-4	-4	-4
Five seconds.		R	-3	-4	0
		R	-2	-4	0
Fade out on strip.		FD R	-1	6	-13
		FD R	0	6	0
		FD R	1	6	0
		FD R	2	6	0
		FD R	3	6	0
		FD R	4	6	0

Table 4 *(continued)*

Pause.		P	5	1	-14
III: Chime a little fainter still.		C	5	-9	-7
Pause for echoes.		P	5	1	7
Fade up to a little less still on strip. Rest in darkness.		FU	5	-10	-9
M discovered facing front at R.		FU	5	-10	0
Pause.]		P	5	1	9
M: Sequel.		V	5	-1	1
[*Pause.*		P	5	1	-1
Begins pacing. Steps a little slower still.	Length 1	L	4	4	3
		L	3	4	0
		L	2	4	0
		L	1	4	0
		L	0	4	0
		L	-1	4	0
		L	-2	4	0
		L	-3	4	0
		L	-4	4	0
	Length 2	R	-4	-4	2
		R	-3	-4	0
		R	-2	-4	0
		R	-1	-4	0
		R	0	-4	0
		R	1	-4	0
		R	2	-4	0
		R	3	-4	0
		R	4	-4	0
halts facing front at R.		H	5	6	-11
Pause.]		P	5	1	13
Sequel.		V	5	-1	1
A little later, when she was quite forgotten, she began to—		V	5	-1	0
[*Pause.*]		P	5	1	-1
A little later, when as though she had never been, it never been, she began to walk.		V	5	-1	1
[*Pause.*]		P	5	1	-1
At nightfall.		V	5	-1	1
[*Pause.*]		P	5	1	-1
Slip out at nightfall and into the little church by the north door, always locked at that hour,		V	5	-1	1
and walk, up and down, up and down, his poor arm.		V	5	-1	0
[*Pause.*]		P	5	1	-1
Some nights she would halt, as one frozen by some shudder of the mind, and stand stark still till she could move again.		V	5	-1	1
But many also were the nights when she paced without pause,		V	5	-1	0

Table 4 *(continued)*

up and down, up and down, before vanishing the way she came.		V	5	-1	0
[*Pause.*]		P	5	1	-1
No sound.		V	5	-1	1
[*Pause.*]		P	5	1	-1
None at least to be heard.		V	5	-1	1
[*Pause.*]		P	5	1	-1
The semblance.		V	5	-1	1
[*Pause.*		P	5	1	-1
Resumes pacing.	Length 3	L	4	4	3
		L	3	4	0
		L	2	4	0
		L	1	4	0
		L	0	4	0
		L	-1	4	0
		L	-2	4	0
		L	-3	4	0
		L	-4	4	0
	Length 4	R	-4	-4	2
		R	-3	-4	0
		R	-2	-4	0
		R	-1	-4	0
		R	0	-4	0
		R	1	-4	0
		R	2	-4	0
		R	3	-4	0
		R	4	-4	0
halts facing front at R.		H	5	6	-11
Pause.]		P	5	1	13
The semblance.		V	5	-1	1
Faint, though by no means invisible, in a certain light.		V	5	-1	0
[*Pause.*]		P	5	1	-1
Given the right light.		V	5	-1	1
[*Pause.*]		P	5	1	-1
Grey rather than white, a pale shade of grey.		V	5	-1	1
[*Pause.*]		P	5	1	-1
Tattered.		V	5	-1	1
[*Pause.*]		P	5	1	-1
A tangle of tatters.		V	5	-1	1
[*Pause.*]		P	5	1	-1
Watch it pass—		V	5	-1	1
[*Pause.*]		P	5	1	-1
—watch her pass before the candelabrum, how its flames, their light…		V	5	-1	1
like moon through passing rack.		V	5	-1	0
[*Pause.*]		P	5	1	-1

Table 4 *(continued)*

Soon then after she was gone, as though never there, began to walk,		V	5	-1	1
up and down, up and down, that poor arm.		V	5	-1	0
[*Pause.*]		P	5	1	-1
At nightfall.		V	5	-1	1
[*Pause.*]		P	5	1	-1
That is to say, at certain seasons of the year, during Vespers.		V	5	-1	1
[*Pause.*]		P	5	1	-1
Necessarily.		V	5	-1	1
[*Pause.*		P	5	1	-1
Resumes pacing.	Length 1	L	4	4	3
		L	3	4	0
		L	2	4	0
		L	1	4	0
		L	0	4	0
		L	-1	4	0
		L	-2	4	0
		L	-3	4	0
halts facing front at L.		H	-4	6	11
Pause.]		P	-4	1	13
Old Mrs Winter, whom the reader will remember,		V	-4	-1	1
old Mrs Winter, one late autumn Sunday evening, on sitting down to supper with her daughter after worship,		V	-4	-1	0
after a few half-hearted mouthfuls laid down her knife and fork and bowed her head.		V	-4	-1	0
What is it, Mother, said the daughter,		V	-4	-1	0
a most strange girl, though scarcely a girl any more…		V	-4	-1	0
[Brokenly.]… dreadfully un—…		B V	-4	17	-18
[*Pause.* Normal voice.]		P	-4	1	17
What is it, Mother, are you not feeling yourself?		V	-4	-1	1
[*Pause.*]		P	-4	1	-1
Mrs W. Did not at once reply.		V	-4	-1	1
But finally, raising her head and fixing Amy—		V	-4	-1	0
the daughter's given name, as the reader will remember—		V	-4	-1	0
raising her head and fixing Amy full in the eye she said—		V	-4	-1	0
[*Pause.*] —		P	-4	1	-1
she murmured, fixing Amy full in the eye she murmured,		V	-4	-1	1
Amy did you observe anything strange at Evensong?		V	-4	-1	0
Amy: No, Mother, I did not.		V	-4	-1	0
Mrs W: Perhaps it was just my fancy.		V	-4	-1	0

Table 4 *(continued)*

Amy: Just what exactly, Mother, did you perhaps fancy this… strange thing was you observed?		V	-4	-1	0
[*Pause.*]		P	-4	1	-1
Mrs W: You yourself observed nothing … strange?		V	-4	-1	1
Amy: No, Mother, I myself did not, to put it mildly.		V	-4	-1	0
Mrs W: What do you mean, Amy, to put it mildly?		V	-4	-1	0
Amy: I mean, Mother, that to say I observed nothing… strange is indeed to put it mildly.		V	-4	-1	0
For I observed nothing of any kind, strange or otherwise.		V	-4	-1	0
I saw nothing, heard nothing, of any kind.		V	-4	-1	0
I was not there.		V	-4	-1	0
Mrs W: Not there?		V	-4	-1	0
Amy: Not there.		V	-4	-1	0
Mrs W: But I heard you respond.		V	-4	-1	0
[*Pause.*]		P	-4	1	-1
I heard you say Amen.		V	-4	-1	1
[*Pause.*]		P	-4	1	-1
How could you have responded if you were not there?		V	-4	-1	1
[*Pause.*]		P	-4	1	-1
How could you possibly have said Amen if, as you claim, you were not there?		V	-4	-1	1
[*Pause.*]		P	-4	1	-1
The love of God, and the fellowship of the Holy Ghost, be with us all, now, and for evermore. Amen.		V	-4	-1	1
[*Pause.*]		P	-4	1	-1
I heard you distinctly.		V	-4	-1	1
[*Pause.*		P	-4	1	-1
	Length 2—3 steps—	R	-3	-4	4
		R	-2	-4	0
		R	-1	-4	0
halts without facing front.		H	-1	6	-11
Long pause.		LP	-1	-15	-14
	Length 2—6 steps—	R	0	-4	15
		R	1	-4	0
		R	2	-4	0
		R	3	-4	0
		R	4	-4	0
halts facing front at R.		H	5	6	-11
Long pause.]		LP	5	-15	-14
Amy.		V	5	-1	-15

Table 4 *(continued)*

[*Pause*. No louder.]		P	5	1	-1
Amy.		V	5	-1	1
[*Pause*.]		P	5	1	-1
Will you never have done… revolving it all?		V	5	-1	1
[*Pause*.]		P	5	1	-1
It?		V	5	-1	1
[*Pause*.]		P	5	1	-1
It all.		V	5	-1	1
[*Pause*.]		P	5	1	-1
In your poor mind.		V	5	-1	1
[*Pause*.]		P	5	1	-1
It all.		V	5	-1	1
[*Pause*.]		P	5	1	-1
It all.		V	5	-1	1
[*Pause*.		P	5	1	-1
Fade out on strip. All in darkness.		FD	5	10	10
Pause.		P	5	1	10
IV: Chime even a little fainter still.		C	10	-9	-7
Pause for echoes.		P	10	1	7
Fade up to even a little less still on strip.		FU	10	-10	-9
No trace of MAY.		N	10	-20	19
Hold ten seconds.		LP, LP	10	-18	-19
Fade out.]		FD	10	10	-16

Table 5. Parsing of *Footfalls* (Second Pass)

<table>
<tr><th>Section I</th><th>Section II</th><th>Section III</th><th>Section IV</th></tr>
<tr><td>-FU</td><td>-FU</td><td>-FU</td><td>-FU</td></tr>
<tr><td>-</td><td>-</td><td>-</td><td>-</td></tr>
<tr><td>*WU</td><td>#SU</td><td>#SU</td><td>≈-FU</td></tr>
<tr><td>*</td><td>1#</td><td>1#</td><td>-</td></tr>
<tr><td>*WU</td><td>#SU</td><td>]</td><td></td></tr>
<tr><td>*</td><td>2#</td><td>*WU</td><td></td></tr>
<tr><td>#SU</td><td>#SU</td><td>*</td><td></td></tr>
<tr><td>1#</td><td>3#</td><td>#SU</td><td></td></tr>
<tr><td>#SU</td><td>#SU</td><td>1#</td><td></td></tr>
<tr><td>2#</td><td>4#</td><td>|</td><td></td></tr>
<tr><td>#SU</td><td>#SU</td><td>#SU</td><td></td></tr>
<tr><td>3#</td><td>5#</td><td>1#</td><td></td></tr>
<tr><td>|</td><td>#SU</td><td>#SU</td><td></td></tr>
<tr><td>|</td><td>6#</td><td>2#</td><td></td></tr>
<tr><td>#SU</td><td>#SU</td><td>#SU</td><td></td></tr>
<tr><td>1#</td><td>7#</td><td>3#</td><td></td></tr>
<tr><td>#SU</td><td>#SU</td><td>|</td><td></td></tr>
<tr><td>2#</td><td>8#</td><td>#SU</td><td></td></tr>
<tr><td>#SU</td><td>#SU</td><td>1#</td><td></td></tr>
<tr><td>*WU</td><td>9#</td><td>|</td><td></td></tr>
<tr><td>*3#</td><td>#SU</td><td>#SU</td><td></td></tr>
<tr><td>|*WU</td><td>10#</td><td>1#</td><td></td></tr>
<tr><td>*|</td><td>#SU</td><td>#SU</td><td></td></tr>
<tr><td>#SU</td><td>11#</td><td>2#</td><td></td></tr>
<tr><td>1#</td><td>#SU</td><td>#SU</td><td></td></tr>
<tr><td>|</td><td>12#</td><td>3#</td><td></td></tr>
<tr><td>#SU</td><td>#SU</td><td>]</td><td></td></tr>
<tr><td>1#</td><td>13#</td><td>*WU</td><td></td></tr>
<tr><td>|</td><td>#SU</td><td>*</td><td></td></tr>
<tr><td>#SU</td><td>14#</td><td>#SU</td><td></td></tr>
<tr><td>1#</td><td>#SU</td><td>1#</td><td></td></tr>
<tr><td>#SU</td><td>15#</td><td>|</td><td></td></tr>
<tr><td>2#</td><td>|</td><td>#SU</td><td></td></tr>
<tr><td>#SU</td><td>#SU</td><td>1#</td><td></td></tr>
<tr><td>3#</td><td>1#</td><td>#SU</td><td></td></tr>
<tr><td>#SU</td><td>#SU</td><td>2#</td><td></td></tr>
<tr><td>4#</td><td>2#</td><td>#SU</td><td></td></tr>
<tr><td>#SU</td><td>|*WU</td><td>3#</td><td></td></tr>
<tr><td>5#</td><td>*|</td><td>#SU</td><td></td></tr>
<tr><td>#SU</td><td>|*WU</td><td>4#</td><td></td></tr>
<tr><td>6#</td><td>*</td><td>#SU</td><td></td></tr>
<tr><td>#SU</td><td>|</td><td>5#</td><td></td></tr>
<tr><td>7#</td><td>|</td><td>#SU</td><td></td></tr>
<tr><td>#SU</td><td>|</td><td>6#</td><td></td></tr>
<tr><td>8#</td><td>|</td><td>#SU</td><td></td></tr>
</table>

Table 5 *(continued)*

#SU	|	7#	
9#	|	|	
#SU	|	#SU	
10#	|	1#	
#SU	|	#SU	
11#	|	2#	
#SU	|	#SU	
12#	|	3#	
|	|	]	
#SU	|	*WU/2*	
1#	|	#SU	
|	|	1#	
|	|	|	
|	|	|	
|	|	|	
#SU	#SU	#SU	
1#	1#*WU	1#	
#SU	*|	#SU	
2#	|	2#	
#SU	#SU	|	
3#	1#*WU	|	
WU/2	#SU	#SU	
#SU	2#	1#	
1#	#SU	|	
|	3#*	|	
|	-FU	|	
|	-	#SU	
]		1#	
WU/2		#SU	
*WU		2#	
≈*|		|	
|		|	
|		|	
#SU		|	
1#		|	
#SU		|	
2#		|	
#SU		|	
3#		|	
≈*		#SU	
-FU		1#	
-		#SU	
		2#	
		#SU	
		3#	
		#SU	

Table 5 *(continued)*

		4#	
		]	
		#SU	
		1#	
		]	
		≈WU	
		]]	
		≈WU	
		]#SU	
		1##SU	
		2#	
		#SU	
		3#	
		#SU	
		4#	
		#SU	
		5#	
		#SU	
		6#	
		#SU	
		7#	
		#SU	
		8#	
		#SU	
		9#	
		#SU	
		10#	
		]	
		-FU	
		-	

Table 6. Parsing of *Footfalls* (Third Pass)

Section I	Section II	Section III	Section IV
-	-	-	-
*	#	#	%
*	#	%	-
#	#	*	
#	#	#	
#	#	%	
%	#	#	
%	#	#	
#	#	#	
#	#	%	
#	#	#	
*	#	%	
%	#	#	
*	#	#	
%	#	#	
#	#	%	
%	%	*	
#	#	#	
%	#	%	
#	%	#	
#	*	#	
#	%	#	
#	%	#	
#	*	#	
#	&	#	
#	&	#	
#	&	%	
#	&	#	
#	&	#	
#	&	#	
#	&	%	
%	#	*/	
#	*	#	
&	%	&	
#	%	#	
#	#	#	
#	*	%	
*/	#	%	
#	#	#	
&	-	&	
%		#	
*/		#	
*		&	
&		&	

Table 6 *(continued)*

#		&	
#		#	
#		#	
*		#	
		#	
		%	
		#	
		%	
		*/	
		%	
		*/	
		%	
		#	
		#	
		#	
		#	
		#	
		#	
		#	
		#	
		#	
		#	
		%	
		-	

Notes

Chapter 1. Introduction

1. I will use this term, which Henning 1988 coined, several times in this work.

2. This video (and there may well be others), k. d. lang's "Constant Craving," off of her 1992 album, *Ingénue*, contains the single-tree set and many of the more memorable scenes from *Godot*, including that in which Didi and Gogo exchange hats (though a third person is introduced in the video), the hanging scene, and even Lucky's speech (in mime). I call this an iconic use of the play, since no attempt is made to identify it with any literary work; the play is simply utilized for its powerful archetypally allusive imagery. Thus it seems Mihalyi's words more than a quarter-century ago were prophetic: "[F]rom a work of art, it *[Godot]* becomes an almost disassociated mythological symbol in its own right" (1966, 329).

3. A quick search of the MLA on CD-ROM reveals a staggering 1,171 articles on Beckett, counting only the years between January 1980 and August 1994. As for books, Indiana University, for example, maintains a collection of 600-odd books *about* Beckett (not including the author's work). Although several of these are duplicate copies, the number is nonetheless remarkable.

4. These include the essays in *The World of Samuel Beckett*, ed. Joseph H. Smith (Baltimore: Johns Hopkins University Press, 1991), as well as parts of Knowlson and Pilling 1980.

5. See, for example, Ruby Cohn's famous 1973 publication, *Back to Beckett*, and Abbott 1990.

6. Examples include Heise 1992, 245–69, and Nealon 1988.

7. A few of these are: Trezise 1990; Connor 1988; Butler and Davis, 1990; J. H. Smith 1991; and Bove 1982, 185–221 (this work , as with others listed, overlaps with the previous category).

8. Though there has not been a great amount of work devoted specifically to this subject, Laughlin 1987 is a strong example of reader/audience response theory directed at Beckett's dramatic work.

9. Garner 1993 is an attempt to revitalize this particular critical slant, as well as to bring it into a dialogue with postmodernist/deconstructivist readings of Beckett's work, readings that often place themselves in opposition to the "old" phenomenological readings. Some other examples of a phenomenological reading of Beckett's work include Chabert 1982; Robbe-Grillet 1965; Lawley 1983; and Gontarski 1985.

10. An interesting occurrence of this occurs in Saltz 1992, when, in chapter 4, he uses *Ohio Impromptu* as example, indicating the "illocutionary force in performance" of L's knocks on the white deal table (p. 222).

11. See, for instance, Helsa 1971 and Dearlove 1982.

12. See, for example Hwang 1993. A less successful work is Alter 1987, which is so abstracted and circular that little of significance to the play (or semiotics, for that matter) is gained.

13. An excellent and far-ranging collection of essays on Beckett and mythological structures appear in Burkman 1987.

14. For example, in *The Theatre of the Absurd*, Martin Esslin compares the child Clov spies in *Endgame* to the Buddha (1969, 50).

15. Foster 1989. Additionally, Doll 1987 makes explicit reference to the Zen koan in relation to Beckett's fiction and drama.

16. Early examples of these include Schlossberg 1973 and parts of E. Levy 1980. Later ones include Montgomery 1991 and Howe 1983.

17. Work like this creates "a narrative (or narratives) which is (are) non-linear, moving back and forth in local eddies and swirls, sometimes against the macro flow of the piece, following now one stream, now another, but always edging towards the alluvial plain where the currents run together" (Hancock, forthcoming, 3).

18. This of course refers to a famous Zen aphorism that claims that those who mistake the pointing finger for the moon itself—those who mistake the dogma and trappings of Zen for its real essence—are doomed to live forever in suffering and illusion.

19. This is not to say, of course, that everyone has the same way of understanding the universe. The generalization is intended merely as shorthand for the causal, dualistic mode of thinking that most Westerners (and indeed, most people) generally maintain.

Chapter 2. Zeno, Zen, and $z^2 + c$

1. Religio-philosophy is an awkward term, but Buddhism, Taoism, and especially Zen cannot be described simply in terms of religion or philosophy. These systems, as should become more clear, combine the mysticism and faith of religion with the speculative reasoning of philosophy. For a more complete study of Zen, there are many fine books in English or in English translation. Among them, the works of the "founding fathers" of Zen, Dogen and Hakuin, are invaluable, as is Suzuki 1949.

2. Though these men, as well as most of the other early Zen (or Ch'an) Buddhists were from China, I have chosen to use the Japanese pronunciation of their names, as these forms are the ones most familiar to the Western reader.

3. This is in opposition to religious Taoism, which focuses a great deal on alchemy and such and is now not much more than an historical curiosity.

4. Because of the unique structure of this work, references are to verse number, as opposed to page number. However, as each verse is approximately one page, this reference system is, for all practical purposes, a page reference.

5. Loy attempts a definition of this important term: "They *[Sunya* and *Sunyata]* derive from the Sanskrit root *su*, which means 'to be swollen,' both like a hollow balloon and like a pregnant woman; therefore the usual English translation 'empty' and 'emptiness' must be supplemented with the notion of 'pregnant with possibilities.' . . . Rather than *Sunyata* being solely a negative concept, however, Nagarjuna emphasizes that it is only because everything is *Sunya* that any change, including spiritual transformation, is possible" (1992, 233).

6. This obviously has important connections with deconstruction theory and Derrida's use of the terms "play" and "slippage" to represent the ultimate indeterminacy of language. Though he generally sticks to the problems of abstracted sender-receiver communication (à la information theory) rather than the slippage between language and object, the question of

what and whether reality of any sort can be conceptualized to some extent follows Derrida's line of reasoning. We will have reason in later chapters to refer again to this comparison.

7. This is a complex issue, however, as the state of satori consists of many levels, and, depending on which Zen school one refers to, satori may begin the moment one really applies oneself to zazen (the quiet seated meditation interposed with periodic questioning from the master). Thus, there is need for instruction and guidance all along the "path" to enlightenment.

8. The similarity between Zen—particularly Dogen's take on it—and Socrates' admonition to live a reflective, examined life is striking; this point has not escaped many modern philosophers who deal with Zen Buddhism.

9. Zazen, or seated Zen meditation (as Zen literally means meditation), is a foundation of Zen itself. Externally, this practice consists of periods of quiet seated meditation punctuated by interviews with a Zen master. The meditation is, however, not intended to be relaxing, as the novitiate must concentrate wholly on a koan (Zen riddle) or other difficult issues; neither is the interview with the master necessarily a pleasant experience—often the student has to be dragged forcibly to the master's chamber, his fear of the questions he will be asked exceeding his willpower.

In his *Shobogenzo*, Dogen gives what is considered the classic definition of the internal focus of zazen—an excerpt of which follows:

> For *sanzen* [or doing zazen as instructed by a master], a quiet room is suitable. Eat and drink moderately. Cast aside all involvements and cease all affairs. Do not think good or bad. Do not administer pros and cons. Cease all movements of the conscious mind, the gauging of all thoughts and views. Have no designs on becoming a Buddha. *(Sanzen)* has nothing whatever to do with sitting or lying down. . . .
>
> Once you have adjusted your posture, take a deep breath, inhale and exhale, rock your body right and left and settle into a steady, immobile sitting position. Think of not thinking. How do you think of not-thinking? Without thinking. This in itself is the essential art of zazen.
>
> The zazen I speak of is not learning meditation. It is simply the Dharma-gate of repose and bliss, the practice-realization [which Kasulis translates as cultivation-authentication] of totally culminated enlightenment. It is the manifestation of ultimate reality. (Waddell and Masao 1973, 122–23)

With the classic rejection of categories so indicative of Zen, Dogen characterizes zazen as seated meditation, which has nothing to do with sitting—the true focus of Zen is not the external state, which like Zen literature is only a guide, but the internal movement toward "without-thinking."

10. Though this is a pre-Zen text, it is one of the most influential of the Buddhist sutras on the Zen sect and, as is obvious from its text, is very much in harmony with Zen thinking.

11. See appendix 1 of Ogata 1959 for a translation of the complete work.

12. Loy considers the paradox of this "non-empty" emptiness: "*[A] self which can never be objectively experienced*, because by definition it is the experiencer, *can just as well be described as Sunya*. However, then this will be not a nihilistic emptiness . . . but a *Sunyata* that can be cherished as the Buddha-nature essence of all things" (1988, 212; emphasis in the original).

13. An example of this is the famous poem by Basho:

Old pond—
and a frog-jump-in
water sound.

Note the concreteness of imagery, the perceiving self reduced to the acknowledgment that the frog's jump creates a "water sound."

14. This is, indeed, what the famous mathematician and philosopher Pierre Simon Laplace postulated was possible. In his own words, a large enough intelligence "would embrace in the same formula the movements of the greatest bodies of the universe and those of the lightest atom; for it, nothing would be uncertain and the future, as the past, would be present to its eyes" (quoted in Gleick 1987, 14).

15. This is related, to some extent, to Einstein's famous indication of the absolute relation between mass and energy: $E = mc^2$.

16. Thus, the famous case of the Schrödinger cat: a cat in a sealed box is either dead or alive. Without our intervention, its death/life quantum state is in flux. But as soon as we *do* something—by opening the box or by some other means of observation—we collapse the quantum state to *either* death *or* life. The experimenter here radically affects the outcome of the experiment.

17. It was this ramification of quantum mechanics and electrodynamics that led to Einstein's famous grievance with this new science: "God does not play dice with the universe."

18. See Gleick 1987, chap. 2, for a complete narrative of this discovery.

19. In fact, there can be many more than six dimensions in phase space: a great deal of mathematics associated with Chaos theory is concerned with multidimensional phase-space objects called manifolds (for many folds) that are stretched and folded like dough to create shapes with highly interesting characteristics (the Lorenz attractor and the Mandelbrot set, which we will deal with in a moment, can both be described by this math). While highly trained and gifted individuals can visualize these multidimensional spaces, it is really the computer, which can operate in any number of dimensions (limited only by memory requirements) through matrix algebra, that enables those less gifted to get a feel for the complex shapes in this multidimensional space. In order to make the situation more intuitive, in our examples, we will deal only with two- and three-dimensional phase spaces, which can be represented on paper.

20. Phase space is actually more general than this, as any time-dependent functions can be mapped onto a phase space. All that is really necessary is that the equations describing this system be reduced to the minimum number of degrees of freedom, or dimensions. In general, each degree of freedom is contained in an equation which is uncoupled, and when all equations are solved the motion of the particle can be traced. In the example of Lorenz's model for weather, there are three dimensions described by the three equations,

$$\frac{dx}{dt} = 10(y - x)$$

$$\frac{dy}{dt} = xz + 28x - y$$

$$\frac{dz}{dt} = xy - (8/3)z$$

where dn/dt is the time derivative (or motion) of a particle in the nth direction based on the position of the particle in the x, y, and z dimensions.

21. It is important to distinguish this as the Newtonian pendulum, as this model is highly abstracted from the behavior of a real pendulum. First, in the main example, we assume no friction, which never happens in the real world, and second (and of much more

import), because even a simple pendulum will, if driven hard enough, exhibit plenty of nonlinear behavior and will trace out a "strange" attractor of the Lorenzian variety. Thus, even the mainstay of Newtonian physics is simply a limited or special instance of Chaotic behavior.

22. I am indebted to Stevens 1989 for performing the complex math of the Runge-Kutta integration of the Lorenz equations, as well as for finding a very elegant algorithm for the iterations—which I made good use of in my program.

23. This experiment can be done using play-doh™, or the like. Simply take two small objects like candy sprinkles, place them next to each other, and stretch and fold the material many times. After enough stretching and folding, the sprinkles will end up in seemingly random places on the surface—yet where they end up is exactly determined by their initial placement and the operations you perform on the material.

24. For more information on this area of the science of complexity and the edge of Chaos, refer to Prigogine and Stengers 1984; Hayles 1990, esp. chaps. 1 and 4; Waldrop 1992; and Lewin 1992.

25. For a rigorous treatment of the subject, see for example Marion 1970, chaps. 3 ("Linear Oscillations") and 5 ("Nonlinear Oscillations"), or Goldstein 1980, chap. 6 ("Small Oscillations").

26. Hale puts the issue thus: "The problem of seeing in an indeterminate world has long preoccupied Samuel Beckett" (Hale 1987, 1).

27. Most of us have been introduced to the complex number plane in high school. It is a two-dimensional plane where the real half of the number is the horizontal axis and the imaginary half is the vertical axis. In general, a complex number takes the form, $x + iy$, where x is the real, y the imaginary, and i is the square root of -1. To find a point on the imaginary plane, we go across x places on the real line, then up y places on the imaginary line. Thus, the number $2 + 3i$ would look something like this:

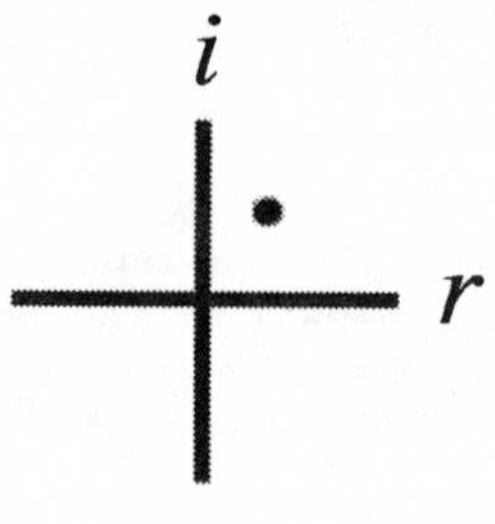

The only real trick to complex numbers is that, if they are squared (as in the Mandelbrot set), when a term containing i is multiplied by itself, the result is the *negative* of the numbers multiplied (as $\sqrt{-1} \bullet \sqrt{-1} = -1$).

28. These pictures of the Mandelbrot set were multicolor representations with medium resolution. The black portions constitute the set of points that do not "blow up" (the actual Mandelbrot set). Each shade of gray represents a group of points a certain "distance" outside the set; in other words, it is only after a certain number of iterations that the points blow up to infinity. At each point, the number of iterations required to force the point outside the set is equated to a shade of gray.

One very important limiting factor in representing the set is the number of calculations that must be performed to generate a decent picture of expansions of smaller portions of the set. The final image in this series of pictures of parts of the Mandelbrot set required upwards of 75 million iterations of the formula, $z \rightarrow z^2 - c$, and took over an hour to generate on a fast home computer. There are several books which contain excellent, highly detailed pictures of the set. See, for example, the plates between pages 114 and 115 in Gleick's book for high-resolution pictures generated by supercomputer. For a slightly less accurate, but beautifully colored picture, see the frontispiece to this work (the inaccuracy of this image results from the choice to reduce the number of iterations done to calculate the portion of the set; this results in a less detailed, more starkly rendered image).

29. For a complete treatment of information theory, see Shannon and Weaver 1949 and Brioullin 1956. Also see Hayles 1990, chap. 2, for the connection between Chaos and information theory.

30. The logic behind Zeno's paradox (altered so as to be additive) is as follows: if we take one grain of sand and drop another on top of it, the two cannot logically form a pile or "heap," as there are only two grains of sand now. This can be made into an equation with the following form: $S_{n+1} = S_n + 1$ (S_n being the grains of sand already on the ground and 1 being the next grain added, producing S_{n+1} grains of sand). As $S_2 = S_1 + 1 = 1 + 1 = 2$ grains does not logically constitute a pile and we can project this equation out for an arbitrarily large value of n, it is logically impossible for the equation—adding one more grain of sand to the group—to produce a pile of sand. And yet, eventually a pile is produced.

31. Additionally, deconstruction and Chaos theory have iteration in common: "repetition and iterability form a central part of Derrida's critique of phonocentrism" (Connor 1988, 126).

32. Phenomenology, however, is not unrelated to our focus in this work: Zen and other forms of Eastern mysticism have been related to the West's phenomenological models in recent books including Nagatomo 1992 and Kasulis, Ames, and Dissanayake 1993. These works indicate a strong relationship between this branch of Western philosophy/psychology and religio-philosophies like Zen in their centralizing the body-as-interface with the world. This foregrounding of the physical body over (as mediator) the mind places phenomenology and Zen (etc.) in stark contrast to much of Western philosophy and religion, which postulates supremacy of the mind.

Interestingly enough, this new overlapping of Eastern mysticism and Western phenomenology also brings Chaos theory into play. Nagatomo 1992 examines a recent theory of the body brought forth by Yuasa Yasuo, which constructs the human body as a series of four quasi-electrical circuits ranging from the "sensory-motor" circuit to the "unconscious quasi-body" circuit. All of these circuits rely on an iterative feedback loop of a sort that controls and directs the body (and mind) in future events. As Nagatomo puts it, "This self-contained system [of circuits] suggests that the body embodies a self-controlling mechanism, that is, biofeedback" (1992, 62). This "biofeedback" is a point of direct contact between Yasuo's phenomenological theory and Chaos theory: as the body here uses an iterative loop to control movement, emotions, and self-awareness, so the fractal form or Chaotic computer program utilizes iterative feedback to control future events and movement.

CHAPTER 3. WAITING IN *GODOT*

1. Interestingly, in light of the connections between Beckett's theater and the Japanese Noh, Paul Claudel states (roughly translated from the French), "In Western drama, something happens, in Noh, someone comes" (1965, 1167). As Yasunari Takahashi points out, however, *Godot* is a negation of both these norms (1983, 99).

2. As described in more detail in chapter 2, the term "lack" is here used technically,

as it is related to the Sanskrit term *sunyata*, or "emptiness." Therefore the lack described here is a feeling of insecurity in the ego when it senses that it may consist of nothing beyond this *sunyata*.

3. As Beckett put it, "I am interested in the shape of ideas even if I do not believe in them. . . . It is the shape that matters" (Hobson 1956, 153). He thus gives precedence to pattern over meaning, a fact which is very interesting in light of Chaos theory.

4. The question becomes, who is trying to remember? Is it the characters within the play, or is it the actors who, during the run of the show, *were* present and doing the same things the night before?

5. Nealon here uses Godot in a limited sense: "he" is equivalent to the modernist ideal of an all-encompassing metaphysics, an absolute conceptual system that self-sufficiently "explains" the multiplicity of life and art. The associative violence of a monistic metaphysics notwithstanding, it seems too limiting to render Godot in such a single-sided manner. More accurately, it is the characters' *waiting* for Godot that attempts to inscribe the fragmented universe within these bounds.

6. As noted in chapter 2, Laplace conceived of a computerlike intelligence that would be capable of "knowing" the course of a deterministic universe for all time.

7. To reiterate, the two main findings of quantum physics (at least for our purposes) derive from the Heisenberg uncertainty principle. The first—that we cannot know all information for a given system—rules out a deterministic universe. The second—that an experiment interferes with the evolution of a system—nullifies the supposed separation between experiment and experimenter (better yet, between subject and object).

8. Once again, a nonlinear equation is one in which a variable is raised to a power greater than 1. A classic example is the equation of a parabola: $y = x^2 + c$, where x^2 is the nonlinear term. Only a very small subset of these equations is completely solvable.

9. This is not completely true, as many great mathematicians have given analytic proofs of Chaos theory's more important findings. The visual/graphical is, however, an extremely powerful experimental tool for this science.

10. *Footfalls*, with its small size and formal structure, allows a more specific look at this equivalence. See chapter 6 for this study.

11. This is evident, for example, in the final moment of each act: the second act "simply exchanges the speakers of the ending of act 1" (Burkman 1986, 50), as Estragon here initiates the exchange, "Well, shall we go? Yes, let's go."

12. This analogy is more comprehensible if we place ourselves in the experiment. If we sit on the rock, it seems permanent and stationary; if we float with the river, the rock rises and vanishes like smoke.

13. See, for example, Houedard 1987 or Buning 1992.

14. This is not to suggest, of course, that there is always this pairing—merely that in an amazing percentage of his plays, this doubling occurs.

15. This mechanical nature is obvious when Pozzo breaks into the beginning of Lucky's "lecture":

> LUCKY: On the other hand with regard to—
> POZZO: Stop! (Lucky stops.) Back! (Lucky moves back.) Stop! (Lucky stops.) Turn! (Lucky turns toward auditorium.) Think!
>
> (28)

At which point, Lucky starts over.

16. Refer to chapter 7, on *Ohio Impromptu*, for a more complete look at the koanlike mirroring that takes place in Beckett's plays.

17. See Gleick 1987, 73, for more on the proof.

18. Yet even this mess has order in it. For one thing, the "noise" is contained within well-defined boundaries; for another, small ordered patches appear spontaneously amid the chaos. Also, as Yorke proved for this type of equation, there is a period three solution at the point indicated.

19. The *Tao Te Ching* is obviously not a Zen text, but, as discussed in chapter 2, Taoist thought directly influenced the development of the Ch'an (Zen) sect.

20. Interestingly, Hayles makes this statement in the context of Chaos theory, not Zen.

21. This point of view makes some sense if we consider that, if I repeat the *exact* message to you many many times, you will gain no new information with each repetition (as the message is completely predictable). Thus, this repeated message, which has *meaning* each time I say it, ceases to carry *information* after the first few repetitions.

22. This speech "offers a vision of the wisdom of the ages become incoherent in the face of a universe that is wasting away, the single surety being that man too 'wastes and pines wastes and pines'" (Burkman 1986, 36; the embedded quotation from Beckett is from Beckett 1954, 29).

23. The devaluation of the allusive will be taken up at greater length—for obvious reasons—in our discussion of *Happy Days*.

24. A Cantor dust, also known as the "middle-third" set, is derived from the simple premise that if we take a line and cut out the middle third, then take each of these two lines and cut out the middle third of each of these, and continue to repeat this on smaller and smaller scales, we will eventually reach a "dust" of fine points separated from their neighbor by apparently random distances. But the distance between sets of points will always look the same, no matter what magnification we view them under. As the computer printer—as well as our eyes—has a limited resolution, we see this dust as a series of points on the paper, but the scale-invariance of the separation is obvious even from this. The set is self-similar because it repeats the same pattern exactly over every scale of magnification. In later chapters we will deal further with Cantor dust.

25. See chapter 6 for a look at how *Footfalls* also follows this self-similar patterning.

26. This legend states that in a far corner of the universe, there is a net, infinitely long and wide, which has, at each of the intersections of the netting, a polished ruby attached (thus there are also an infinite number of these rubies). Because of their polished translucence, each ruby in the net reflects and absorbs within it every other ruby in the net, thus reflecting all other points of the net. The purpose of this legend is to demonstrate that every point in "being-time" reflects every other—in an acausal manner. It is thus an error to view each moment as separate and causal.

27. Due to a failure of language to describe this state of dynamic presence, there seems to be no other choice but to use the loaded term, need—however, need in this sense must be understood as being without desire, merely existence (though actually there is also a great deal of need in the normal sense of the word).

28. Interestingly, Kolve 1967 has done a similar job of relating the final moments of *Godot* to Christianity's Holy Saturday (between Good Friday and Easter Sunday), a day when nothing can be known with certainty any more, a day when doubt takes over the faithful one's being.

29. This state, I will show, grows more and more explicit in Beckett's later plays.

Chapter 4. End of Zeno's Game?

1. Most notably, Hamm quotes Prospero directly after thwarting his father's request for a sugar-plum: "Our revels now are ended" (Beckett 1958, 56). See Drew 1993 for a much more detailed study of the intersection of the two playwrights.

2. As noted in chapter 3, Beckett's plays often provide physical manifestation of existential dilemma. Thus, supposedly opposite characteristics obtain for pairs of characters, distinctions that are, however, destabilized in any essentialist sense.

3. This reading is, of course, similar to the psychological reading of *Endgame* (see, for example, Kenner 1961), in which the characters are parts of a single "mind." Here, however, the characters are not parts of some whole, but simply fragments of being that exist within the confines of the "shelter."

4. Susan Maughlin, for example, states that Clov is a "nearly full-grown" character creation of Hamm's (1987, 91).

5. Pountney makes a similar observation, but with a focus that is important to our later analysis of this metaphor: "Certain *limited* actions recur, with a deliberation which has caused them to be compared with the moves in a game of chess" (1988, 50; my emphasis). It is the concept of an iteration of a limited palette of actions which links *Endgame* not only with a game of chess but also with the iteration of a formula in Chaos theory.

6. Although this psychological model of *Endgame* falls outside the scope of this work, there will be occasion to utilize some of this metaphor's important results. For an early observation of the import of this metaphor on the play, see Kenner 1961, 155.

7. See chapter 2 for more on this topic.

8. As noted in chapter 2, entropy is the tendency a system has to convert energy into a "useless" form where no usable work can be performed with it. Thus, according to the classical paradigm, in a largely entropic system little work can be performed and little can be created.

9. A partial explanation for the paradoxical nature of order arising from highly disordered systems which are obeying the second law of thermodynamics is found in the constant influx of energy any arbitrary system—a tree, a planet, the solar system—receives from outside.

> In the real world, atoms and molecules are almost never left to themselves, not completely; they are almost always exposed to a certain amount of energy and material flowing in from the outside. And if that flow of energy and material is strong enough, then the steady degradation demanded by the second law [of thermodynamics] can be partially reversed. Over a limited region, in fact, a system can spontaneously organize itself into a whole series of complex structures. (Waldrop 1992, 33)

Though this summary still begs the question of *how* a system organizes itself, it is important to note that for *Endgame*, the consequence is that entropy and decay are by no means a one-way path to death and disorder.

10. Helsa goes on to add what he calls references to tennis to his list of gaming metaphors: "'Deuce': existence is like that point in tennis where advantage is to neither player and the game is at a stalemate" (1971, 151). The reference to "deuce" can also, however, act as a continued reference to a game of cards like poker: references to a deuce are made near other card references, and the metaphor works just as well in the sense of being dealt a bad hand in poker (a deuce, or two, being the lowest card around). Though in the French, Hamm uses the term "égalité" (French for a deuce in tennis), the English version allows us to add another level to Hamm's reference. We may thus note that in the domain of metaphor and allusion as well, the play both moves toward and away from closure of meaning.

11. Other religions obviously follow this pattern as well. In original Christian teachings, for example, it is noted that a rich man has less chance of getting to heaven than a camel has of passing through the "eye of a needle"—a strong motivation for renouncing one's material belongings.

12. Loy contrasts the "Eastern" doubt with the Cartesian doubt that lies at the heart of modern Western philosophy:

> It would be interesting to contrast this "great doubt" with the Cartesian doubt that stands at the beginning of modern Western philosophy. Briefly, the main difference seems to be that Cartesian doubt is something the self *has*, whereas the great doubt becomes something the self *is*: the self becomes so preoccupied with its *koan* that it literally "forgets itself" in its puzzlement. So Cartesian doubt has the effect of reifying the sense of self, while the great doubt leads to the evaporation of that sense of self. (Loy 1988, 207)

13. While denial of causality may seem an indirect contradiction to the absolute causality of Chaos theory, we have seen in chapter 3 how these two views of the universe actually maintain the same relationship to the absolute: whether everything is completely relative or absolute, the variance, or bifurcation into opposites, cannot exist. Thus, whether "reality" is absolute or relative, distinctions into polarities are mere illusions—as long as we maintain that *everything* be essentially one or the other (they thus are effectively the same vision of the universe, merely under different guises).

14. Likewise, the characters themselves are "condensed and overdetermined. . . . Similar to the figures who people our dreams, they have absorbed meanings, signs, and properties from other characters as well as pure psychological or aesthetic functions" (Schwab 1984, 198).

15. The two are related through their "burial," and in their elegiac reverence of "yesterday," or "the old style." This relationship is interesting precisely because Nell is one of the first female characters in Beckett's drama, and Winnie, in the next major play Beckett writes, is the first of Beckett's leading stage women (excepting Maddy Rooney from the radio drama, *All That Fall*—though this, to some extent, is justified, as she is never physically manifested). Thus, parallels between the half-submerged Nell and her equally disabled husband and the sinking Winnie and her husband reveal a trend in Beckett's drama toward exploration of the unique interaction with the world pioneered by these two women.

16. The full text of Nell's quote, which contains the line, "But it's always the same thing," is also very interesting in light of information theory: repetition of anything, even a joke at which "we laugh, with a will, in the beginning," eventually loses its "surprise," or information value. As the joke is repeated, information is sacrificed, and "we don't laugh any more."

17. Nell's disappearance is made more explicit in early typescripts of the play. In typescript 1 (in The Ohio State University Library rare books collection), Nell explicitly dies at the end of act 1, her ash bin removed from stage before act 2 starts.

18. ". . . Hamm and Clov realize they are actors, that dialogue keeps them upon the stage; at times they fear the introduction of subplots, at others they speak of asides" (Bair 1990, 467).

19. It is interesting to question whether this fictional madman might be linked to a biographical source like Bram van Velde, on whom Beckett wrote an article, *La Peinture des van Velde, ou: le monde et le pantalon*, which contains in its title the joke Nagg tells in *Endgame* (Bair 1990, 347). Though an intriguing possibility, as a link like this might associate Beckett with Hamm (or Clov, as has been suggested), speculation like this would lead us too far afield.

20. The "halfway point," as we will see with other plays (notably *Footfalls* and *Ohio Impromptu*) is very significant for Beckett's drama, and, for a writer who creates works with the high degree of structure of Beckett's work, this placement is most likely conscious.

Endgame, even more than others, is carefully planned and laid out. Bair, for example, comments that *Endgame* was "Begun as an intellectual exercise" and that "This play marks the beginning of his [Beckett's] preoccupation with dramatic exactitude, his need to specify every nuance and gesture that may take place on his stage" (1990, 464).

Chapter 5. *Happy Days,* Minutes, Hours

1. From the manuscript and typescript collection held at The Ohio State University Library.

2. This is more specifically a "leftover" from the "old style" in the early manuscripts, in which a visible alarm clock is utilized as a means of waking Winnie. The obvious social implications of alarm clocks (getting up at a proper time to go to work, for example) create a more explicit contact with the world that "used to be" for the characters than does the vaguer, yet more horrifying "bell" that wakes her in the final version.

3. The original, as Beckett wrote out fully in a production notebook for *Glückliche Tage* (see Pountney 1988, 250), being Ophelia's lines from *Hamlet*: "O, woe is me / T'have seen what I have seen, see what I see!" (III.i.160–61).

4. The term *chaos* is here being used in a very different sense than elsewhere in this (and Lao Tzu's) work. Instead of using the term to indicate the richer a priori void that surrounds the moral and physical dichotomies, in this quote chaos stands for the disharmonious state of mankind when living far from the true path or Tao.

5. As Esslin points out, Beckett felt that "habit and routine was the cancer of time [and] social intercourse a mere illusion" (1969, 14), indicating Beckett's disgust with the way people hide—their heads buried like ostriches in the sands of time (cf. *Murphy*)—from the true horrors of life.

6. This "code of conduct" is, in many ways, specifically patriarchal. Thus, as we will explore later, Winnie is object as well as subject in this world.

7. Winnie's actions here in fact are something like a miniaturized version of Clov's ladder episode at the beginning of *Endgame*.

8. To some extent, this reduction of scale has already started in the banana routine that opens *Krapp's Last Tape*.

9. Hayles says of Feigenbaum's discovery of the universality of the approach to chaos, "The startling aspect of Feigenbaum's work was his discovery that despite the different operations performed by different nonlinear functions . . . their iterated paths approached chaos at the same rate and showed the same characteristic patterns of period doubling" (1990, 153). Thus, on whatever scale or in whatever system, Chaos arises in pretty much the same fashion.

10. These actions recall those of the narrator in *The Unnamable*, who sees characters and stories floating before his mind's eye.

11. For example, Winnie's cycling around sorrow in her quotations—"woe woe is me" (10) and "oh something lasting woe" (14)—and the reduction of the "quality" (or fame) and length of her quotations—by the end, she is quoting tiny, nearly unrecognizable fragments of Charles Wolfe.

12. Actually, the Koch curve is more often generated from a triangle (and thus the figure is often termed the Koch "snowflake"), but, as a line segment is effectively one side of a triangle, and the picture generated is easier to understand and looks more like an earthly shoreline, I have chosen to model the figure in this fashion. Also, as I am most interested in the shape of the boundary line formed by the Koch curve, I have chosen to use only the upper two-thirds of each triangle instead of filling in each triangle completely.

13. Mandelbrot defends this similarity, stating that an actual coastline is constructed

by self-similar actions (erosion, tidal movement, etc.) that "naturally" have noise in them, and thus each real coastline is a unique intermixture of constant forces over all scales and random fluctuations in these forces (Mandelbrot 1983, 210).

14. In a level 6 Koch curve (which has 4,096 line segments) with only a 1 percent chance of one type of noise (far less than in the pictures above), the chance of repeating the figure exactly would be about 1 in 7.5×10^{17}. In other words, I would have to redraw the figure nearly 80 quadrillion times in order to have a realistic chance of reproducing the same pattern. If I could draw one curve every second, it would take about 24 million years to have a good statistical chance of redrawing the exact figure. Statistics like this indicate why human beings, whose genetic codes are all extremely similar, never look alike.

15. This random, generative power of quotation is an essentially positive aspect of language according to deconstruction: "Every sign, linguistic or non-linguistic, spoken or written (in the usual sense of this opposition), as a small or large unity, can be *cited*, put between quotation marks; thereby it can break with every given context, and engender infinitely new contexts in an absolutely nonsaturable fashion" (Derrida 1982, 320).

16. Beckett's notes for *Glückliche Tage*, which he directed at the Schiller Theater, Berlin, in 1971, provide the full line of poetry. See Pountney 1988, 250, for a facsimile of these notes.

17. All quotations from "Ode to a Nightingale" are from Abrams 1986, 819–22.

18. This of course brings to mind Clov's statement, "Then one day, suddenly, it ends, it changes" (Beckett 1958, 81), which, as noted, concerns the paradoxes inherent in trying to causally connect a "life."

19. It would carry us too far afield to explore fully the complex interaction between *Happy Days* and "Ode to a Nightingale," but this little fragment of analysis indicates the value of rereading the poem in terms of the play, as well as the other way around.

20. This reference is also confirmed by Beckett's notes for *Glückliche Tage*. See Pountney 1988, 250, for a facsimile of these notes.

21. The use here of a narrative scream followed by one on stage seems a definite precursor of Mouth's screams in *Not I*.

22. The paradox is as follows: Ulysses sets out on a voyage across the ocean in his ship, which just happens to be carrying replacement lumber for all the parts of the boat. As he and his crew sail along, first one, then another, piece of the ship becomes rotten from the water and is replaced by the fresh lumber they are carrying on board. Over time, all of the ship's original parts rot and are switched with the fresh parts. When, finally, Ulysses returns home, is he sailing the same ship in which he left port? Given that all of the cells in the human body are replaced about every seven years, can we be the same people today we were seven or more years ago?

23. Kant, in *A Prolegomena to Any Future Metaphysics*, formulates this concept of "being as perceiving" in a very clear fashion. Taking a positivist attitude about the conscious mind's workings (in stark contrast to the more skeptical Buddhist attitude), Kant indicates how, by laying down an arbitrary mental grid of time and space on the flow of the universe, we create meaning out of what is otherwise meaningless to us.

24. Actually, this claim is not entirely true for Winnie, as her use of the "old style"—the term "day," for example—already begins the process of conceptual categorization, since she thus places the present moment into a context of some deterministic succession of "happy days."

25. This identification of Zen and Chaos theory cannot be made naively: Chaos theory is still firmly rooted in the world of cause and effect, as well as the traditional Western thought that gives rise to it. Zen, on the other hand, would not only do away with causality but also with the notion of the self entirely (though on the other hand we have seen in previous chapters how these differing views merge). In this instance, both systems do agree

that the world is much "larger" (i.e., impossible to conceptualize) than is commonly thought, while at the same time, its "mystery" (or large-scale behavior) is intuitively obvious if perceived properly.

26. From typescript 1 of "Happy Days," contained in The Ohio State University Library rare books room.

27. At the same time, however, this rigid daily schedule is akin to the Buddhist monk's life in zazen, where sitting in meditation happens during large portions of the day. Thus, Winnie's routine produces nicely ambivalent signals about the dynamic interplay of the two modes of seeing the world around her.

28. One famous Zen anecdote is based on this taboo: "Two Zen monks came to a river which a woman was trying unsuccessfully to cross. The older of the monks, without hesitation, picked the woman up, carried her across the river, and set her down on the other side. After the two monks had walked on several miles, the younger monk turned to his elder and said, 'I can't believe you picked that woman up back there!' The first monk, on hearing this, laughed and said, '*I* put her down on the bank of the river—*you're* still carrying her!'"

29. Being an unconscious object of the male gaze is quite different from achieving a state of "preconsciousness," or nirvana. In the first, the female is excluded from any possible subjectivity, existing as an essentially inanimate object. In the second, subjectivity encompasses all distinctions, and there are effectively no objects. Winnie once again splits these two visions: "Winnie does admittedly display a habituated accommodation to societal pressures upon women to please the eye, amongst other requirements. Yet, though attentive to her bodily appearance, she clearly privileges to a greater extent her mental faculties . . ." (Bryden 1993, 88).

CHAPTER 6. ITERATIVE *FOOTFALLS,* "HOWEVER FAINT THEY FALL"

Portions of this chapter are adapted from Kundert-Gibbs 1995.

1. See Brater 1987, 60ff. for a more complete discussion of this image.

2. From a conversation between Billie Whitelaw and Beckett, August 1986. Quoted in ibid., 60.

3. There is, however, certainly a bow toward the (absence) of this relationship in *Not I*, in which Mouth bears a similar anger toward her mother for "sparing" her the "love such as normally vented on the . . . speechless infant" (Beckett 1984c, 216).

4. This is not to say, of course, that I have completely sidestepped the psychological (or even biographical), merely that the focus is shifted toward one of present images.

5. In his article, "Visual Fields in Beckett's Late Plays," Garner places too much emphasis on the visual in this play. Though he is correct in finding that words, for Beckett, are "increasingly subordinated to visual modes of address" (1987, 350) throughout this period, he draws the erroneous conclusion that "*Footfalls* is a drama of light . . . and of the imperceptible shadings which merge it with darkness" (358). It is obvious from the heightening of the aural element, as well as the importance of the "surrogate audience" positioning of the listener(s) that if *Footfalls*, as well as the other plays of this period, is a painterly "composition" (349), it is one done in aural as well as visual brush strokes.

6. This decentering occurs physically as well as metaphorically. In *Footfalls* and Beckett's other later plays, staging is always somewhat off-center (May's strip being "a little off center audience right" [Beckett 1984b, 239], for example). In *Quad*, the crux of the play rests in the four characters' need to avoid the center, or "danger zone" of the square they tread (Beckett 1984f, 293); and in *Ohio Impromptu*, we will find that even the distinction between center and "off-center" is blurred.

7. See Doll 1987, 74, for her work with Eliade, which focuses mostly on the temporal end of ritualized action.

8. This correlation is made all the more plausible by the close link between *That Time* and "Tintern Abbey" (Acheson 1987, 129).

9. Conversely, all time is redeemed in the sense that collapsing the object-existence of future and past negates such concepts as original sin and predestination (Boëthius, in his *Consolation of Philosophy*, argues this case at length).

10. This is an extrapolation of Eliade's work, as he never mentions Zen Buddhism in this context.

11. For Eliade, this implies a continual, continuous movement from the death of the "profane condition" to an "emerging" birth into the sacred (1957, 201, 69).

12. We have already seen how Mandelbrot "proved" that the length of one's ruler drastically affects the length of what one measures (a coastline, say); thus length is not invariant over scaling functions in a Chaotic system. The nonconservation of mass follows a similar line of reasoning.

13. The Cantor dust is generated by removing the middle third of a line segment, then removing the middle thirds of each of the resulting lines, and so on. Eventually, there is a "dust" of infinitesimally small points. The set has infinitely many points, but a total length of zero (see Gleick 1987, 92–93). Interestingly, this scheme of a discontinuous dust of points has been used recently by astrophysicists to explain the nonhomogeneous nature of the universe. Also see Hayles 1990, 155ff. for further discussion of fixed point symmetries and the Cantor dust.

14. This concept is, of course, related to the ancient Taoist (more generally, Chinese) idea of synchronicity, as related in the *I Ching* (Book of changes), which Carl Jung introduced to the West. In this framework, all events and objects, from smallest to largest, are linked acausally, each reflecting in some deep way all others. Thus the random (or chaotic) act of casting a diagram is a valid way of perceiving the flow of the universe, as this act mirrors goings-on in the rest of the universe.

15. This reference from a lecture by Carl Jung that Beckett attended has been so heavily used by critics, it almost needs no citation. However, for those interested, see Brater 1987, 64, or Knowlson and Pilling 1980, 222.

16. As Knowlson points out, the chime, fade-up and fade-down, each lasting an equal seven seconds according to Beckett's own notes (Anna McMullan 1993, 103), gives a progressive, cyclic structure to the entire play:

> The form of the play therefore becomes that of a series of circular revolutions, moving from one phase of absence to another, gradually fading away into less and less sharp definition and moving towards silence, stillness, and deepening darkness. (Knowlson and Pilling 1980, 226)

17. My specific metaphor. See chapter 6 for more extended use of this metaphor.

18. We will return shortly to deal with the "fictional," or narrative, element of the play.

19. I use the term *undramatic* more in the sense that the mother-daughter pair was not considered fit subject for theater than that the relationship was supposed to be in some metaphysical sense dull (though the two concepts must certainly be related).

20. As we will see, these problems are not fundamentally different than those facing the characters we see in the traditionally male role; instead, it is the focus that has shifted, necessitating and potentiating a new approach.

21. The Japanese position is effectively that the stage is "but a world" instead of the other way around. This reversal meshes well with our previous work about the universalizing tendencies of "lessness" in *Footfalls*.

22. The centrality of this relational context to Eastern thought is clearly revealed in Herrigel's master's statement: "[W]e would say that it [a child] was playing with [his toys] . . . were it not equally true that the things are playing with the child" (1953, 30).

23. The irony of writing these lines is not lost.

24. For a more detailed account of the evolution of this decomposition of *Footfalls*, please see the appendix.

25. If work revealing the underlying structure of the play seems somewhat unfounded and arbitrary, one need only consider with what mathematical precision Beckett himself planned permutative passages in his novels (including the famous "stone sucking" scene in *Molloy* and numerous passages in *Watt*), as well as how carefully he calculated timing and the number of revolutions May walks in *Footfalls* (see Pountney 1988, 283–86).

26. To visualize this pattern better, think of driving on a road with bumps spaced out on the road. As you drive along, you will encounter one bump, then another one second later, then another three seconds later, then another one second later, etc.

27. Thus, in order to filter out noise, one must establish a system of redundancy which "hops" the noisy bursts (see Gleick 1987, 91–92). This fact is utterly crucial to the workings of the modern, computer-dependent world: from fax machines and modems to hard drives and computer RAM, dependable data storage and transmission rely on accommodating this scale-invariant geometric relationship between order and disorder.

28. Notably, Billie Whitelaw discusses how her mother, shortly before dying (though not of Parkinson's disease), would also frantically pace the halls and then sit motionless for long periods of time (Beckett 1985).

29. This remarkable fact actually demonstrates the interdisciplinary paradigm shift taking place from the 1960s through the 1980s. In the main text (originally written in the early 1970s), Sacks wrestles, with a great deal of frustration, with patternings of behavior and overdriven response behavior for which he can find no model. When, in revisiting the subject in the late 1980s, Sacks utilizes Chaos theory, he is able to explicate his earlier patients' behavior with remarkable precision. During this same period, response to Sacks's work progressed from vilification to lionization, as others around him began to understand and to accept the new paradigm of Chaos theory. Even in a science as removed from fundamental physics as medicine, similar shifts were taking place in the way doctors perceived their universe.

30. This article, which presents the results of a study done in the early 1990s, utilizing the "theory of dynamical systems" to study various irregular movements, concludes that "the parkinsonian tremor is nonlinear and deterministic, even *chaotic*" (Gantert, Honerkamp, and Timmer 1992, abstract).

31. There is a bit of confusion about the number of steps in published versions of *Footfalls*. Beckett, during rehearsals for the first production, altered the number from seven to nine, and subsequent versions of the play should include this alteration. *The Collected Shorter Plays of Samuel Beckett* dictates that May's paces be nine (in the stage directions), but doesn't adjust the number of steps V counts as her daughter paces.

32. This is virtually a restatement of one of Beckett's favorite quotes (coined by Bishop Berkeley), *Esse est percipi*, which he uses in emblematic fashion in *Film*.

Chapter 7. What Is the Sound of *Ohio Impromptu*?

Portions of this chapter appeared in Kundert-Gibbs 1997.

1. As Takahashi has noted, one is reminded by this minimalization and abstraction of Japanese Noh theater, which reduces to essential movements and energy states a vast range

of human emotion and action. In this form of theater, "nothing happens, everything has already happened . . . but someone emerges out of an unknown country" (1993, 260). Here, as with Beckett, stillness and memory (often in the third person) are primary dramatic "actions."

2. Though I will not perform the same quasi-rigorous formulation of *Ohio Impromptu* as I did with *Footfalls*, there is good reason to believe that the superstructure of this play as well is effectively a strange attractor. Thus, the large surprise encoded in R's response to what he reads (as well as what he reads itself) shifts the play from one "arm" of a Lorenz-like attractor (if we assume a similar shape) to another.

3. As discussed briefly in previous chapters, an important Western parallel to this Zen (and Chaotic) re-visioning of the universe is the Husserlian (and post-Husserlian) theory of phenomenology. As noted, Garner has attempted to revitalize the use of this out of favor philosophy for the study of Beckett's drama, citing the problem of "scriptocentrism" that generally pertains to textual (structural *or* deconstructive) studies of Beckett's plays. In opposition to a linguistic study based on dissecting pieces of dramatic texts to show how they fit within a conceptual framework, "Phenomenology is the study of givenness . . . , of the world as it is lived rather than the world as it is objectified, abstracted, and conceptualized" (1993, 448); this is true whether the world is ours or the one we see on the stage.

4. This is (Kasulis's translation of) Dogen's term for the process of enlightenment, which *is* sitting in zazen. As previously discussed, Dogen, founder of the Soto sect of Zen, based his philosophy of zazen (or seated meditation) on the observation that zazen should not be understood as a means toward enlightenment—a means to an end (which causes waiting)—but instead should be considered enlightenment itself (if it is practiced correctly). "Consequently, the hallmark of Dogen's Zen is *shikantaza*—'nothing but sitting' or, more simply, 'just sitting'" (Kasulis 1981, 67). This twist on the practice of zazen implies that satori, or enlightenment, is a state that gradually builds up in the novitiate, the sudden "burst" or shock of awakening so familiar to Westerners (mostly from Rinzai stories) being only a final step in the long process of enlightenment. Although this difference between Soto and Rinzai schools of Zen is apparently small, it is very important, as the Great Doubt and Great Death are seen in different contexts. For Rinzai, the school that utilizes the koan as a cornerstone of its enlightenment process, the step from novitiate to enlightened one is very large, as the ego-consciousness is thrust off pretty much all at once. For Soto Zen, on the other hand, the years of practice a student goes through have already partially enlightened the novitiate, and thus (though the koan is sometimes utilized in Soto as well), the final movement to enlightenment is less dramatic or shocking. Being eclectic here, I consider the ostensibly long-term process of character enlightenment to have been achieved more or less in the Soto manner, while the audience's shorter, more deeply shocking (potential) movement toward enlightenment effectively arrives by way of the more intense Rinzai Great Doubt.

5. One can achieve this state of enlightenment accidentally—through a prereflective response to an intense aesthetic experience or an emergency situation, for example—as it is "the return to the normal human condition" (Deshimaru 1982, 55).

6. In this article, Doll notes the similarities between the koan and Beckett's later plays.

7. Suzuki has an appropriately metaphorical warning for such overzealous conceptualization: "Let the intellect alone, it has its usefulness in its proper sphere, but let it not interfere with the flowing of the life-stream. . . . The fact of flowing must under no circumstances be arrested or meddled with; for the moment your hands are dipped into it, its transparency is disturbed, it ceases to reflect your image which you have had from the very beginning and will continue to have to the end of time" (1949, 19). Like the river in R's narrative, we should be content to experience life's "joyous eddies."

8. Most, if not all of these hypotheses have been circulating throughout the critical literature for years.

9. The Yin-Yang, an ancient Oriental symbol, operates like the river-Isle image. It indicates at once the duality of the universe (the separate black and white halves of the circle) and its ultimate unity (the white and black dots on the opposite-colored fields, and the fact that the black and white halves are contained within a single circle). Things that our Western culture has taught us to be distinct, separate entities, even simple things like hot and cold, are in reality both two and one. They are two in the sense that they are not, in our usual frame of reference, conceptualized as "the same," and from a causal framework it is generally easier to think of them as separate or polar opposites; and they are one in the sense that it is only our mental activity—our consciousness—that separates them. As Kasulis puts it, the Zen master's teachings are usually aimed at making explicit "the relativity of all conceptualizations—even those which constitute the doctrines of the Buddhist tradition itself" (Kasulis 1981, 13). Under this radical relativity, even Buddhism's own teachings ultimately must be secondary to immediate experience—a point that, we will find, is also important to *Ohio Impromptu*.

10. A Westerner, D. E. Harding, who found Zen through an accidental encounter with the enlightened state, speaks in words that sound as if they could have come from the "worn volume" when he describes his experience: "What . . . happened was something absurdly simple. . . . For once, words really failed me. I forgot my name, my humanness, my thingness, all that could be called me or mine. . . . It was as if I had been born that instant, brand new, mindless, innocent of all memories" (1986, 1–2). In other words, he found himself free from the mental grid within which we normally try to force the ever changing world, and became one with everything as his "I-ness" dropped away. As Harding puts it, he was still himself, but he was no longer himSelf. What seems a complex paradox to the logical, conscious mind is, as Harding says, "absurdly simple" when the forebrain stops trying to figure it out. The listener and the reader are two and they are one; it is that complex—and that simple.

11. I use this term *interfering* here and hereafter in its technical sense: the interplay, constructive and destructive ("positive" and "negative"), between differing wave forms. An example would be ripples in a pond, which can merge to create larger waves or which can cancel each other, creating nodes of stillness.

12. A facsimile of the holograph, as well as of all the typescripts, is in the appendix of Beja, Gontarski, and Astier 1983.

13. Following the conventions set up in the book, "Bracketed words and phrases indicate deletions by S. B.; a blank space enclosed in parentheses within brackets indicates an indecipherable deletion" (ibid., 191). The full text of the poem is as follows:

I am out on leave. Thrown out on leave.
Back to time, they said, for 24 hours.
Oh my God, I said, not that.
Slip [into] on this shroud, they said, lest you catch your death of cold again.
Certainly not, I said
This cap, they said, for your [death's head] skull.
Definitely not, I said.
The New World outlet, they said, in the State of Ohio. We cannot be more
    precise. *Pause*.
Proceed straight to [Lima] the nearest campus, they said, and address them.
[Address] whom? I said.

The students, they said, and professors.
Oh my God, I said, not that.
Do not overstay your leave, they said, if you do not wish it to be extended.
Pause.
What am I to say? I said.
Be yourself, they said, [you're ( )] stay yourself.
Myself? I said. What are you insinuating?
[Yourself before, they said.]
Pause.
[And after.]
[*Pause.*]
[Not during? I said.]

(Ibid., 191–92)

14. Actually it is/was two: an older island upstream, which became part of the *Port du Gros-Caillou*, and a newer, man-made *Allée des Cygnes*. In this image, then, any simple linearity of past and present is effaced (see Astier 1982, 336–37).

15. Again, in Chaotic systems, it is this "roughness"—not length, mass or time—that is conserved.

16. To explicate the double entendre here: first, a nonrational (fractional) dimension is the characteristic of a fractal, or Chaotic form; and second, the attainment of this nonrational state is what Zen advocates and what L and R (etc.) apparently achieve by the end of the play.

17. Dark matter in the universe has been postulated for several decades (and discovered recently) as a means of "weighing down" the expanding universe sufficiently to cause its pieces eventually to fall back together, creating a cyclical series of "Big Bangs," regenerating the (a) universe in a constant, tidal motion. As this dark matter has been discovered, it has been found to be dispersed in a Chaotic manner: it is inconsistently and discontinuously placed about the universe, but on every scale it "looks" the same in its dispersal.

18. More accurately, the Julia set is a different expansion of the basic equation on the complex plane which is iterated to produce the Mandelbrot set: $z \rightarrow z^2 - c$. For Mandelbrot's set, we move the value of c around the complex plane, each time starting z at the value, $0 + i\,0$. For the Julia set, on the other hand, we take a single value of c (and thus one point in the Mandelbrot set), and vary the initial value of z over a certain range. Thus, while produced from the same equation, Julia and Mandelbrot sets are expanded along different "dimensions."

19. This, of course, is the punch line of the famous koan in which Joshu responds to the question, "Does a dog have Buddha-nature?" with a strident *"Mu!"* The commentary that follows this brief koan is as follows:

> *Mumon's comment*: To realize Zen one has to pass through the barrier of the patriarchs. Enlightenment always comes after the road of thinking is blocked. If you do not pass the barrier of the patriarchs or if your thinking road is not blocked, whatever you think, whatever you do, is like a tangling ghost. You may ask: What is a barrier of a patriarch? This one word, Mu [negative prefix], is it.
>
> This is the barrier of Zen. If you pass through it you will see Joshu face to face. Then you can work hand in hand with the whole line of patriarchs. Is this not a pleasant thing to do?
>
> If you want to pass this barrier, you must work through every bone in your body,

through every pore of your skin, filled with this question: What is Mu? and carry it day and night. Do not believe it is the common negative symbol meaning nothing. It is not nothingness, the opposite of existence. If you really want to pass this barrier, you should feel like drinking a hot iron ball that you can neither swallow nor spit out.

Then your previous lesser knowledge disappears. As a fruit ripening in season, your subjectivity and objectivity naturally become one. It is like a dumb man who has had a dream. He knows about it but he cannot tell it.

When he enters this condition his ego-shell is crushed and he can shake the heaven and move the earth. He is like a great warrior with a sharp sword. If a Buddha stands in his way, he will cut him down; if a patriarch offers him any obstacle, he will kill him; and he will be free in his way of birth and death. He can enter any world as if it were his own playground. I will tell you how to do this with this koan:

Just concentrate your whole energy into this Mu and do not allow any discontinuation. When you enter this Mu and there is no discontinuation, your attainment will be as a candle burning and illuminating the whole universe.

Has a dog Buddha-nature?
This is the most serious question of all.
If you say yes or no,
You lose your own Buddha-nature.

(Reps 1975, 89–90)

It is easy to see from the rewards of this state of mind why the state of satori, or enlightenment, is so eagerly sought after in the East.

Also note that the negative symbol, *Mu*, appears in the title of the collection in which this koan appears.

20. As far as I know, this is not a canonical koan, but it certainly destabilizes the sense of self-in-reality, and thus seems to me a fairly good approximation.

21. As an aside, we might note that this image of birth so important to Beckett's work is refracted in the physical image of the Isle midriver, adding yet another level on which the play operates:

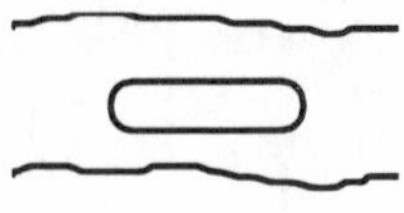

The "Birth" of the Isle of Swans

Like a child being infinitely born, the Isle is poised forever to be set in motion down the flowing river around it.

Chapter 8. Conclusion

1. Since "there are many right answers and there are also none. . . . For the koan itself is the answer" (Reps 1975, 86).

2. Note how this reiterates Zen's rejection of absolute authority or dogma, as noted by Kasulis above.

Appendix. Evolution of the Decomposition and Phase-space Diagram of *Footfalls*

1. The biggest problem with resolution in this process is the lumping of all spoken words into V's, as the subtle interplay of language is essentially removed. However, I did not deem it worth the extraordinarily difficult task of parsing the language to improve the mapping; while this certainly can be done, I feel my crude results give sufficient evidence as they stand.

2. By section, there are 41 static vs. 8 movement; 36 static vs. 4 movement; 63 static vs. 5 movement; and 3 static vs. 0 movement.

3. As noted in chapter 5, the spacing starts out like this: 1, 3, 1, 9, 1, 3, 1, 27.

4. A ∂event-type is the "amount" of change from one event to the next (or $\partial E/\partial t$). This and the position of May gives the mapping a built-in time dependence.

5. The +16 being the first sixteen "bars" of the next section, to which this adjoins.

Works Cited

Abbott, H. Porter. 1990. "Late Modernism: Samuel Beckett and the Art of the Oeuvre." In *Around the Absurd: Essays on Modern and Postmodern Drama*, edited by Enoch Brater and Ruby Cohn, pp. 73–96. Ann Arbor: University of Michigan Press, 1990.

———. 1991. "Reading as Theatre: Understanding Defamiliarization in Beckett's Art." *Modern Drama* 34, no. 1: 5–22

Abrams, M. H., ed. 1986. *The Norton Anthology of English Literature.* Vol. 2. 5th ed. New York: W. W. Norton.

Acheson, James. 1987. "The Shape of Ideas: *That Time* and *Footfalls*." In *Beckett's Later Fiction and Drama*, edited by James Acheson and Kateryna Arthur, 115–35. New York: St. Martin's Press.

Alter, Jean. 1987. "Waiting for the Referent: Waiting for Godot?" In *On Referring in Literature*, edited by Anna Whiteside and Michael Issacharoff, 42–56. Bloomington: Indiana University Press.

Astier, Pierre. 1982. "Beckett's *Ohio Impromptu*: A View from the Isle of Swans." *Modern Drama* 25, no. 3:331–41.

Bair, Deirdre. 1990. *Samuel Beckett: A Biography*. New York: Summit Books.

Beckett, Samuel. n.d. "Fin de Partie." Manuscripts and Typescripts. The Ohio State University Library rare books collection. Columbus, Ohio.

———. n.d. "Happy Days," Manuscripts and Typescripts. The Ohio State University Library rare books collection. Columbus, Ohio.

———. 1949. "Three Dialogues with Georges Duthuit." *Transition* 49, no. 5:97–103.

———. 1954. *Waiting for Godot: A Tragicomedy in Two Acts*. New York: Grove Weidenfeld.

———. 1958. *Endgame: A Play in One Act. Followed by Act Without Words: A Mime for One Player*. New York: Grove Press, Inc.

———. 1961. *Happy Days*. New York: Grove Press.

———. 1971. *Théatre I: En Attendant Godot, Find de Partie, Actes sans Paroles I et II*. Paris: Les Éditions de Minuit.

———. 1981. *Ill Seen Ill Said*. New York: Grove Press.

———. 1984a. *Film*. In *The Collected Shorter Plays of Samuel Beckett*, 161–74. New York: Grove Press.

———. 1984b. *Footfalls*. In *The Collected Shorter Plays of Samuel Beckett*, 236–43. New York: Grove Press.

———. 1984c. *Not I*. In *The Collected Shorter Plays of Samuel Beckett*, 213–23. New York: Grove Press.

———. 1984d. *Ohio Impromptu*. In *The Collected Shorter Plays of Samuel Beckett*, 283–88. New York: Grove Press.

———. 1984e. *Play*. In *The Collected Shorter Plays of Samuel Beckett*, 145–60. New York: Grove Press.

———. 1984f. *Quad*. In *The Collected Shorter Plays of Samuel Beckett*, 289–94. New York: Grove Press.

———. 1984g. *Rockaby*. In *The Collected Shorter Plays of Samuel Beckett*, 271–82. New York: Grove Press.

———. 1984h. *That Time*. In *The Collected Shorter Plays of Samuel Beckett*, 225–35. New York: Grove Press.

———. 1985. *Rockaby: A Play by Samuel Beckett*. Film. Directed by D. A. Pennebaker and Chris Hegedus. With Billie Whitelaw and Allan Schneider. Albany: State University of New York Programs in the Arts.

Beja, Morris, S. E. Gontarski, and Pierre Astier, eds. 1983. *Samuel Beckett: Humanistic Perspectives*. Columbus: Ohio State University Press.

Booth, Wayne. 1961. *The Rhetoric of Fiction*. 2d ed. Chicago: University of Chicago Press.

Bove, Paul. 1982. "Beckett's Dreadful Postmodern: The Deconstruction of Form in *Molloy*." In *De-Structuring the Novel: Essays in Applied Postmodern Hermeneutics*. Troy, N.Y.: Whitston Press.

Brater, Enoch. 1987. *Beyond Minimalism: Beckett's Late Style in the Theater*. Oxford: Oxford University Press.

Brillouin, Leon. 1956. *Science and Information Theory*. 2d ed. New York: Academic Press.

Browder, Sally. 1989. "'I Thought You Were Mine': Marsha Norman's *'night, Mother*." In *Mother Puzzles: Daughters and Mothers in Contemporary American Literature*, edited by Mickey Pearlman. New York: Greenwood Press.

Bryden, Mary. 1993. *Women in Samuel Beckett's Prose and Drama*. Lanham, Md.: Barnes & Noble.

Buning, Marius. 1992. "Allegory's Double Bookkeeping: The Case of Samuel Beckett." In *Samuel Beckett Today*, edited by Marius Buning, Sjef Houppermans, and Daniele de Ruyter, 69–78. Amsterdam: Rodopi.

Burkman, Katherine H. 1986. *The Arrival of Godot: Ritual Patterns in Modern Drama*. Rutherford, N.J.: Fairleigh Dickinson University Press.

Burkman, Katherine H., ed. 1987. *Myth and ritual in the Plays of Samuel Beckett*. Rutherford, N.J.: Fairleigh Dickinson University Press.

Butler, Lance St. John, and Robin J. Davis. 1990. *Rethinking Beckett: A Collection of Critical Essays*. New York: St. Martin's Press.

Calderwood, James L. 1986. "Ways of Waiting in *Waiting for Godot*." *Modern Drama* 29, no. 3:363–75.

Carey, Phyllis. 1987. "The Ritual of Human Techné in *Happy Days*." In *Myth and Ritual in the Plays of Samuel Beckett*, edited by Katherine H. Burkman, 144–50. Rutherford, N.J.: Fairleigh Dickinson University Press.

Chabert, Pierre. 1982. "The Body in Beckett's Theatre." *Journal of Beckett Studies* 8 (Autumn).

Claudel, Paul. 1965. *Œuvres en prose*. Paris: Gallimard.

Cleary, Thomas, trans. 1989. *The Book of Balance and Harmony*. San Francisco: North Point Press.

Cohn, Ruby. 1973. *Back to Beckett*. Princeton: Princeton University Press.

———. 1990. "The Femme Fatale on Beckett's Stage." In *Women in Beckett: Performance and Critical Perspectives,* edited by Linda Ben-Zvi, 162–71. Chicago: University of Illinois Press.

Connor, Steven. 1988. *Samuel Beckett: Repetition, Theory and Text*. New York: Basil Blackwell.

Creel, Herrlee G. 1970. *What is Taoism? And Other Studies in Chinese Cultural History*. Chicago: University of Chicago Press.

Culik, Hugh. 1993. "Neurological Disorder and the Evolution of Beckett's Maternal Images." In *Critical Essays on Samuel Beckett*, edited by Lance St. John Butler, 366–73. Critical Thought Series, vol. 4. Brookfield, Vt.: Ashgate Publishing Company. Originally published in *Mosaic* 22, no. 1 (winter 1989): 41–53.

Dearlove, J. E. 1982. *Accommodating the Chaos: Samuel Beckett's Nonrelational Art*. Durham, N.C.: Duke University Press.

deLauretis, Teresa. 1984. *Alice Doesn't: Feminism, Semiotics, Cinema*. Bloomington: Indiana University Press.

———. 1987. *Technologies of Gender: Essays on Theory, Film and Fiction*. Bloomington: Indiana University Press.

Derrida, Jacques. 1982. *Margins of Philosophy*. Translated by Alan Bass. Brighton: Harvester Press.

Deshimaru, Taisen. 1982. *The Zen Way to the Martial Arts*. New York: E. P. Dutton.

———. 1985. *Questions to a Zen Master*. New York: E. P. Dutton.

Doll, Mary. 1988. *Beckett and Myth: An Archetypal Approach*. Syracuse, N.Y.: Syracuse University Press.

———. 1987. "Rites of Story: The Old Man at Play." In *Myth and Ritual in the Plays of Samuel Beckett*, edited by Katherine H. Burkman, 73–85. Rutherford, N.J.: Fairleigh Dickinson University Press.

Drew, Anne Marie. 1993. *Past Crimson, Past Woe: The Shakespeare-Beckett Connection*. New York: Garland.

Elam, Keir. 1980. *The Semiotics of Theatre and Drama*. London: Methuen.

Eliade, Mircea. 1957. *The Sacred and the Profane: The Nature of Religion*. Translated by Willard R. Trask. New York: Harper & Row.

Eliot, T. S. 1963, 1980. *The Complete Poems and Plays: 1909–1950*. New York: Harcourt Brace Jovanovich.

Esslin, Martin. 1969. *The Theatre of the Absurd: Revised Updated Edition*. New York: Doubleday & Company.

———. 1971. *Brecht: The Man and His Work*. New rev. ed. New York: Doubleday & Company.

Foster, Paul. 1989. *Beckett and Zen: A Study of Dilemma in the Novels of Samuel Beckett*. London: Wisdom Publications.

Gantert, C., J. Honerkamp, and J. Timmer, J. 1992. "Analyzing the Dynamics of Hand Tremor Time Series." *Biology-Cybernetics* 66, no. 6:479–84.

Garner, Stanton B., Jr. 1987. "Visual Field in Beckett's Late Plays." *Comparative Drama* 21:4: 349–373.

———. 1993. "'Still living flesh': Beckett, Merleau-Ponty, and the Phenomenological Body." *Theatre Journal* 45, no. 4:443–60.

Genette, Girard. 1980. *Narrative Discourse: An Essay in Method*. Translated by Jane E. Lewin. Ithaca, N.Y.: Cornell University Press.

Gleick, James. 1987. *Chaos: Making a New Science*. New York: Viking Penguin.

Goldstein, Herbert. 1980. *Classical Mechanics*. 2 ed. Reading, Mass.: Addison-Wesley.

Gontarski, S. E. 1985. *The Intent of Undoing in Samuel Beckett's Dramatic Texts*. Bloomington: Indiana University Press.

Hale, Jane Alison. 1987. *The Broken Window: Beckett's Dramatic Perspective*. West Lafayette, Ind.: Purdue University Press.

Hancock, Alan. Forthcoming. "Chaos in Drama: The Metaphors of Chaos Theory as a Way of Understanding Drama Process." *The National Association of Drama in Education, Australia*.

Harding, D. E. 1986. *On Having No Head: Zen and the Re-Discovery of the Obvious*. Boston: Arkana.

Hayles, N. Katherine. 1990. *Chaos Bound: Orderly Disorder in Contemporary Literature and Science*. Ithaca, N.Y.: Cornell University Press.

———. 1991. "Complex Dynamics in Literature and Science." In *Chaos and Order: Complex Dynamics in Literature and Science*, edited by N. Katherine Hayles. Chicago: University of Chicago Press.

Heise, Ursula K. 1992. "Erzahlzeit and Postmodern Narrative: Text as Duration in Beckett's *How It Is*." *Style* 26, no. 2:245–69.

Helsa, David H. 1971. *The Shape of Chaos: An Interpretation of the Art of Samuel Beckett*. Minneapolis: University of Minnesota Press.

Henning, Sylvie Debevec. 1988. *Beckett's Critical Complicity: Carnival, Contestation, and Tradition*. Louisville: University Press of Kentucky.

Herrigel, Eugen. 1953. *Zen in the Art of Archery*. Translated by R. F. C. Hull. New York: Vintage Books.

Hobson, Harold. 1956. "Samuel Beckett, Dramatist of the Year." *International Theatre Annual* 1:153–55.

Houedard, Dom Sylvester. 1987. "'What's a Door Doing Here?': A Squint at Beckett's Layered Question." *The Review of Contemporary Fiction* 7, no. 2:49–54.

Howe, Fanny. 1983. "The Contemporary Logos." In *Code of Signals: Recent Writing in Poetics,* edited by Michael Palmer, 47–55. Berkeley, Calif.: North Atlantic Press.

Hutchings, William. 1991. "*Waiting for Godot* and the Principle of Uncertainty." In *Approaches to Teaching Beckett's "Waiting for Godot,"* edited by June Schlueter and Enoch Brater, 26–30. New York: Modern Language Association of America.

Hwang, Hoon-sung. 1993. "One Mirror is 'Not Enough' in Beckett's *Footfalls* and *Ohio Impromptu*." *Modern Drama* 36, no. 3:368–82.

Iser, Wolfgang. 1981. "The Art of Failure: The Stifled Laugh in Beckett's Theatre." *Bucknell Review: A Scholarly Journal of Letters, Arts and Sciences* 26, no. 1:139–89.

Kaltenmark, Max. 1969. *Lao Tzu and Taoism*. Translated by Roger Greaves. Stanford, Calif.: Stanford University Press.

Kasulis, T. P. 1981. *Zen Action/Zen Person*. Honolulu: University Press of Hawaii.

Kasulis, T. P., Roger T. Ames, and Wimal Dissanayake, eds. *Self as Body in Asian Theory and Practice*. 1993. Albany: State University of New York Press.

Kenner, Hugh. 1961. *Samuel Beckett: A Critical Study*. New York: Grove Press.

Klaver, Elizabeth. 1991. "Samuel Beckett's *Ohio Impromptu, Quad*, and *What Where:* How It Is in the Matrix of Text and Television." *Contemporary Literature* 32, no. 3:366–82.

Knowlson, James, and John Pilling. 1980. *Frescoes of the Skull: The Later Prose and Drama of Samuel Beckett*. New York: Grove Press.

Kolve, V. A. 1967. "Religious Language in *Waiting for Godot*." *Centennial Review* 11:102–27.

Kundert-Gibbs, John Leeland. 1995. "'Revolving it all': Mother-Daughter Pairs in Marsha Norman's *'night, Mother* and Samuel Beckett's *Footfalls*." In *Marsha Norman: A Casebook*, edited by Linda Brown. New York: Garland Press.

———. 1997. " 'What is a Birth Astride a Grave?': *Ohio Impromptu* as Zen Koan." *Modern Drama* 40, no. 1 (Spring): 38–56.

Lao Tzu. 1988. *Tao Te Ching*. Translated by Stephen Mitchell. New York: Harper Perennial.

Laughlin, Karen. 1987. "'Looking for Sense . . .': The Spectator's Response to Beckett's *Come and Go*." *Modern Drama* 30, no. 2 (June):137–46.

Lawley, Paul. 1983. "Counterpoint, Absence, and the Medium in Beckett's *Not I*." *Modern Drama* 26:407–14.

Levy, Eric. 1980. *Beckett and the Voice of the Species: A Study of the Prose Fiction*. Totowa, N.J.: Barnes and Noble.

Levy, Shimon. 1990. *Samuel Beckett's Self-Referential Drama: The Three I's*. New York: St. Martin's Press.

Lewin, Roger. 1992. *Complexity: Life at the Edge of Chaos*. New York: Macmillan.

Loy, David. 1988. *Nonduality: A Study in Comparative Philosophy*. New Haven: Yale University Press.

———. 1992. "The Deconstruction of Buddhism." In *Derrida and Negative Theology*, edited by Harold Coward and Toby Foshay, 227–53. Albany: State University of New York Press.

Lu K'uan Yü [Charles Luk], ed. 1961. *Ch'an and Zen Teaching*. Translated by Lu K'uan Yü. First Series. London: Rider & Co.

Mandelbrot, Benoit B. 1983. *The Fractal Geometry of Nature*. New York: W. H. Freeman.

Marion, Jerry B. 1970. *Classical Dynamics of Particles and Systems*. 2d ed. New York: Academic Press.

Maughlin, Susan. 1987. "Liminality: An Approach to Artistic Process in *Endgame*." In *Myth and Ritual in the Plays of Samuel Beckett*, edited by Katherine H. Burkman, 86–99. Rutherford, N.J.: Fairleigh Dickinson University Press.

McMullan, Anna. 1993. *Theatre on Trial: Samuel Beckett's Later Drama*. New York: Routledge.

McMullan, Audrey. 1987. "The Space of Play in *L'Impromptu d'Ohio*." *Modern Drama* 30, no. 1:23–34.

Mihalyi, Gabor. 1966. "Beckett's 'Godot' and the Myth of Alienation." *Modern Drama* 9, no. 3:277–82.

Milton, John. 1962. *Paradise Lost: A Poem in Twelve Books*. Edited by Merritt Y. Hughes. Indianapolis: Bobbs-Merrill.

Montgomery, Angela. 1991. "Beckett and Science: Watt and the Quantum Universe." *Comparative Criticism: A Yearbook* 13:171–81.

Mulvey, Laura. 1975. "Visual Pleasure and Narrative Cinema." *Screen* 16, no. 3:6–18.

Nagatomo, Shigenori. 1992. *Attunement Through the Body*. Albany: State University of New York Press.

Nealon, Jeffrey. 1988. "Samuel Beckett and the Postmodern: Language Games, Play and *Waiting for Godot*." *Modern Drama* 31, no. 4:520–28.

Ogata, Sohaku. 1959. *Zen for the West*. Westport, Conn.: Greenwood Press.

Pountney, Rosemary. 1988. *Theatre of Shadows: Samuel Beckett's Drama, 1956–76, from "All That Fall" to "Footfalls," with Commentaries on the Latest Plays*. Totowa, N.J.: Barnes & Noble.

Prigogine, Ilya, and Isabelle Stengers. 1984. *Order Out of Chaos: Man's New Dialogue with Nature*. New York: Bantam Books.

Reps, Paul, ed. 1975. *Zen Flesh, Zen Bones: A Collection of Zen and Pre-Zen Writings*. Translated by Paul Reps. Garden City, N.Y.: Anchor/Doubleday.

Robbe-Grillet, Alain. 1965. "Samuel Beckett, or 'Presence' in the Theatre." In *Samuel Beckett: A Collection of Critical Essays,* ed. Martin Esslin (Englewood Cliffs, N.J.: Prentice Hall.

Roof, Judith. 1987. "A Blink in the Mirror: From Oedipus to Narcissus and Back in the Drama of Samuel Beckett." In *Myth and Ritual in the Plays of Samuel Beckett*, edited by Katherine H. Burkman, 151–63. Rutherford, N.J.: Fairleigh Dickinson University Press.

Sacks, Oliver. 1990. *Awakenings*. New York: Harper Collins.

Saltz, David. 1992. "The Reality of the Theater Event" Dissertation, Stanford University.

Schlossberg, Edwin. 1973. *Einstein and Beckett: A Record of an Imaginary Discussion with Albert Einstein and Samuel Beckett.* New York: Links Books.

Schopenhauer, Arthur. 1969. *The World as Will and Representation.* Translated by E. F. J. Payne. Vol. 1. New York: Dover.

Schwab, Gabriele. 1984. "On the Dialectic of Closing and Opening in Samuel Beckett's *Endgame*." *Yale French Studies* 67:191–202.

Shakespeare, William. 1957a. *Hamlet Prince of Denmark*, edited by Willard Farnham. In *The Pelican Shakespeare*, edited by Alfred Harbage. New York: Penguin Books.

———. 1957b. *The Tempest*, edited by Northrop Frye. In *The Pelican Shakespeare*, edited by Alfred Harbage. New York: Penguin Books.

Shannon, Claude E., and Warren Weaver. 1949. *The Mathematical Theory of Communication*. Urbana: University of Illinois Press.

Simon, Richard Keller. 1982. "Dialectical Laughter: A Study of *Endgame*." *Modern Drama*: 25, no. 4:505–13.

Smith, Huston. 1986. Introduction to *On Having No Head: Zen and the Re-Discovery of the Obvious,* by D. E. Harding. Boston: Arkana.

Smith, Joseph H., ed. 1991. *The World of Samuel Beckett.* Baltimore: Johns Hopkins University Press.

Spencer, Jenny S. 1989. "Marsha Norman's *She-tragedies*." In *Making a Spectacle: Feminist Essays on Contemporary Women's Theatre*, edited by Lynda Hart, 147–68. Ann Arbor: University of Michigan Press.

Stevens, Roger T. 1989. *Fractal Programming in C*. Redwood City, Calif.: M & T Publishing.

Stryk, Lucien, ed. 1968. *World of the Buddha: An Introduction to Buddhist Literature*. New York: Grove Press.

Suzuki, Daisetz Teitaro. 1949. *Essays in Zen Buddhism: First Series.* New York: Grove Press.

Takahashi, Yasunari. 1983. "Qu'est-ce qui arrive? Some Structural Comparisons of Beckett's Plays and the Noh." In *Samuel Beckett: Humanistic Perspectives*, edited by Morris Beja, S. E. Gontarski, and Pierre Astier, 99–106. Columbus: Ohio State University Press.

———. 1993. "The Theatre of Mind—Samuel Beckett and the Noh." In *Critical Essays on Samuel Beckett*, edited by Lance St. John Butler, 257–61. Critical Thought Series, vol. 4: Brookfield, Vt.: Ashgate Publishing Company. Originally published in *Encounter* 58 (April 1982): 66–73.

Trezise, Thomas. 1990. *Into the Breach: Samuel Beckett and the Ends of Literature.* Princeton: Princeton University Press, 1990.

Waddell, Norman, and Masao Abe, trans. 1973. "Dogen's *Fukanzazengi* and *Shobogenzo Zazengi.*" *The Eastern Buddhist*, n.s., 6, no. 2:115–28.

Waldrop, M. Mitchell. 1992. *Complexity: The Emerging Science at the Edge of Order and Chaos.* New York: Simon & Schuster.

Winnett, Susan. 1990. "Coming Unstrung: Women, Men, Narrative, and Principles of Pleasure." *PMLA* 105, no. 3:505–18.

Yampolsky, Philip B. 1971. *The Zen Master Hakuin: Selected Writings.* New York: Columbia University Press.

Index

p20 "Hun Dun" Chinese Chaos character p49
<- whirling water

p24 wei-wu-wei "doing-not doing"
p25 Colors/Rainbow/Categories
p26 Zen-neither religion/philo